360
A FULL CIRCLE

DAR BRYANT
&
ANNALEE BANKS

eLectio Publishing

Little Elm, TX

www.eLectioPublishing.com

360: A Full Circle
By Dar Bryant & Annalee Banks

ISBN-13: 978-1-63213-292-5

Published by eLectio Publishing, LLC
Little Elm, Texas
http://www.eLectioPublishing.com

Printed in the United States of America

5 4 3 2 1 eLP 21 20 19 18 17

The eLectio Publishing creative team is comprised of: Kaitlyn Campbell, Emily Certain, Lori Draft, Court Dudek, Jim Eccles, Sheldon James, and Christine LePorte.

Publisher's Note

The publisher does not have any control over and does not assume any responsibility for author or third-party websites or their content.

Dedication

If a single person who has given up all hope thinking they are doomed to a life of crime and addiction reads or hears my story and realizes that it's never too late, and no matter what you have done, no matter who you are or where you've come from, that you, yes YOU can still turn your life around, this book is not in vain. You, yes YOU, can live a fulfilling and rewarding life. You, yes YOU, can be proud again of your accomplishments. If one person understands this message, then my time spent in that crazy life and the time I put into writing this book will have not been in vain.

This book is dedicated to my father, that he may find redemption. This book is dedicated to all who hurt deep inside, who feel lost with no way out. This book is dedicated to those who are in prison or about to go to prison unless they change the path they're on. This book is for the families who suffer and feel helpless and devastated as they watch their loved ones spiraling down the wrong path. This book is for YOU. There is hope. There is ALWAYS hope through God.

CONTENTS

Dedication 1

Acknowledgements v

Prologue...vii

Chapter 1 Roxana Junior High School 1974..................................... 1

Chapter 2 Roxana Senior High School 17

Chapter 3 Business Ventures 37

Chapter 4 The Band 1983... 51

Chapter 5 The Band The Wedding The Baby!............................ 57

Chapter 6 Alisha The Coliseum 75

Chapter 7 1988 TJ Nikki.. 89

Chapter 8 1989 Phoenix Chris 103

Chapter 9 Belleville, IL Second Move to Phoenix.......................... 111

Chapter 10 Barry Randy Sonny 131

Chapter 11 Laughlin: 1993 145

Chapter 12 Lake Havasu December 1993 157

Chapter 13 Mohave County Jail Prison March 1994- 1996 177

Chapter 14 Val 203

Chapter 15 Adderall 221

Chapter 16 Arrested 239

Chapter 17 Prison Is Prison And So It Begins 253

Chapter 18 Home at Last "That Bible" 275

Chapter 19 Throw It All Out There! 303

          March 2015... 304

Epilogue.. 311

          Annalee: A Little about Darwyn and Me 315

          Annalee: A Little about Zach and Me.............................. 317

Acknowledgements

For years, my sister Sherri has encouraged me to write this book, patiently sitting with me for hours on end encouraging me, questioning me, and listening to me while recording sections of this story. I know it wasn't easy for her to take in the insanity of her big brother's dark years. Sherri, I am so sorry for putting you through this, and I want to thank you for lifting me up and helping me through reliving my crazy life.

Thank you to one of my dearest friends, Annalee Banks, who listened to hours of recordings, turning them into a flowing, readable script. Thank you to Gary Pippins for editing our work.

Honestly, there are so many people who deserve recognition, but I can't even begin to list them all. For the sake of the reader, I've shortened this book to certain key events in my life. To those I didn't mention or just briefly talk about, it only means you were not directly involved in the craziness of the incidents that I chose to put in writing.

To all four of my children, I love you more than you will ever know, but I talk about you very little in this book. I am close to and absolutely love all my nephews, cousins, aunts, and uncles, but I don't talk about any of you in this book. I do want you all to know that even though you are briefly mentioned or not a part of this book at all, you were definitely a *huge* part of my life, a part of the family who loved me and helped me, never giving up on me, and I want everyone who reads this book to understand that. I want all of my family to know I love you! Thank you!

To my mom and stepfather, my grandmother and my siblings, I cannot express in words how much love I have for you, and I cannot thank you enough for your unconditional love that helped make this story's ending possible.

A profound thank you to Pastor Mark for administering the final push toward telling my story. To everyone at the River of Life Church, thank you for your continued love and support!

I have not revealed all the details of my dark years even to those closest to me. They will learn through reading this book also. This is difficult for me as I'm sure it will be for all of you who truly love me. To those of you, I apologize profusely for dragging you along this life, and I thank you a million times for never giving up on me.

Mom, I'm sorry I made you cry. I cannot thank you enough.

Grandma, You're the *best!*

Father God, *thank you!*

Prologue

I am about to reveal the story of my life even though the final chapter hasn't happened yet as, through God's grace, I'm still alive! All I can do is start from where it began, taking you through the summer of 2016. I've wanted to write this story for a while and had originally planned on waiting a few more years, but it has been lying heavy on my heart to proceed with it now, and if there's one thing I've learned through all of this, it's which inner voice to listen to, which I now recognize as my Father God. That voice told me to *write*, so I sat down and I wrote.

On the surface, I'm just an average, middle-aged family man living a quiet and very rewarding life in a small Illinois town in the Riverbend area along the banks of the Mississippi River. The very same area I grew up in, the very same area I fled from, and the very same area I've returned to.

I am a devout Christian involved in the ministry of my church. I grew up in church, but when I was fourteen years old, I ran as far away from God as I could. Somehow, I miraculously and unbelievably made my way back.

I am fortunate to live in the same area as most of my family. I'm just a regular guy who has been immensely blessed with this family's love. I've only revealed to them some of my past—they don't know my entire story. No one on this planet except God has ever heard my entire story…until now.

In my early years, I was quite the visionary—an adventurous, ambitious, and very driven individual, a dreamer always wanting more for myself. I started, owned, and operated several of my own businesses, from a small chain of family-owned video stores to a video production company. I managed rock bands and owned a nightclub.

During those years, I appeared to have it all together and seemed to be on my way to certain success. I was respected in the community, had friendships and relationships that I value to this day, and was blessed to be in on several ground floor opportunities. All of this I accomplished by the age of twenty-five.

Within a few years, I went from a successful young business man who partied with his friends to someone who partied heavily every single night, hung out in nightclubs with bands, partied with porn stars in Chicago, and manufactured and dealt drugs.

I started dabbling in the occult from metaphysics to Wicca. I lived a wild and free life—or it felt like it at the time. I felt I was on top of the world, but it was only a life of decadence, rock 'n' roll, money, sex, and drugs. In reality, that false feeling of being on top of the world was actually me losing myself. During those years, my life was so empty, so void of everything that was truly me, and I quickly became a slave to that lifestyle.

I didn't realize it at the time, or maybe I did but didn't care or just didn't know how to find myself again. These things, disguised behind some crazy, horrid, fake reality that I was on top of the world, were slowly killing me, holding me in their clutches and sending me further down the rabbit hole.

There came a time when I was no longer respected by my former peers but highly respected by my new peers. There's a drug enabling me to carelessly turn from my old peers glorifying in the status quo of my new peers. There came a time when I was considered the lowest of the low by my normal circle of friends and all of society while still being highly praised and sought after by my new circle of friends. That same drug allowed me to feel comfortable in my new world and led me to become an outlaw to the extreme.

Handcuffed standing in front of the judge, I was once described by a prosecutor as "a one-man crime wave." These words still ring in my ears today. During the '80s and '90s, I was involved in everything—drug trafficking, drug manufacturing, counterfeiting, fraud, racketeering, and more.

I wasn't surprised when I learned I was on Arizona's Top Ten Most Wanted list. I became a major target of the DEA, was interrogated for several crimes including murder, was involved in a shootout, overdosed several times, and have had more near-death experiences than I care to count.

My world crashed in on me one day, and I was busted, convicted, and had to serve prison time, causing years of my life to be taken. Looking back, I can see I was a prisoner long before I went to prison.

A part of me knew what the outcome would be, what the end result would be—either be caught or die. After having successfully escaped police apprehension eighteen times, I had acquired a false sense of security, thinking I was smarter than they were, but deep inside, I knew my successful escapes couldn't last forever.

My story spans four decades, and I feel the purpose of writing this book is not to glorify the lifestyle I lived but to demonstrate God's love. You see, if not for God's grace, I would not be here today. I owe not only God but also the many people in my life who love me and were praying for me when I didn't have enough sense to pray for myself.

You are about to read my story. As disturbing as it may be, I have described the events as they happened. To do anything less would take away from true understanding. Am I proud of my story? Yes and no. I am not a single bit proud of the decisions I made that led me down a path that hurt my family and almost killed me, but I am *so* proud of what God has done with my messed-up life, turning it into something purposeful and magnificent. Yes, I am very proud of the end of my story.

I have tried not to sugarcoat incidents, maintaining accuracy to allow access to all readers. This was difficult, but for those who have lived a similar life, you will be able to fill in the ugly blanks. To those who haven't, consider yourself spared. To further spare the innocence of readers, I have removed the vile, vulgar, foul language that accompanies this lifestyle. This book would have been twice as long had I left the actual dialect in as it was truly spoken.

Those who grew up with me, you will recognize locations, characters, and incidents. Remember that all of these things happened, but I have condensed actions to a few characters to make this book flow easier while still maintaining its accuracy and getting the main point across. If you recognize a character, don't assume they are a actual part of all incidents of the same character I wrote about in this book.

I have also decided to keep some incidents to myself for right now. In this book, I do not discuss any of my actions with the occult or incidents that happened because of my association. That's an entire book in and of itself.

I did not write this book to preach to anyone. I promise this is not a preachy book…this is just my story.

Today, I am the person and the man my grandmother and mother always dreamed and prayed I would be. I went from a small-town Christian boy to one of the top most-wanted criminals in Arizona to a small-town Christian man. The pages that follow are the story of my 360-degree journey.

Many of the names in this book associated with my story have been changed and incidents condensed to a few characters to protect identities. (How ironic is that?)

Chapter 1
Roxana Junior High School
1974

Today is my first day of eighth grade. Warm rain spits on me as I wait at the corner for the school bus, wearing my dark blue polyester pants and white button-down shirt. Mom says I should always dress nice, so this is what I wear every day.

I reach up and unbutton the top three buttons of my shirt. She had just buttoned them right before I walked out the door, but it's too tight on my neck. I hate standing here waiting for the bus, and I hate school.

Up until last year, Mom drove the three of us to and from school every day. She still drives my little sister and brother, and I must admit I'm a little jealous of that. Sherri's ten years old and Tim is eight. Outside of school, all we do is go to church. My parents and Grandma raise me with very strict old-school Pentecostal rules that I do try to follow. I'm not allowed to hang out with anyone other than my church friends, and we are not allowed to go to the movies or swim in public swimming pools. I've always been an awkward, scrawny, blond-haired, blue-eyed kid who wears dress clothes daily. I just don't fit in with the other kids. They make fun of me—a lot. The teacher taking roll calling out my name, Darwyn Bryant, in front of everyone might have something to do with it. I don't know. Last year was terrible. Seventh grade is the year where all the grade school kids go to the same school together for the first time. So instead of just the few kids I've always had making fun of me, they all joined forces last year, and it was horrendous!

My birthday is September 1, and soon after, school starts. I never look forward to my birthday because I know what follows—nine months of teasing, harassing, and torment. I'm tired, I hate school, and I don't want summer to end, but I stand here on the corner because this is what I'm supposed to do. I guess I'll just do what I do every year—make no eye contact, pretend I don't hear them taunting

1

me, and walk as far away from them as fast as I can. I pretend it doesn't hurt me, but their cruel words do penetrate. Sometimes I wake up late at night hearing them again and again. I try to make it stop. Ugh! June can't get here fast enough.

There's the bus. I wipe sweat from my hands on the sides of my pants and catch myself scratching the back of my fresh buzz haircut. I try my best to stand tall and look like I don't care, like I'm not nervous. Does it show? I can't let them see my fear. They'll eat me alive again.

I flinch when the bus doors clang open. Here goes. Walking down the aisle of the bus searching for a seat, I realize something amazing has happened to me over the summer. I have grown about a foot, and everyone is forced to look up to me. To *me!* I literally now tower over everyone! I find an empty seat halfway down, slide toward the window hoping not to be noticed, and am immediately pulled back to last year and back to the mindset of dreading this school year. I really don't want to be here and cannot stand the idea of attending another year of school. Last week's discussion with Mom over letting me stay home this year didn't work. I keep telling her what an evil place this school is, but she just smiles and tells me it's fine, that I'm making too much of it.

Mom and Dad run a produce market in town. Hanging out at the market over the summer, I met and became friends with Tony Walters who lives close to the market. Tony is a hippie—I guess a freak is what everyone at school would call him. He has long, scraggly hair and smells like a strange-smelling smoke. Mom doesn't like him because of this, and she tells me to stay away from him, but I think he's a great guy. During summer break while hanging out at the store, I told Tony about my seventh-grade year, to which he responded, "Don't worry. Just find me when you get to school. I'll be out front. I'll introduce you to some people before class. You'll be fine."

The bumpy ride comes to an end, and the bus pulls up at good old Roxana Junior High School. I'm surprisingly unscathed. I get off the bus and immediately walk to a group of students who are smoking on the sidewalk at the front of the school. I don't smoke, but I want to look cool, so when I find Tony, I place my thumbs in my polyester pockets and look around, nervously rocking back and forth on my heels. All the other guys out front have hair down to their shoulders, and I find myself scratching the back of my burr head. I quickly slide both hands all the way into my pockets, bend one knee, tap my foot. I feel stupid, so I straighten my legs and wipe the sweat from my hands on my pants, sheepishly trying my hardest to appear cool as he introduces me to a few of his friends. Tony is a good guy. Even through my incredible discomfort, he makes it a point to make me feel that it's all good. The school bell rings, triggering everyone to give each other wide-eyed, annoyed looks. They quickly drop their cigarettes and lean forward, twisting their feet back and forth to put them out beneath their shoes before hustling toward the school doors. I walk over hundreds of butts before entering the school on my way to first-hour class. As always, I head to the back of the room, wanting to disappear into the shadows. A kid with long, dark hair also sitting in the back strikes up a conversation with me. His name is David Edwards, and come to find out, he lives in Rosewood Heights, my neighborhood. David and I spend the entire class talking, laughing, and cutting up in the back row. I have no idea what Mr. Rolland or any of the other three teachers that were unfortunate enough to have the both of us in class taught that day. I'm just glad to have met a friend. We eat lunch together and even hang out after school.

Surprisingly, the first week of school is great! David and I are hanging at his house on a school night when he cracks opens a quart of beer, takes a long draw, and looks over at me, asking if I want one. I have never drunk alcohol before in my life, but hey, you know, I'm a year older now, and it's a new life. We each down a quart, and suddenly I feel better than I have ever felt in my life! All my inhibitions, my worries, my stresses are gone. David is doing a fantastic job picking out the song "Simple Man" by Lynyrd Skynyrd on his acoustic guitar. Maybe it's the alcohol—I don't know—but I'm having a great time listening to him play. Every day after school, I tell Mom I need to go to David's to work on homework, but we never do homework. We drink beer and listen to music. I've always been a good kid, so mom trusts me. She doesn't check. One day, David scores some weed from his older brother. I've never smoked pot before. I try it, but I'm not impressed. It put me to sleep, so I say no the next time he offers.

I am making new friends, learning new things, and entering a world I never knew existed. It's all good! A few months into school, I'm hanging out on the sidewalk when Brad Russell walks up and asks if we want to buy some pills. He pulls out a small vial filled with little tiny purple pills, one dollar apiece. I look over to Tony and ask, "What is that?"

"Purple microdot."

"What is it?"

"I tell you what! You'll have a *blast!* Just one time...try it."

I look back at Brad and then down at the vial and think there's no possible way that that little purple thing can hurt me. So I take it. David does too.

The bell rings. David and I give each other annoyed looks, drop our cigarettes, stepping on them with a twist as we head off to class. I sit quietly staring at the teacher. I'm a little nervous waiting for something to happen because of the pill, but not sure what. Forty-five minutes into class, I look over at David. He looks back, and we laugh hysterically, uncontrollably. We can't stop laughing as we watch Mr. Rolland's face melt, something that at any other time would seem like a scene from a horror movie. We laugh so hard we can hardly breathe. Mr. Rolland wants us out of class, so he sends us to the principal's office.

Mr. Walters doesn't know what to think as we cannot stop laughing. He tells us to sit outside his office with the secretaries. We entertain ourselves for hours watching desk drawers open and close by themselves, papers rattle then take flight, pencils scratch on paper then rise up and fly away, typed letters march out of books then jump to the ground and march out the door, floor tiles rise, hover, and trade places, the wood trim around the door close in on people

4

walking through, people walk by, melting and dissolving into each other. Some stop and talk to us, and their voices are loud and clear one second and then *bam*, they're a million miles away and all I hear are distorted sounds coming from their distorted mouths. The sound of the secretary's typewriter turns into a great musical beat, and the ceiling lights cast beautiful colors on everything. With all these things, we hear distortion and clarity, see lights shooting from them, streaks and colors melting, rolling, twisting, turning, marching across our brains vertically, horizontally, and squiggly, all beautiful, funny, and scary rolled up into one, and it's hysterical! I am having an absolute blast. I love this!

Every morning, David and I have our dollar bills ready for Brad to bring his vial over so we can purchase our purple microdot for the day. I have talked Mom into buying some new clothes. My polyester church clothes lie in the bottom of my bedroom drawer as I tuck my Marlboros into the front pocket of my new black T-shirt that hangs loosely over my stiff, brand-new Levi 501 blue jeans. I throw on a Levi jacket to hide the cigarettes in my pocket from Mom and flip my long blond hair outside the collar. For the first time, I'm comfortable at school and finally fit in.

We are halfway through the school year, and the front sidewalk has turned into a farmer's market for selling drugs. I buy anything I want out front, and there is still so much I don't know about. Daily, students walk up and down the sidewalk pushing their products.

"Got joints here, four for a dollar!"

"Get your speed here, four for five dollars!"

Whatever drug or smoke I want, I can buy before school on the front sidewalk. I become comfortable with this even though I'm told drugs are bad. If that were true, if drugs are so terribly bad, why is everyone, I mean *everyone*, doing drugs? It's just normal school activity. I experiment smoking different things and popping different color pills every morning, eager to get to school and try something new or again experience an old favorite. My body acclimates to this way of life easily. I learn what all that weird stuff in the glass counter at Gladrags is used for. I feel strong, even powerful, and have never before in my life felt so connected to a group of people.

A guy I've seen around but have never talked with before walks up and starts talking to David and I before school. He has long, scraggly, light brown hair and blue eyes and wears an army jacket and ragged blue jeans. David introduces him to me as Zach Banks. I find out that he is in my fifth-hour history class with Mrs. Keller. Mrs. Keller is crazy, that's all I can say, crazy. Even though the school year is almost half over, I have never seen Zach in that class because he apparently skips school a lot. We hit it off, and Zach decides to attend class with me today.

Walking down the hall during passing period and heading to Mrs. Keller's class, I notice Zach standing by the boy's bathroom next to her room. He opens up his army jacket and shows me a pint of Jack Daniels he has stashed in an inside pocket and asks, "I'm going to hit this. You want to hit this with me?"

We slip into the bathroom and in seconds finish off the entire pint of Jack. Instead of going to class, we have a better plan. Zach walks into a stall, removes two toilet paper rolls from the wall, and flings them at me. Flying across the bathroom, I knock them into the sink, turn on the faucet, and completely soak them with water, laughing at the thought of what we're about to do. Zach holds the dripping wet toilet rolls out from his sides as he walks out of the bathroom. I hold Mrs. Keller's door open. I can see her sitting at her desk looking toward the back of the room with her stiff bright red hair all piled up on top of her head when—*Zoom! Zoom!*—two soaking wet rolls of toilet paper fly past me, seconds apart, perfectly nailing Mrs. Keller spot on! In a second, Zach is gone. I am too.

One thing I learn about Zach early on is that he is very agile and very fast. He can jump, sprint, throw, and do anything faster and better than anyone I have ever met in my life. From this moment forward, I have a very small circle of close friends. David, Zach, and I are inseparable.

It's turning out to be a great year! I go to school daily but am learning only about drugs, alcohol, and how to cause mass chaos in school halls. Between the three of us, we think, organize, and pull off pranks without getting caught. Zach doesn't care if he gets caught — he's lucky enough to not have parents to deal with. David and I have parents at home, so we do our best not to get in too much trouble — well, not to get caught anyway.

One evening, I accidentally spill lighter fluid on my jeans, and for some unknown reason, I light my jeans on fire just to see what happens and learn that lighter fluid will burn off quickly without burning or damaging my jeans. This amazes me! I repeat this a few more times, testing it with the exact same results. The next morning, I tell my friends about it before school, and on a dare after drinking Jack and popping a microdot, I pour lighter fluid from my cigarette lighter up and down both sides of my blue jeans while at the end of the school hall, light myself on fire, and run the length of the hall screaming. It causes a great disruption, burns out quickly, and then I calmly walk to class as if nothing happened. It's a *hit!* My friends love it, so I repeat it a few more times until, well, the frayed edge on the back hem of my jeans really does catch fire. My leg heats up, and it starts to burn my skin. Terrified, I stop running. When repeated slapping and stomping doesn't work, I frantically run to the bathroom in search of water while flames shoot from the bottom of my right pant leg. I slam into the side of the stall and shove my foot in the toilet. I have decided the fire show is over — no more fire dares.

Zach has no parental supervision, none whatsoever. He has stowed away above a friend's garage for weeks and in basements of others without parental knowledge. He jumps around from place to place a lot to avoid his guardians, and they don't really look for him. Zach recently moved in with his grandpa who lives on Sixth Street in Roxana right next to the high school. It's great! We leave school and go back to Zach's house to get high, hang out, and listen to music. Sometimes we go back to school, but most the time not. His grandpa sits at the kitchen table in a wifebeater, smoking a cigarette, and just grunts when we walk in. He doesn't even look away from the TV sitting on his dresser in the bedroom just off the kitchen. An array of newspapers, *Playboys*, and overflowing ashtrays are scattered across the table. Zach's room is off to the left of the kitchen. His mattress is on the floor, and there are Led Zeppelin posters plastered all over his bedroom walls. He has a very nice stereo in the corner of his room with a great selection of albums in a Peaches crate on the floor and next to it a decent selection of drugs in a wooden stash box. His grandpa doesn't even know my name or ask who I am. Whatever we say to him, he just grunts without even looking at us, so we come and go as we please. He never questions us about why we aren't at school in the middle of the day, what we are doing, or where we are going.

"Bye, Grandpa. We're leaving."

"Hgggggh." He grunts as he takes a long drag off his cigarette.

That is the coolest thing ever, not to have anyone question where you're going or why you aren't in school. Zach is one of the luckiest guys on the face of the planet.

David, Zach, and I wreak havoc daily at school, but we are smart enough to pull off our pranks in a hallway or classroom where no one knows us. That way when students are questioned about "incidents," we are long gone, and they couldn't turn us in if they wanted to. Mr. Smith is chasing Zach and I down the hall, but we are far enough ahead of him that when we turn the corner, Zach has time to grab a fire extinguisher hanging on the wall. He sprays foam all over the floor, making the teacher giving chase slip and slide into the lockers as soon as he turns the corner. I guess he wasn't expecting that. We stop briefly to watch, feeling proud of ourselves, before running away laughing, already looking for the next thing to do.

It's snowing outside, but the front sidewalk market is full of business as usual. The three of us make a few snowballs apiece and hide them in our pockets, waiting for the bell. The bell rings, and there are the usual annoyed looks, dropped cigarettes, and twisting ankles. We walk inside and head down a different hallway, throwing snowballs into classrooms and smashing them hard and high on the wall so they explode upon impact with the fallout hitting everyone around. Then we calmly go straight to class, sit down, and act surprised when people come in talking about it.

It's not all fun and games, though. Third-hour study hall is held in the auditorium. Multiple classes meet here with only one teacher in charge. The room is large and set up for stadium seating to better view the stage for school plays, talent shows, and whatever else they do. There is a desk on the floor in front of the stage for the teacher who monitors the room during study halls.

Zach and I always sit and talk with a couple friends, Tonya Layman and Abby Milford. We have sat and talked with these two girls since the beginning of school. A substitute teacher walks in and attempts to take roll call. He decides since it's a study hall, we shouldn't be talking. He's going to split us up, putting one of us in each of the four corners of the auditorium. Zach and I aren't going for it. After words fly back and forth, we walk out, telling him where to go. The girls stay. Zach and I aimlessly wander the halls for a while trying to find something to entertain us. We walk back down the hallway in front of the auditorium, and Tom runs out into the hall to fill us in on what's happened since we left. Apparently, the sub didn't get our names before we left, and no one, not one single person in the entire auditorium, will rat us out. This infuriates the sub, so he is making study hall miserable on everyone, threatening detentions and just not leaving anyone alone trying to get someone to give him our names. It's time to have another talk with this guy.

We walk down the sloping aisle of the stadium toward the front to speak with him, and words start flying back and forth when we're halfway there. There are probably over one hundred students in study hall, and everyone stops what they're doing to watch. Zach and I don't walk out this time. This time, as the substitute speaks, as I speak, as Zach speaks, we continue to get louder and closer to him until our noses almost touch. We don't back down one bit, piercing him with four angry blue eyes. The sub becomes uncomfortable, backs up, and turns to walk behind the desk, nervously fiddling with some papers. Zach and I stand there for a few moments quietly, staring intensely at him. When he doesn't look back up or say anything more, Zach and I look at each other, shrug our shoulders, and walk back to Tonya and Abby. Uninterrupted this time, we talk for the remainder of study hall.

Eighth grade has become a *great* school year. I've made good friends, I no longer dread coming to school, and I no longer dread being around other people. I am having fun. I fit in. I feel good about myself, and that's all that matters to me right now.

Eighth grade ends as great as it began, and summer vacation comes faster than it ever has before. Mom is happy that I'm happy. She doesn't have a clue what really went on during school. She wouldn't have liked it very much. She knows I've made new friends, and she is relieved I no longer complain or beg her to let me stay home. She hasn't met Zach yet, but she loves David. From the very first time meeting my parents, David has always been exceptionally polite to them, so both Mom and Dad love David.

During summer vacation, David and I sleep in late and spend warm, humid days fishing, drinking, smoking, and getting high in the woods along the creeks that wind through our neighborhood. We strap our supplies to dirt bikes and explore different areas, sometimes spending the days alone and sometimes running into and partying with others doing the same. We aren't old enough to drive yet, so we don't see Zach. He lives down the hill by the school.

I'm half asleep when the phone rings and I hear Mom yelling it's for me. David is on the other end telling me to come over. I throw on a pair of gym shorts and walk into the kitchen to get a bowl of sugar frosted flakes. It's a hot, humid morning, and I almost drop the sweaty glass bottle pouring milk in my bowl. Crunching my flakes at the kitchen table while Mom talks to me, I grunt a few times, paying no attention to what she's saying but pretending I do. It's too early in the morning to think. Mom leaves for work, and I shower, get dressed, and head out the door. David's parents are both gone when I arrive and find him sitting in the living room. He looks at me with a huge grin on his face and holds up a set of keys.

"What's that?" I ask.

He whispers, "My sister left her keys in her car."

10

David just turned fifteen. I won't turn fifteen until September. We cannot get our driver's licenses until we turn sixteen. Neither of us has ever driven a car before, but we are quite good on dirt bikes. This could be fun.

David continues, "I've already called Maggie and Tara. We're going to pick them up and hang out at the levees, maybe get lucky!"

It's a great plan. Steal his sister's car, drive to South Roxana, and get lucky with a couple of blondes. I'm in! We climb into his sister's white 1969 Grand Torino, and I am surprised at how well David drives. South Roxana is about fifteen miles down the hill from us on the other side of the Roxana High School. He is driving slowly, stopping at all the stop signs, staying in between the lines, and doing everything like he knows what he's doing. We make it all the way to South Roxana, pick up the girls with no problems, and head toward Poag Road.

Protecting the low-lying local communities from flood waters from the Mississippi River and its many creeks and canals are tall levees with gravel roads on top. The locals use these levees, depending on the season, for sledding, flying kites, or for easy access in and out of the surrounding woods adjacent to the waters. It's a perfect place to throw out a blanket, get high, and get lucky. The girls are in the car, and David decides to show off a little as we turn off Poag Road onto one of the levees. He punches the gas pedal to the floor, and the engine roars, sucking us back in the seat and shooting gravel out from the tires as we fly down the levee and fishtail around an S curve! David loses control of the car, and we're thrown to the right. The car careens into a ditch on the left and crashes sideways into a telephone pole. The girls are screaming, and I almost pee my pants. We come to an abrupt stop, and everything goes dead silent. A few seconds pass as we all take inventory of our body parts. Then I hear David whisper, "Oh crap!"

The girls jump out of the car screaming, *"Are you crazy! You tried to kill us!"*

David and I sit in the car solemnly watching those short shorts and halter tops walk angrily back down the levee toward their hometown. When they are out of view, we look at each other, wondering what to do next.

David turns the key a few times while stepping on the gas pedal, but the car won't even try to start. I smell gas. We get out and walk around it, scratching our heads and realizing now just how much trouble we are in.

David looks at me and asks, "Man, do you think maybe it would be okay if I come and stay at your house for a little while?"

We take off walking down the levee in the same direction as the girls toward South Roxana. Half an hour later, we find a pay phone at the gas station in town and call his big brother Jim. Jim lives in Wood River with his wife, so he's here in five minutes. We drive back out to look at the car. The three of us circle the car as Jim speaks in a quiet, serious voice, "Man, you guys are *dead!*" Shaking his head, he investigates all the car's damage and repeats, "You guys are *so* dead! I'll tell you what. I'm going to take you home and not say anything. When Dad gets home, you are going to have to deal with this on your own."

We climb into his car and drive home.

I don't feel like going anywhere. I want to stay home by the phone in case David calls. I spend the evening just waiting—waiting for the shoe to drop, waiting for the phone call and wondering what is happening over at David's this very minute. I sit sideways on my bed, tapping my head against the wall to the tune of "Black Water" by the Doobie Brothers, and the phone rings. I turn the music down and listen as I have done with every phone call this evening. It's seven o'clock, and this is the call I've been waiting for. Dad answers, and I listen to his one-sided conversation.

"Hello?

"Well, hello, Mr. Edwards. How are you?

"Uh-huh.

"Uh-huh.

"Huh."

I sit in my room visualizing my escape because I can't come up with a good enough reason to make this any better. I hear dad compassionately say, "Aww, Mr. Edwards, you don't want to do that."

I cannot come up with a story that will get us out trouble for stealing and crashing a car. Dad really likes David, and I continue to listen to him talk to David's dad, calmly telling him, "He's your son. You don't want to do that. You need to think about this."

The only thing I have in my favor is the fact that I was not driving the car and it does not belong to anyone in my family.

Dad hangs up the receiver and yells my name. As I walk out of the bedroom and up the stairs, his compassionate voice has turned to a slightly louder stern voice. "What were you guys thinking?" he says quickly.

I just stand there looking at him. I've got nothing to say to help me out of this one.

He continues with genuine concern in his voice. "I wouldn't want to be in David's shoes right now."

I ask him what's going on with David, and he won't talk about it. I'm waiting for the belt, but instead of the belt, Dad slowly turns and leaves the room with a worried look on his face. The conversation is over. We never talk about it again. David does get a phone call through to me later that night. Apparently, his dad beat him up pretty bad and kicked him out of the house. His dad is an older man and an alcoholic who loses his temper easily. In the evening after work, I've watched him many times throw down tumbler after tumbler of scotch. David stays with us a few days, giving his mom time to talk his dad into letting him go back home.

Next week is my fifteenth birthday and the beginning of ninth grade. This year, I look forward to my birthday and am ready to get back and see my friends at school. Huh...first time I've ever thought that. David and I ride the bus together and immediately head to the front of the school, and there's Zach on the sidewalk. We start right where we left off last year, doing all the crazy stuff we love to do. It's even better this year—all of our older friends now have driver's licenses, so we meet in front of the school to buy what we need, pile in cars, and take off for the day.

We drive around town, do some acid, drink some booze, smoke a little weed, and head up the Great River Road. The Mississippi River is on one side of the road, and on the other side are tall, steep, jagged bluffs with trees growing out the sides. We pull over and decide to climb a two-hundred-foot bluff and act a fool. The bluff we climb is steep, solid rock with no trees. We have no inhibitions. We're high, we climb, we scream, we hang looking out across the road and river. We don't scream because we're scared. We scream and holler just because we can.

The Blue Pool sits further on down, off to the bluff side of the Great River Road. Local rumor is this pool is bottomless. The story is that in an effort to fill it, many things have been dumped in this pool never to resurface or be seen again—for instance, train cars. *Train cars!* It has been told that years ago, it was a popular swimming hole for locals, but after a few people dove in from the top of the bluffs never to be seen again, they fenced it off and no one is allowed to swim here anymore. It's a strange and beautiful area, and the fence is easy to climb. The Blue Pool isn't very big and is surrounded by tall bluffs on two sides. It got its name because even though it's a matter of a few feet away from the largest, muddiest river in the United States, the Blue Pool's water is crystal clear and reflects the blue skies beautifully. When placing your hand in the Mississippi River, you cannot see your fingers after an inch of submersion. Sitting along the side of the Blue Pool, you can see ragged stone lining the pool many feet underwater, a continuation of the bluffs deep into the pool. This pool is always a mystery and exciting to be around especially when you're high. It's a great place to party.

We seldom go to school anymore other than to meet out front. If the weather is nice, we drive down the River Road and party along the bluffs, swim in the Blue Pool, or cross in the ferry to party along the only sandy beach on the Mississippi River, Royal Landing. It's not a natural sandy beach. Someone years ago had the idea to haul tons of sand in, and it turned out pretty decent. We're always tripping or higher than a kite. When the weather is bad, we walk into other schools—Wood River, Jerseyville, Alton, Edwardsville—pretending we belong there, stirring up as much trouble as we can before running out the door. No one in these schools knows us, so we freely run the halls hollering, yelling, and cussing at anyone and everyone unfortunate enough to encounter us before making a quick exit, laughing at the thought of them trying to figure out which of their students did this. We drive away knowing there will be no repercussions. We do it for no reason other than we are high and we are bored. It's a good time.

Shell Shack is our main hang out. It's a small burger joint across the street from the school. Bobby's dad owns it and runs it, and they both live there. They sell burgers, fries, soda, candy, and any drug available in the area. We have a system worked out—someone is always assigned to watch the school, and when Mr. Walters, the high school principal, is spotted walking across the street toward us to check to see who's skipping school, Bobby's dad lets us exit through the back door so the principal can't catch us. Our guard is watching, and we're eating burgers and candy when Jack comes in and shows us these small foil packets with four little white pills inside. Each pill has a white cross in the center. I ask him what it is, and he answers, "Check it out. It's speed, white crosses. One dollar a pack."

"Do I take one or two or…"

"Take all four! That's why we packed them four in a pack, dummy. It takes four of them to really do anything to you."

I give Jack a dollar, rip open the foil, and throw back all four pills, chasing them with soda and some fries. Within twenty minutes, I know this is my drug. I have never felt so on top of the world in my entire life. My energy level is incredible. I can do anything and say anything, and nothing bothers me. This is it! This is what I've been looking for!

The next day at Shell Shack, I buy five packets from Jack. I want to make sure I have enough to last the week. I rip open the foil packet and down four white crosses with a beer. Twenty minutes later, and not the same high, so I pop two more. Yesssss, there it is. I no longer want purple microdots or any of the other drugs. I spend all my money on white crosses. This is all I want, all I need.

To keep the high I crave, I have to keep increasing my dose. I'm up to twenty pills a day. Mikey stops in Shell Shack to show us his small black pills, so I ask him, "What's that?"

"Black Beauties."

"Do I take four?"

"*No!* No. Just take one."

I place that black beauty in my mouth, swallow, and I am zinging for the next twenty-four hours straight, nonstop. The three of us buy and take them daily.

Zach says, "You know, I've figured it out. You can live on three dollars a day."

I ask him, "How's that?"

"One dollar for a black beauty, one dollar for a pack of cigarettes, and one dollar for a burger and coke. That's all you need in life."

Chapter 2
Roxana Senior High School

Occasionally I do attend some classes, hoping to move up a grade at the end of the school year with the rest of my class. My favorite class is Mr. Gerome's craft class. This class is held deep in the belly of the school basement. It's dark and windowless. Large pipes hang above our heads from low ceilings, clanking loudly as they heat and cool. I hear a click, immediately followed by the sound of a spark hitting gas. A few bright lights shine straight down on the craft tables. My first impression is that it's a strange place to hold a class, but after our initial shock, everyone in the class finds the surroundings calming, and here we relax and learn to cut, carve, paint, and assemble things out of leather.

I've been working on a leather case to hold my pinch hitter. The teacher doesn't care or even ask what it's for or about the shape of the leaves I carve into the front of it. Honestly, the way it smells back around the dark entryway to Gerome's office—of which he has instructed us *never* to enter—I think he knows exactly what I plan to use my project for and probably has made one for himself. He gives me an A. I take it home and put it to good use. I'm not the only student who made one.

We all like Mr. Gerome. He leaves us to work, allowing us to talk as much as we want, so we always listen when he does occasionally speak. He is quiet, easygoing, very mellow, and funny. He answers our questions and gives us great ideas for our projects, but mostly he just sits quietly shaking his head and laughing at our open table conversations. He'll quietly slip back to his office, thinking we won't notice him leave, and every time he returns, we can smell smoke. We ask him every single time what he's smoked back there, and every single time, his face turns bright red, almost as red as his hair as he gives up some lamebrain crazy answer. It's like clockwork, and we all look at each other grinning as we work on our projects. We can

17

smell what he's smoked. We really can, and we know what we smell. It's not cigarettes.

Kat, Mikey, and Annalee all sit at my table. Annalee is a cute, dark-haired thing who is usually very quiet, but in this class at this table, we all feel comfortable and talk openly, including her. Maybe it's the dark, quiet room or the relaxation of beveling leather to create anything that comes to mind with a very chilled teacher or the smell that encircles us from the teacher's office. I don't know…but we just talk about everything as we work at that table together, nothing off limits. Because of this, we all become good friends.

I have never once seen Annalee out front on the school sidewalk or in Shell Shack. She does spend a lot of time in the library and is even a student library helper during third hour. She's kind of a little goody two-shoes who stays away from the business out front, so I take some of my cigarette breaks in between classes behind the school with her instead of out front.

The school adopted an idea of putting a smoking area behind the school on school property by the catwalk. The catwalk is an enclosed hallway on the second floor used to get from the main building to the science building. They painted a thin yellow line on the concrete around a small area against the back of the school off to the side of the catwalk and now call it our new smoking area in hopes of allowing us to get a quick smoke and back to class on time. Annalee and I are sharing a cigarette out back when David and Zach walk up. I talk with them, and she just stands there listening and watching, not saying a word. The bell rings, there are the annoyed looks and twisting legs, and off to class we go.

Next time I attend crafts class, she questions me about David and Zach. She doesn't like them and reams me up and down about hanging out with those kind of people.

I'm now old enough to apply for a worker's permit, so I go around town filling out applications at every local restaurant, finally landing an interview with a dude they call Slick. Slick manages an IHOP (International House of Pancakes) in Wood River. He hires me!

David and his brother along with Zach and Kraig all have jobs there, so I am excited to start work.

My first day on the job, I walk in and am greeted by Annalee. She works here as the hostess. This is going to be fun! As usual, my friends and I minus Annalee sneak in the food storage room to pop acid and get high during work. Kraig and David are fired within the first week, and Zach quits soon after to work at Bacon's down the road for more money than he makes bussing tables at IHOP. Even though he's only fifteen, Zach's kind of on his own and needs the extra money.

Over the next few weeks, Annalee gets a good look at my friends and my life and as I really live it, not just me working on projects during my occasional visits to crafts class. I think she's shocked and a little disgusted with me. I don't really care. I like her, and she's a good friend, but I'm having too much fun with David and Zach to care about what Annalee thinks. Other than the dirty looks she throws my way when I walk to the back to get high, we have a blast working together.

Who knew that frill picks could fly so perfectly when blown through a straw? Frill picks are fancy little toothpicks with curly colorful strings on one end that are used to hold a sloppy sandwich together while serving. David's brother Jim is the main cook, and all the busboys always crack Annalee and the other girls up when we walk past the grill and shoot Jim's chef hat full of colorful frill picks. His chef's hat is a large puffy paper hat that rises about a foot off the top of his head, so if we shoot them just right, they perforate the top of his hat, and he doesn't even know it. Annalee tells us we shouldn't do that, that we might hit him in the eye, but we ignore her and make bets on how many we can shoot in his hat before he notices and removes them.

Frill pick torpedoes are best shot during rush hour. Jim is so busy behind the grills, ovens, and fryers making pancakes with smiley faces, frying bacon and eggs, heating up spaghetti dinners, sizzling steaks, and deep frying French fries trying to get everyone's orders out on time. He and his wife have a newborn baby, so he takes his job seriously. At fifteen, nothing in my life is serious right now. I do my job as best I can while high. I do my best to keep everyone laughing—that's what I'm good at. I like my life. I know how to have a good time.

Rush hour comes to an end, and Jim, completely exhausted, stops to take a breath and look around. We laugh at his hat that has about twenty frill picks dangling from all directions along the top of it, wiggling and threatening to fall as he turns his head to look back and forth from one of us to the other. It is pretty funny. Even Annalee laughs but then collects herself and throws us a stern *stop it* look. Customers walk through the door, and she turns to them, smiles, grabs a few menus, and seats them, throwing me a warning look over her shoulder.

Even though I'm just fifteen, Mom and Dad let me drive myself to work because they don't like my late hours. IHOP is open twenty-four hours seven days a week, and my parents are usually in bed by the time I get off work at 10:30 on weeknights and midnight on weekends. I drive an old green 1966 Plymouth Belvedere grandma car that I tricked out with hijacker shocks, cut off the wheel wells, and put on giant L70 tires with deep craters. It sits like a grasshopper. Sitting in the back seat is difficult. It's jacked up so high you have to push on the back of the front seat to not fall forward. Totally cool car!

Annalee is ten months older than I am and just recently got her driver's license. She shows up at work in her dad's new car. It's a beautiful 1971 deep red Plymouth GTX muscle car with a black race stripe running down each side. After work, I ask her if I can drive it. A quick "No!" with a dirty look and we're cruising around drinking a quart of beer as I settle for just a passenger ride. Well, I drank most of the beer—she only had a swallow or two. When you drive a car like this, and you sit at a stop sign waiting for the light to change with that powerful V-8 engine purring, rumbling, vibrating under your hood, just waiting for you to give it gas, and then someone pulls up beside you eyeing that beautiful car and revs their engine, you *have* to show them who's boss. You *have* to! That's what I do after work now. I ride around with Annalee in her dad's muscle car, and *no one* has beat us out of a stop light yet. We're always a couple car lengths ahead by the time we stop at the next light. Annalee just barely smiles as she stares ahead concentrating and waiting for the next light to turn green, and I'm hollering, ready to race again. We have fun, but she sure is quick to throw me a dirty look when I ask to drive it. I just want to race it one time, just once.

It's Friday night at IHOP, and rush hour should hit in about thirty minutes, so I slip in the back to pop a few extra pills to get me through the shift. Rush hour is when all the local bars close around 2 a.m. and all the hungry drunks come here, packing every table along with the waiting room and lining up outside sometimes for hours. It gets crazy.

Annalee and the other girls are out front filling water glasses with ice, wiping off menus, and wrapping silverware in napkins and throwing them in a tub. Jim is checking his supplies behind the grill and asks me to run upstairs to grab a few extra rolls of paper towels. I feel a little strange, but I blow it off and bolt up the stairs. The next thing I know, I'm looking up at Annalee, and she isn't happy. I'm confused. I shut my eyes and then look up again. She's still there, and I can tell by how fast her hands and her mouth are moving that she's yelling at me, but I still can't make out what she's saying. She's a foot above my face but sounds miles away. My senses slowly come back, and I hear, *"I told you to stop that stuff! You're gonna kill yourself! What do you think you're doing? Stop hanging out with those people or you're gonna die!"*

All senses are back and functioning. I jump up and head to the stairs, patting Annalee on top of the head and telling her she's cute when she's mad as I walk past her. I completely ignore her cries—we have work to do. No time for yelling. Honestly, I don't want to hear what she has to say. I don't want to hear that crap. I like my friends. I'm having fun.

Another school year comes and goes. Annalee sideswipes a stop sign in front of East Alton, a hit-and-run with her dad's car, so he sells it before I get the chance to race it. She'd have eventually let me race it. I know because I wasn't planning on giving up.

What a rough night at work. We were swamped with hungry drunks from one until five in the morning. I normally get off at six, but with the longer than usual rush, I stayed to help clean up and didn't get to leave until now — it's 7 a.m. I'm exhausted and drenched in sweat and grease from working in the galley. Because of the massive bar rush, I had to help Jim keep up with food orders along with helping bus tables, and I'm covered in a layer of grease and smell like an old, cold French fry. Grease coats my hair, my clothes, my skin, and my paper hat full of frill picks that I throw in the trash on my way out the door. I can't get away from the smell as it fills my lungs with every breath even as I walk outside to my car. I hate to get in my car smelling like this. I'll have to clean the smell out later. I need a shower and some sleep.

Climbing in my old jalopy, I light a cigarette and take a long, slow drag as I drop the shift down and take off. Cigarette smoke temporarily hides the grease stench and makes me feel a little better. When I pull into my driveway, I can hear Mom and Dad arguing in the living room from my car. I pull a couple bennies out of my pocket and stare at them. I consider popping them, backing out, and heading somewhere for the day so I don't have to go in and face them or listen to them argue. It bothers me—I really don't want to go inside.

Mom and Dad's produce market burned down a while back, and Mom, who usually doesn't argue, is starting to take up for herself. They both still have other jobs working for a grocery store. It's bad around here, really bad, and it seems to be getting worse. Sitting in the car listening to them, I decide to head on in anyway, so I push the bennies deep into my pocket, finish my cigarette, kill the engine, walk in quietly, and head straight downstairs to my sanctuary, falling into bed as they continue to fight. They didn't even notice me, and that was my plan. I want to sleep, but they're too loud. It's early morning, and they're already this heated. What will the rest of the day bring?

I've always viewed my dad as a vile man. We've never been close. His handling of David and me crashing the car surprised me. I just knew he was going to kill me that night, but he was actually pretty civil about it, one of the only times I can remember him being civil about anything. Over the years, I've watched him treat Mom bad, but she always just took it. I'm not used to her standing up to him. Mom isn't usually the type to argue. She's always upbeat, positive, and encouraging and Dad's the opposite. Everything seems to be changing, and I'm not sure where I fit in, what I should do, or how I should react to these changes.

I can't sleep through their arguing, and I need to wash off the smell of pancake batter and bacon grease, but I'm not about to go upstairs to shower while they're still arguing. Sitting at the edge of my bed, I wait, hoping one of them will leave or at least shut up. I just want to sleep. Clueless on how to make this better, I decide there's nothing I can do and lie back down, hoping my exhaustion will be stronger than the sound of their voices. Then something on the bookshelf beside the bed catches my eye.

Lying on the bookshelf in plain view right next to my stash box is a Bible. I haven't seen that Bible in years. How did it get there? Mom and Dad's voices are slowly silenced as my thoughts pull me back to when I was nine years old.

My grandmother, whom I love dearly, gave me a Bible the day I was baptized. I sure would like to eat one of her amazing breakfasts and pass out in her quiet house right now. Reaching over to pick up the Bible, I think about Grandma, her cooking, and our many talks. She gave me a simple six-inch by nine-inch black leather King James Bible with a copper zipper. Listening to the clicking sound of the zipper, I slowly open it to expose the pages inside. It's been years since I've seen this, held this, opened this Bible. I read her inscription on the first page: "From Grandma Ruby. 1969."

23

Gazing at Grandma's inscription, I'm immediately taken back in time to the church I was raised in, saved in, baptized and filled with the Holy Spirit in all by the time I was nine years old. My uncle was our pastor and Grandma, our family's solid rock, a devout servant to the church and the Lord. Church was my life from back then all the way until eighth grade. That's when my uncle died. That's when Mom and Dad quit going to church. That's when I quit going. Mom and Dad said they quit because they had to take care of the produce market on Sundays, but who knows. So much has changed in the last few years, and it just keeps changing.

Grandma never stopped going to church, and she still calls me every Saturday night without fail asking me to go to church with her on Sunday morning. Even though right now God is the furthest thing from my mind, I sometimes concede and go just to make her happy. Besides, I get to enjoy the *best* breakfast in the world on those Sunday mornings. Every Sunday that I attend service with Grandma, she invites me over before church for a fantastic breakfast she's prepared for me with all the biscuits and gravy, bacon and eggs, French toast and grits I can eat. Plus, eating this huge breakfast always gives me a great excuse to leave church early — it's perfect! Halfway through the service, I look over at Grandma, pat my bloated belly and whisper to her, "I ate too much, Grandma. I can't stay any longer."

She gives me a disappointed look, yet I know she's pleased I enjoy her cooking so much that I eat to the point of getting sick. Truth? I don't know if it's even possible to eat myself sick. I can seriously put away some food. I don't really need to leave. It's just that church makes me feel uncomfortable, plus I need a cigarette. This excuse works, so I keep using it. Leaning over, I place the Bible back on the shelf and, with a deep sigh, lie down on my bed in my grease-soaked clothes and fall into a deep, relaxed, and peaceful sleep.

I wake up around four in the afternoon and find myself home alone. Mom and Dad are gone, and Sherri and Tim are at Grandma's — just another typical summer day. Showering off the grease, I get dressed and head down to Kevin's house, a buddy of mine who lives a block down the street. We met about a year ago. Even though we only live a block from each other, the dividing school district line separates us, so he and everyone on his side of the line attends Wood River High School, and those on my side of the line go to Roxana High School.

Kevin is different from any of my other friends. He's clean-cut, has short hair, and dresses more like he's going to college at Harvard or Yale than Wood River High School. He's polite and well-spoken, so of course Mom loves him. She wouldn't if she really knew him. What she doesn't realize is that Kevin is one of the biggest drug dealers in the area. There's not a time I go to Kevin's that I can't get whatever drug I want—acid, coke, speed, benzedrine, dexedrine, biphetamine. He has it all. He also deals in pot, a *lot* of pot! I don't like smoking weed, so I seldom do—except when I go to Kevin's. This summer, I have spent hours hanging out at Kevin's popping pills, dropping acid, and smoking weed. What else is there to do?

Kevin asks me if I want to take a road trip with him. He tells me it's a four-day trip to the Florida Keys. Of course, I want to go! The Florida Keys! Isn't this what summer's about? I call off work, and we head south.

Kevin has a shipment to pick up in the Keys, and he needs someone trustworthy to ride along. I feel privileged he trusts me. As we pass the Gateway Arch heading south down highway 55 through St. Louis, Kevin lights a doobie, and we begin to talk. He tells me stuff I kind of already know from just living in this area, but I didn't really understand it all until now. Apparently, Kevin is the youngest runner for an organization called "The Company." This organization employs around 200 people. They have their own trucking company and their own airplanes along with a few small airports. Their business? Running drugs, lots and lots of drugs. Their headquarters are in my hometown.

The people running The Company are local businessmen, one of them a bank president. They have kids I go to school with, which explains the market in front of school. Drugs are very accessible at my school and, I'm finding out, much more accessible at Roxana High School than any other area school. The reason for this run is that the shipment is small but very valuable, and they feel that sending a plane would be an unnecessary risk. The more I listen and learn, the more nervous I become.

As we approach the Florida Keys, I sit up straight, staring forward down the highway. Unbelievably, the land disappears, and before I know it, all I see is the vast, beautiful blue ocean waters with a highway heading out to what looks like…nothing. I'm used to seeing land on the other side of a bridge, and as I push myself up from my seat straining my eyes to see, I can't see the other side. This highway, this bridge is headed right into the ocean with no land in sight. Feeling a little uneasy yet exhilarated from this phenomenal view, I look side to side at nothing but ocean! It feels like we're skimming across the water's surface. Then I see it on the horizon. Thank God! Land!

Soon after driving onto dry land and then exiting the highway, we turn onto a dirt path, kicking up a trail of dust before pulling up to a run-down clapboard house next to a huge warehouse. Two armed Cubans immediately walk out of the house and wave us toward the warehouse as large garage doors open, and Kevin drives inside without hesitation. Two more Cubans are waiting inside, which unnerves me, and I look over at Kevin, who is completely calm and confident. He's done this before, but I haven't. I'll admit that I'm a little scared.

Staring at Kevin and trying not to make eye contact with the Cubans, I'm surprised when he opens his car door and gets out. With no smiles, the Cubans look from Kevin to me, and I reluctantly and awkwardly follow Kevin's lead. After they frisk us and search our car, they're satisfied we're clean.

Motioning us to follow, we are surrounded and escorted further into the warehouse into a room located in the back corner. Upon entry, I see a table with no chairs in the center of the room, and my knees almost give out when I look around to all four corners of the room. In each corner, a Cuban guard stands at attention, watching our every move, an assault weapon slung over his shoulder. Struggling to keep my cool and not throw up, my brain spins this scenario in my head, trying to warn me. I'm in the Florida Keys, off the main road and down some dirt path, in an old crappy warehouse surrounded by eight armed Cubans. I am literally going to puke.

A ninth armed man walks in, tossing a book on the table. Kevin picks it up, thumbs through the pages, and pulls out a single sheet. On this sheet of paper are one hundred divided squares, each with a small cartoon character printed on it. In the middle of each little cartoon character is a tiny green dot. I watch in amazement as I roll this around in my mind. One hundred little cartoon characters per page. One little green dot in the center of each, which means each page contains one hundred hits of Mr. Natural, the latest strain of LSD.

I've been around enough to know about it and have even tried a few different strains—purple microdot, orange sunshine, and now Mr. Natural. Watching Kevin flip through the book, counting pages, I silently count with him. One hundred separate pages of cartoon characters have been slipped into every few pages of this book! I may not get good grades in math class, but it's not because I don't know math, it's because I don't attend class. That's *ten thousand* hits of acid! It sells for five dollars a hit back home. Do you realize how much this book is worth?

Kevin looks up at the guy who brought in the book and tosses him the car keys, saying, "In the trunk under the spare."

Three of the guards walk back to our car and return with an envelope full of one-hundred-dollar bills while the other six stare at Kevin and me. Through all of this, Kevin seems fine while I continuously wipe my sweaty hands on the sides of my shorts. I'm ready to leave—now. The guy who brought in the book slowly counts the money. When he's done, he starts all over again, slowly counting each one-hundred-dollar bill. I watch and count each one with him. This envelope contains one hundred, one-hundred-dollar bills. That's only one dollar a hit for what I know will sell for five dollars a hit back home. My mind is spinning, thinking, analyzing, figuring, and I realize just how profitable this drug dealing can be.

Back at the car, I watch Kevin toss this $50,000 book into a gym bag along with five other school books—algebra, history, economics, statistics and English—and a change of gym clothes. Since we partied a little on the drive down from Illinois, we thoroughly clean out our car, making sure there are no roach clips, roaches, or stray pills lying on the seats or floorboards before leaving the warehouse. We check our wallets and our pockets, and I down my last few bennies. This way, if we get pulled over, the cops will have no reason to search us. If they do open the trunk, all they'll find is a gym bag with textbooks, gym clothes, and our overnight clothes. For an added touch, we stop along the coastal waters and throw a couple pairs of ocean-soaked swimming trunks in the backseat. I am glad to be back in the car and out of that warehouse.

Heading north across the never-ending floating bridge toward home, I ask a few questions, and Kevin fills me in on The Company and those involved. I'm overwhelmed by his answers and quit asking questions. This is way more information than I care to know, and the scary thing is, I know all these people. For years, I've known these people, from the head honchos to the runners to their hit man. Oh man, I know them all! I arrive home changed forever.

David, Zach, and I pile into my green grasshopper jalopy and drive aimlessly around, ending up in Bethalto. I keep a leather slapjack with a lead inner club under my car seat. I'm not a violent person—I carry it so that if someone starts something with me, I can protect myself. Pulling into a convenience store, we encounter a kid about our age. We've had a little to drink and smoked a bit, and Zach yells something at this kid from the backseat window. The kid didn't like what he heard, and trying to act tough, he turns to David, who is in the passenger seat, and insults him. In an instant, David grabs my slapjack, jumps out of the car, and coldcocks this kid across the face. I don't like fights and avoid conflicts at all costs, so I stay in the car and watch wide-eyed and open-mouthed. As the kid fights back, Zach jumps out, grabs him, and throws him head first against the brick wall of the store. The kid falls to the ground, and David and Zach quickly jump back into the car. I peel out, feeling the need to get out of Bethalto, fast. This surprises me, but at the same time, nothing surprises me anymore.

Back at Shell Shack, I'm in the bathroom taking a leak when I hear a commotion out front. It sounds like tables and chairs being knocked over. Then David and Zach start yelling. Finishing quickly, I step out of the bathroom and see the kid from Bethalto along with a guy who's twice our age. I guess I should have thought twice about parking my lime green grasshopper directly out front. This guy is ticked. He's hollering, yelling and throwing chairs and tables aside trying to get at David and Zach.

David reaches into his pants pocket and pulls out a knife as this guy angrily clears a path toward him. He grabs David's knife, trying to disarm him, and winds up slicing his own palm open. David didn't want to cut him. David didn't try to cut him. Nevertheless, blood pours from his hand, and David and I seize the opportunity to bolt out the front door. Two blocks down the road, Roxana police officer Anders pulls us over and carts us to the police station. Zach stays at Shell Shack and is picked up by another officer, but en route to the police station, he kicks out the back window of the police car and escapes. After a pretty good chase, he's apprehended again and delivered to the police station in handcuffs. David, Zach, and I along with the kid and his friend are all at the police station pointing and yelling at each other while the police try to figure it all out. The older guy jabs his finger toward us, screaming at the police that he wants to press assault charges against the three of us. A ray of hope surges through me as I listen to the police explain to the this guy, "You went into a high school hangout after some sixteen-year-old kids. You better hope *their* parents don't press assault charges against *you!*"

Our parents and Zach's guardians are called to pick us up. Mom and Dad are not happy with me. I never see that Bethalto kid again.

It's my first year of high school, my sophomore year, and finally, even though I've already been driving for months, I will get my official legal driver's license. To get my license, I have to pass at least five classes this semester. I hate PE but attend because it's an easy grade. I want my license.

I've been having some issues with one of the jocks in PE class. At Roxana, we are classified as belonging to one of three categories. Jocks are the burr-headed kids that play sports and think they're something. Not all of them but most of them are cocky and pretty much stupid. They push people around just because they can and always get away with it because if they're caught and get in trouble, they can't play sports, so this makes teachers look the other way when they act up. Nobody wants to lose a game. They are for the most part the bullies of the school. Then there are the freaks—that would be me. These are the kids with long hair who are out front buying and selling drugs. For the most part, they keep to themselves and only become violent when pushed. At that point, they will band together to protect each other. I mean, how many people do you know that will smoke a joint then be mean to someone? They might steal someone's Ding-Dong off the lunch table, but they don't usually get physical with anyone. Some of the freaks are pretty smart, and some we have to take care of. The fruits are the smart kids. They attend school regularly and actually listen and make good grades. They are placed mostly in classes without the other two groups, therefore they only associate with each other. They keep busy doing homework and participating in school plays and other activities I know nothing about. I don't pay much attention to them. They're harmless and leave me alone, so I do the same with them.

Even though these last few years I have wreaked havoc, hollered, yelled, and cussed people out, I am not a violent person. I have never ever assaulted anyone and don't plan on doing so. The incident in Bethalto bothers me sometimes when I think of it. I just want to have fun. Now Zach, he doesn't think twice about hitting someone for looking at him cross-eyed, and he always manages to walk away without a scratch. Not me. I will do anything to avoid physical confrontations.

There's a jock named Dennis who's been trying to start something with me for a while. I do my best to avoid him, but he's in my PE class, and I need this grade. He's mean, ignorant, and a fool. I mind my own business in PE but also try to be aware of where he is to be prepared for his daily shoves. I hate to be caught off guard. It's never good.

PE is out on the football field today, and Dennis is standing about fifteen feet off to my left side, repeatedly tossing a football up in the air. I turn my head the other way to see who tripped over a hurdle running track, and Dennis throws his football as hard as he can, nailing me right in the crotch. In a split second, I'm nauseous and on my knees in excruciating pain. My brain plots my revenge, running through a million ways I'm going to make this guy disappear. Fighting to stay on my knees, I'm dizzy and trying to catch my breath and not puke in front of the entire PE class while he and his cronies laugh at me. This guy will pay. The bell rings, and everyone runs toward the school while I pick myself up and limp back to the locker room again, saying and doing nothing to him as always. This guy will pay? Only in my dreams. He's the quarterback on the football team. Yes, he can throw a football, but what a moron.

My only class with Dennis is PE, but now because I didn't confront him on the football field or in the locker room, he makes it a point to find me in between classes. He not only continuously shoves me but also hits me in the back of the head. I've become his main target. He uses me to get laughs from his punk friends. He's a typical jerk jock, and I try to ignore him and blow it off. I keep hoping he'll just get bored and stop until one day I'm walking up the concrete steps on the east side of the school, and he comes around the corner, sees me, and sprints up the steps behind me, provoking me with insults as I continue forward, ignoring him. When I step onto the landing, he knocks me forward with a hard shove.

Reflexes take over, and I turn and shove him right back full force, throwing him off balance. Standing at the top of the concrete steps, I watch as he teeters backward, fighting gravity and struggling to keep from falling head first down the stairs. Looking into his eyes, I see fear. He looks into my eyes and sees months of built-up hate, revulsion, and loathing for him. As I glare at him for that split second, it runs through my mind, *This guy's going to die.* Quickly reaching out, I grab the front of his shirt mid-fall before he hits the steps. Out of panic trying to save himself, he grips my arm. Realizing that at this very moment, I have complete control, I stare at him intensely as I hold him dangling over the steps. I can let go and walk away, letting him fall back on his head, or pull him up to safety. Part of me is yelling, "Just let the fool go! Let him fall!"

I jerk him up and shove him against the wall on the landing, glaring at him as I lean down so close our noses almost touch. I have a lot to say, but I can't seem to get a word out. Shaking my head, I release him roughly and walk away. Today, we both learned what I'm capable of. He never harasses or even speaks to me again.

Thanksgiving isn't full of thanks this year. Mom and Dad continually become more toxic and more argumentative, and I'm starting to fear for her safety. Mom has been a solid rock in my life. She is always upbeat and happy, but lately, she's just beat. Dad, he's an ass, plain and simple. He's an ass to me, to my little sister, to my little brother, and especially to Mom. Everything, literally everything, is Mom's fault, from the gutters full of leaves to the bathroom drain that needs cleaned to the grass growing in our yard. Mom tries her best to make up for Dad's asinine behavior, but it doesn't stop the pain he causes us while in his presence. The older I get, the more I realize just how strong my mother is to remain so loving, so attentive, so understanding and kind—not only to the three of us, but also to Dad—under such horrendous treatment from him. This makes me despise him even more.

Coming home from work Thanksgiving weekend, I walk in to Dad verbally berating and abusing Mom again. I can't take anymore. As always, I quietly sneak in, heading straight downstairs to my room. Growing angrier by the minute, I pace back and forth, hating that I do nothing yet not knowing what to do. Anger, fear, resentment, and humiliation surge through me as I pace. Then I notice they've stopped. Dad's left the house. I charge up the steps and plead to Mom, "You *have* to get away from him, Mom! He's going to hurt you!"

Waiting for Mom to reprimand my attitude, I'm surprised when she reaches out, touches my arm, and in a calm, confident voice says, "Hopefully he will be the one who leaves. That would make it easier."

Turning from me, she walks through the kitchen into the laundry room and takes a load of laundry out of the washer and places it into the dryer as if nothing happened. Standing there dumbfounded, I watch her for a second then shrug my shoulders and decide to adopt her attitude and go about my day.

Mom and Dad don't slow down and are at it daily. It's Christmas Eve. Every Christmas Eve, Grandma spends the night with us so we can all spend Christmas morning together. We love having her around. Mom and Dad act more normal in her presence. It's 5 p.m., and Dad leaves to pick Grandma up while Mom is busy with last-minute Christmas stuff. Grandma calls around six-thirty asking if we've forgotten her. "Absolutely not!" Mom tells her, wondering where Dad is.

While on the phone, she turns to ask Sherri, Tim, and me if we've heard from Dad. No, none of us have. We wait. Seven o'clock rolls around, and still no Dad. We wait a while longer, then Mom sends me over to pick Grandma up.

Dad doesn't come home Christmas Eve. Dad doesn't come home Christmas morning. Dad doesn't come home for Christmas dinner. Dad doesn't come home the day after Christmas or the day after the day after Christmas. Dad never returns home again. He walked out of our lives, just like that, on Christmas Eve. No good-byes, no reasons, no I'm sorry, no I love you and it's not your fault. Nothing. My little sister and brother are devastated, and I watch Mom be strong for them. Me? I am relieved and vow to myself to take care of all of them. I feel this will be easier without his presence. It's one less person to protect them from.

Now Steve is trying to start fights with me at school. He's not as mean as Dennis but equally annoying. He likes to fight and is known to taunt people until he gets his fight. I'm his latest target. I try ignoring him and hoping he'll move on because again, I don't want to fight. I don't want to fight him. I don't want to fight anyone. I don't like to fight.

I'm walking to the front of the school to leave when Steve walks up behind me and shoves me into the heavy glass doors. I've had it. I'm jacked up on speed, and my reflexes take over. As I turn to face him, I swing my hand around as hard as I can, hoping to make contact somewhere, and I do. The side of my hand hits hard on the front of his neck. I just karate chopped this guy in the throat, full strength. I didn't plan it. He provoked me. I stand looking down on him as he grabs his throat. He's turning red, and I'm wondering if he can breathe. I don't want to just walk away if he's really hurt, so I continue to stand and watch him, wondering if I should go get help. Tears well up in his eyes, and when he can breathe again, he starts to cry like a little girl. I feel powerful at this moment, realizing that no one will ever step on me or bother me again if I just start taking up for myself.

New life rule—I won't start a fight, but if I'm forced into confrontations, I will do what I have to do. Steve never even looks at me again.

Mr. Moretti, the high school assistant principal, doesn't appreciate my new persona, but I do. I'm halfway through my junior year, and no one has bullied me this year. *No one!* Zach and I have raised hell in school and outside of school. We've literally terrorized the staff to the point a couple of them quit.

Moretti calls me into his office, shuts the door, and looks up at me. "I've had it with you, punk!" he tells me. "Just you and me, right here! You think you're so bad! Let's go for it!"

He's serious. This educated adult man who used to be a golden glove boxer back in his day wants to fight me? Unreal! I don't know what to do, so I just stand there shocked. I stare down at him, thinking, *You're just another dumb jock. This wouldn't be an issue if I were a jock.*

He continues, "Get out of this school and don't ever come back!"

I don't want to fight him. So I turn around and walk out of Roxana High School, and I don't ever go back. I find out that David and Zach had a very similar conversation with him that day. Just like that, our high school days are over.

Chapter 3
Business Ventures

Mom introduces me to Wayne, a man she's been dating for a while. I don't know what to think of him, but Mom seems cheerful again. It's been years since I've seen her happy. Wayne is so different from Dad. He appears to be very attentive to Mom and treats Sherri and Tim well. They deserve that. I think she's in love with him, and to see her so content, that's all that matters to me.

Since I'm not in school anymore, Mom suggests I apply at the grocery chain where she and Wayne work. Dad used to work there too but quit soon after he left us. They hire me, and I drive straight to IHOP to put in my two-week notice. I'm a little excited because now that I can work full time, I'll bring in more money, and Mom needs help feeding all of us with Dad gone. It'll be nice to make some money without being covered in grease and frill picks.

Starting as a stock clerk, my job is to keep the shelves stocked. It's rigorous work but it keeps me occupied, and I like it. The money's great and so is the view as I notice the new girl that just got hired bagging groceries. Normally, I take a few cases of product on a two-wheeler out of the storage room, but today I find myself flexing my muscles to impress this new girl.

I carry one case at a time propped up on my shoulder and head straight up the aisle in front of the checkouts where she's working. She seems extremely shy, almost scared and unsure of herself, as she's bagging groceries for a mouthy old lady. First day on the job is never fun. This lady is giving her an earful as she nervously tries to figure out how to pack her items.

Setting the case down, I lean over and whisper, "Here, let me help."

She stares up at me with a relieved look while I finish bagging the woman's groceries and send her on her way. "The first day is always the worst," I tell her.

I explain the best way to bag groceries, and she laughs, saying, "Who would have thought bagging groceries could be so complicated?"

"It gets easier, I promise. By the way, I'm Darwyn. What's your name?"

Through a slight grin, she reminds me, "You already know my name. It's Ann. You asked earlier this morning when I walked in the door."

"Oh yeah. Okay, you got me. Yes, I did ask, and it's nice to meet you again, Ann Grace Sanders"

"Hey, that's not fair! I don't know your middle name," she says, laughing.

"And you're not going to, either!" I tell her over my shoulder as I walk back to the stockroom. No way am I going to tell her my middle name is Earl.

Ann is sixteen and very tiny, maybe only 5'5" with long brown hair hanging down to her butt. She has beautiful brown eyes above her high Cherokee cheekbones. She's very cute!

I do my best to take breaks when she does and eventually get enough nerve to ask her to grab a bite to eat after work. She flat out refuses. Not letting that stop me, I continue talking with her during breaks trying to win her over. I can feel us getting closer and becoming more than just friends, but she still won't go out with me. I keep asking her to no avail. This intrigues me!

Tuesday night, I notice Ann taking a break, so I take mine as well. Surprisingly, she asks, "What are you doing Sunday?"

Looking down at her with raised eyebrows and a crooked grin, I think to myself, *I'll be passed out Sunday morning after partying all of Saturday night, and I'll wake up just in time for tae kwon do practice at five.*

But she has such a sweet smile, so I tilt my head and say quizzically, "Nothing. Why?"

I'm feeling proud of myself. *Yes! I'm in! I'm finally in!*

Without batting an eye, she asks, "Would you like to go to church with me?"

Wait a second. This isn't quite what I had in mind, but I do see it as a way in, so I jump on it and agree to go to church with her.

Since we've made plans for Sunday, Ann is more open with me during breaks. I learn she's the daughter of an Assembly of God pastor, and she can't date anyone without her parent's approval. So this Sunday, I am attending an Assembly of God church service to suck up to the pastor and his wife, hoping I'll be allowed to date their daughter.

Up to this point in my life, I have never had a steady relationship with a girl. Don't get me wrong, I've had girls, many girls, girls I've hooked up with at parties. Ann's different. She's a nice girl.

Knowing how much Grandma worries about me, when I listen to Ann tell me all this, I'm thinking of just how happy Grandma's going to be. I want this girl—she's beautiful and kind and comes from a nice family. She's perfect for me, and God knows I need someone good in my life.

Sunday morning, I fall into an old routine I remember well. I shower, shave, comb my hair, and put on my polyester pants and button-up shirt. I look just like the good boy I was raised to be. My new routine—I pop a couple bennies, hide my cigarettes in the glove compartment of the car, and throw out my best smile and polite manners to win over Ann's parents so we can date. It works! I'm in!

The longer Ann and I date, the more I find myself spending less time with my friends. Ann grounds me, and that's a good thing. I still pop speed daily, but now I don't use it to get high and act a fool. I use to maintain my energy level. I can't function without them. I have a job and a woman now. I need the energy speed gives me to work and make enough money to take Ann out and hopefully move out on my own, but mostly to buy more speed. Ann doesn't use drugs, so I never mention or talk about drugs with her. It's best she doesn't know.

Mom and Wayne soon marry, and we all move a few blocks away into a new home. Ann and I have been dating for months now, so I ask her to marry me, and she accepts. The wedding is set for February, one month after she graduates high school and one week after she turns seventeen. I'm nineteen. I really love this girl. I've never been in love before. Since she's so young, her parents have to sign court documents for her to legally get married, and they're okay with that. Her mom is scared to death she's going to get pregnant. The one thing Pentecostals don't do is have sex or get pregnant before marriage. Plus, it will just make things easier—with our incomes combined, we can afford our own place.

The wedding is a traditional wedding in her family's church. I really didn't have much to do with it other than show up and say "I do" when instructed. Her sister and mom along with my grandma took care of all the arrangements. Ann is absolutely stunning in the hand-stitched wedding gown Grandma sewed for her. Watching this beautiful woman walk down the aisle toward me, I start getting nervous. *What am I doing? I can't be the man a woman like Ann needs me to be! I can't possibly be the man for her!*

I watch Ann, my bride, walk down the aisle to me, and she has no clue who or what I am. I've become exceptionally good at hiding my addictions from the ones I'm closest to, and I feel guilty for marrying this woman knowing I can never properly take care of her.

Soon after the wedding, the grocery store we work at closes. Ann and I are married and living in an apartment, and now neither of us has a job. I didn't see this coming. We search for other jobs, and Ann lands a department store clerk position. Me, I find a job selling Kirby vacuum cleaners. I hit up my friends and family and quickly learn that I am quite good at this. I pull in $28,000 my first year!

Late one evening, I get a call. "Hullo?"

"Hey! Did you hear?"

"Hear what?"

"The DEA busted Kevin last night. It's all in *The Telegraph*."

> *The largest drug smuggling operation in this country's history was taken down yesterday. Ricky Thorp was head of The Company, said to be more profitable than General Motors. Headquartered in the heartland outside St. Louis, Missouri, The Company, organized in 1976,*

grew into an enterprise with about 250 employees. Separate executive branches were set up to buy airports, lease of warehouses, and give polygraph tests to prospective employees. Thorp put in place a $2,000,000 bail fund. In just two years, The Company had acquired thirty-three airplanes, three airports, and warehouses stretching over seven states. The FBI states that The Company's profits were about $48,000,000. More than a hundred of its employees have been arrested. Thorp has eluded capture, and his whereabouts are unknown.

It was a long way from Wood River, Illinois where Thorp grew up. For thirty years, Thorp's uncle, Larry, sixty-two, had cut hair at Thorp's Barber Shop in Wood River, a town of 12,449 that lies in a secluded nook of the Mississippi River.

In the high school yearbook, Ricky Thorp's nickname was "Road Rocket." His pastime was "cars and girls." His ambition was to "become a playboy." He was a good enough wrestler to go to the state finals his senior year in 1965. He hung around with other guys on the wrestling team—James Dugan, Jim Stassi, and Ryland Dare.

"It shocked everybody because these kids grew up in good middle-class American homes and were athletes," Larry Thorp said. "Ricky was just like my own boys. He went to First Baptist Church and enjoyed family picnics."

My friend Kevin is one of the one hundred arrested during the sweep while Thorp, their ringleader, got away. I'm worried. Where will I buy my drugs?

Zach turns eighteen and receives almost $20,000 from an insurance policy from his mom's death. Ten years ago, long before I knew him, she was in a head-on collision with a diesel truck at the top of the middle levee out on highway 111 in South Roxana. She was a passenger, and the driver was drunk. Zach buys a new car, a car stereo, pays a deposit and rent on a trailer, and gets new furniture and a brand-new Kirby vacuum cleaner from me.

After tae kwon do class, I stop by to see Zach's new place. David and a bunch of the old gang are there along with people I've never met. Zach's home is now the party place, the place to go and see everyone. With the daily traffic in and out of his trailer, the vacuum I sold him is perfect for keeping his shag carpets clean. He doesn't have a job and just parties 24/7, living off his insurance money, but after a year, his money runs out. He picks up a job and moves into a dirty basement apartment next to Ken and Joe's tavern that he calls Heartbreak Hotel.

For the next two years, I continue selling vacuums, making almost thirty grand a year, but as it turns out, you can only sell so many vacuums in one area. After a few good years of saturating the playing field, along with a declining economy, I am forced to look for other work.

Mom calls with an idea. "Hey, what do you think of opening a video store?"

"What's a video store?" I question.

She explains, "I went into a video store that opened about a month ago in St. Louis, and the place was so packed I had a hard time looking around."

She goes on to explain, "They sell video cassette recorders that you hook up to your TV to watch movies in your own home!"

She tells me this as if I have been living under a rock or something. Video recorders have been out for a while, but few people own them, and I didn't know they had stores.

"This store rents and sells VCRs and has a huge selection of movies on tape. You have to go check it out, Darwyn!" she says excitedly.

"Why?"

"Because you have to make a living, don't you? This video thing, I think it's going to take off!"

I think about it and realize it really could be a good idea. Right now, there are no video stores in the Metro East area, on the Illinois side of the river where I live. I tell Mom, "Okay. Let's do it!"

Mom and I talk about it and decide she will put up fifteen thousand dollars, and I will do all the work. We rent a little building at the corner of 111 and Edwardsville Road in Wood River, Illinois. On our first day of business, our store, Fantasy Video World, has only three VCRs, forty movies, and no people. On day two, we have a handful of kids who come in thinking we are a video arcade, and I have to tell them we aren't, but I ask them to tell their parents to stop in. Few people around here even know what a VCR or VHS is. I'm a little concerned, thinking this is going to bomb quickly, and my stepdad's going to kill Mom for spending thousands on this place. He told her right from the beginning not to do it, that it would fail! I have to make this work!

After closing up the store on the second failed day, I visit some local police officers and firefighters I know and give them coupons for six months' worth of free membership along with six months of free movie rentals with a purchase of a VCR. Since no one knows how to hook up the VCRs to their TVs I advertise free installation.

The third day of business, I'm traveling to my new customers' homes to install VCRs and show them how to work their new equipment. Overnight, business booms, and I'm selling up to twenty VCRs a day! We are the only game in town, and now I can't keep up. I hire Dave and Mikey. Dave and I met selling Kirby vacuums together and quickly became good friends, so I know he'll be a good employee. Mikey is a friend from high school who's great with people. He'll be good too.

By the end of the week, we double our movie selections, and we quadruple them the second week. The end of the year rolls around, and we now have over three thousand movie titles and a full line of VCRs and TVs.

Business grows rapidly, so the following year, we open two more stores. Mom and I now own and operate three stores—the original in Wood River, one in Granite City, and one in Godfrey, all within a thirty-minute drive from each other. Growing fast, we quickly become the number-one Quasar Panasonic dealer in the St. Louis metro area. We're selling entire lines of video equipment, VCRs, VHS, TVs, cameras, and recording equipment. Everyone, from experienced videographers to an average grandma wanting to film her grandchildren, is interested in this new technology. Who doesn't want to watch a movie in the privacy of their own home at their convenience? This technology is changing everyone's lives, especially mine. To keep up with my busy life, I now pop twenty bennies a day.

Zach purchased a VCR a year or so ago, and I usually see him on weekends when he stops by to rent a movie. His grandfather is retired from a local union and managed to get Zach into the same local. He's now working steady, moved out of Heartbreak Hotel, and making a decent living. David married, and I don't see him much, but he seems to be doing fine. Imagine that…three juvenile delinquents expelled from school, all working and making good money. Two of us are married, but Zach, I can't imagine him ever getting married.

Fantasy Video World quickly becomes number one in our area, mainly because we are the only distributor of adult films within a thirty-mile radius. Sectioning off a small area in the back of each store for these movies, we buy, rent, and sell hundreds of adult films a month. They quickly become the bulk of our profits. Charging twenty-five dollars a year for membership, we also charge five dollars a day for movie rentals, and people are happy to pay. The only other alternative for adult movies in this area is the Cameo movie theater in Alton. The Cameo shows XXX movies on Fridays, but not many people want to sit on those upholstered seats that smell like smoke and urine after a Friday night porn flick.

It doesn't take long before we have the attention of VCX, VCA, and other companies who manufacture and distribute adult films. I get a call from one of my distributors informing me that we are not only number one in the area but number one in southern Illinois. He then invites me to an adult movie convention in Chicago. Everyone involved in the adult film industry will be there. This show is for the owners of video stores so the adult film companies can sell their latest releases and promote their newest stars. Sure, I'll be there! I RSVP for Dave, who is now one of my store managers, and me. The cost is fifty dollars to attend, but because of our high rental and sales, we get in free.

I love Chicago, but I'm excited to attend this convention even more than visiting the city. From the time we walk in, we are having a blast, meeting porn stars and viewing their latest releases. Rob, the representative of VCX, asks to meet with us and gives us a special thank you for our success. Because we are the number-one purchaser of their films in southern Illinois, we are VIP guests.

"Meet John Holmes." Rob introduces us to a *huge* guy who stands about 6'7". I haven't had to look up to anyone since I turned fourteen.

I'm thinking, *Holy crap! This is the king of porn himself!*

Looking down at me with hollow eyes and smiling slightly, he quietly asks, "What are you guys doing tonight?"

Dave speaks up with unashamed enthusiasm, "Looking for a party!"

John looks to Rob, and speaking in a monotone voice, he says, "Great! Rob, give them the address and pass code."

John turns away to talk to a stunning, scantily clad blonde-haired beauty. Rob hands me a business card with an address and pass code printed on it. Sliding it deep into my back pocket, I wander around wide-eyed and in awe, drinking, partying, and popping different colored pills while porn stars entice me to stop at their booths, view their videos, and buy their films. They are very convincing.

Later that night, Dave and I use the card to get into the party, and within minutes, we are introduced to the biggest in the business — Seca, Vanessa Williams, Marilyn Chambers, Tracy Wards, Ron Jeremy. All the kings and queens of the porn industry are here. I'm attracted to and spend a long time with a cute little blonde, Shauna Grant. To me, Shauna just doesn't seem like she belongs here. We sit and talk a long time, and I find her extremely timid and shy. She seems sad — nothing like she appears in her movies. We party through the night drinking, snorting coke, and dropping speed. Someone talks me into a tap of MDMA (methylendoxymethamphetimine), so I am flying higher than ever before. Things are getting crazy, very crazy, and I've lost all control, but I just roll with it. What else can I do?

My senses are maxed to the extreme, and my mind rolls with constant visions of films I've viewed all evening as the very same intoxicating woman in these films surround me. I watch them breaking off in small groups, easily slipping out of their clothing and tossing it on the floor. I'm up for anything! My head spins as Alexis X and Pamela Louise approach me. They grab me, kiss me, touch me. I'm at their mercy as they drag me down into their pit of seduction. I notice we're being filmed, but I don't care. All my inhibitions are gone. I'm too far in to stop.

Someone rouses me out of my stupor. I must have passed out. I don't know how that's possible with all the stimulants I have in my system, but someone is shaking me, trying to wake me up, telling me it's time to leave. Completely confused, I touch my chest and immediately start looking around for my shirt. My feet—those aren't my socks! I can't remember anything about last night, but I slowly look around and think maybe it's best I don't remember. My head pounds as I stagger, trying to stand up. Yes, it's time for me to go. Gathering my clothes—or what I can find of them—I trip over naked bodies on my way to the door. I glance around, looking for Dave, but I can't find him. I have no idea what happened to him last night. Dressing as I go, I head out the door without him.

Just outside the door, three limos are lined up. I start to walk past them to find my way back to the hotel when a driver steps out of one, opens the back door, and waves me inside.

"Huh?" I stutter.

I'm waiting for someone important to get out when he looks at me and says, "Sir, where should I take you?"

Still not getting it, I look around. Seeing no one else, I turn to him and ask, "You talking to me?"

He nods. "Yes, sir. I'm instructed to take you wherever you need to go."

This is crazy! I climb in the back of this huge limo, and he drives me back to my hotel, stopping a few times along the way so I can puke. Hanging my head out the back door, hurling on Michigan Avenue, I look up at the driver thinking he's got to be annoyed with me, but he seems unmoved, as if my vomiting out the back of his limo is perfectly normal.

Back in my hotel room, I'm worried about what happened to Dave last night, so I dial his room. He answers, half asleep and obviously still drunk. "What the heck happened last night?" I ask.

He chuckles. "We'll talk on the train. Right now, I gotta go puke."

On the train ride home, we decide that what happened in Chicago stays in Chicago.

The next day at work, my business partner, who is also my mother, asks, "How'd it go?"

Nope, not going there. No way can I ever tell her what happened, so I innocently say, "Fine. I lined up some good deals on about one hundred and fifty videos. They'll be arriving soon."

One month later, I'm at work going through the mail when I notice a letter with a return address of Las Vegas, Nevada. In the corner of the envelope is a funny little logo of a rabbit smoking a cigarette, so I open it. Inside is a release form asking for my permission to use the footage of me in Chicago with Alexis and Pamela in an upcoming release. In return, they'll send me five hundred dollars. Along with this release form is a handwritten note inviting me to come in person and talk to them about future endeavors. The signature? Ron Jeremy.

Blood rushes to my head as I guiltily look around, instantly tearing the letter into tiny pieces and shoving them down to the bottom of the trashcan before anyone notices. My wife, my mother, Grandma, no! No one must *ever* find out about this. Time to take the trash out.

I realize after that trip to Chicago, seeing the inside of the adult movie business, and partying with them, it's not my thing. Okay, it was exciting, and I had fun, but honestly, there is a definite sadness hovering over that type of business. I never want to be the kind of person that others look at with disgust. Besides, I have other plans and better things to do. I have decided to start my own video production studio. I have no interest in being in a porno, but the money I could make producing one is enticing.

As I begin plans to open my own production studio, I want to stay local. I find a great place to rent down by the Mississippi River at Mineral Springs Mall in Alton. Mineral Springs is an old historic hotel turned into a mini boutique mall. Right now, it's starving for business. The agreement is that I will wait until all the boutiques close for the evening before I run my business. That's perfect as the stores close at six and don't open again until eight the next morning. For what I plan on doing, we'd never work during those hours anyway. I don't think the owner would be renting to me if he could rent to another retailer, but it looks like I'm the only game in town right now.

After determining how many rooms I need for my studio, I end up renting thirty percent of the mall. I now have a huge rustic setup for my studio, including separate rooms for a recording studio, a rehearsal room, a talent agency, and an office. I purchase all the equipment I need and immediately start shooting local commercials, business seminars, and wedding ceremonies. My dream, though, is to shoot live music performances.

Even though I started the studio with porn in mind, I just can't bring myself to pursue it. I have no knowledge of the production, manufacturing, packaging, and marketing of that genre. Music is my true love. In addition, if I ever became bold enough to make a porno and Grandma found out, it would absolutely kill her—if she didn't kill me first.

Zach walks into the video store. It's been a while since I've seen him. "Wow!" I say. "I haven't seen you for months, man. How've you been?"

"Good," he says with a strange smile on his face.

I don't know what to make of it, so I ask, "What's up?"

Zach has a habit of stammering a bit then just spitting it out when he has something he wants to say but doesn't quite know how. "I… Me and…" he says and then blurts out, "I'm getting married."

Staring at him, I wait for him to laugh and tell me he's joking. When he says nothing, I ask, "You're joking, right?" He's waiting for my reaction. *Is he serious?* "What? When? How? Who? I didn't even know you were dating anyone! Who is she?"

"It just kind of happened."

"*Who?*"

"Annalee."

I'm speechless. There is only one Annalee I know of. It can't be the same Annalee who wouldn't let me race her dad's GTX, the same Annalee who chewed me out *numerous* times for being Zach's friend…but I can tell he's serious! "Holy crap! How'd that happen, bro? Isn't she already married?"

"Well, technically yes, but that marriage has been over a long time, and they haven't even lived in the same house in over a year. We started dating and decided to get married, so she's getting divorced. Saturday morning we're going to the East Alton courthouse to finalize her divorce and then to the Edwardsville courthouse to get married that afternoon."

I can't help but laugh as he explains this. I'm not laughing at him—I just find it ironic that of all the women in the world, he's marrying Annalee! I'm making plans to further engage my video production studio, and movie plots randomly run through my head. If this were a scenario in a movie I'd have deemed the plot unbelievable but here it is, two of my best friends who went to school and worked together and wouldn't even look at each other let alone talk, are now getting married. You can't make this stuff up.

I couldn't be happier for them. Digging for my wallet, I throw my credit card on the counter as I reach over to shake his hand. "Man, congratulations. Take this for a night in St. Louis on me. Have fun."

Zach and Annalee elope Saturday afternoon at the Edwardsville courthouse, five hours after her divorce. After the ceremony, we celebrate at Vanzo's across the street from the courthouse, toasting to many happy years. Zach, delinquent number three, is now married and stepfather to a three-year-old.

Fantasy Video World started with an idea and fifteen thousand dollars. Within the first two years, our three video stores combined grossed over $1.3 million in sales, employing eight and funding the opening of my studio, Fantasy Production Studio. I've decided to turn over the video stores to Sherri and Mom so I can give the production studio my undivided attention.

On my way to the studio, I hear on the radio that John Holmes has been diagnosed with AIDS. Shauna Grant, the shy blonde bombshell who seemed so out of place at the Chicago convention shot herself in the head. She didn't survive. She was only twenty years old. No, I can't take my studio there, not to a place with such an undercurrent of sadness. Calls continue to come in offering money for the release of those tapes filmed in Chicago. I never return their calls.

Chapter 4
The Band 1983

Ann doesn't have a clue about my lifestyle. She knows I work long hours and bring home good money. She knows I have a lot of energy, but she doesn't understand what fuels my energy, and I don't plan on telling her anytime soon.

With Mom and Sherri taking care of the video stores, I spend my time researching video production. Currently, Mom, Sherri, Dave, Mikey, Tim, and his girlfriend are doing a great job with the stores, but we need to hire someone to fill my vacancy. Mikey suggests hiring his neighbor, Cat.

Cat is a cute little blonde with a spirited personality. She is all about a good time, and anyone in her presence is going to have fun. We quickly become good friends, and I learn she is stuck in a ridiculously bad marriage. My marriage is on a slippery slope also.

I make it a point to stop by the video store before going home for the evening so I can spend a few hours with Cat on the nights she's working. I feel I can tell her anything, regardless of how stupid it is. She doesn't judge or ridicule me. Others are starting to think we're an item, but we're not. We're just really good friends. I know this probably doesn't make sense, but we are such close friends that I'd never sleep with her. With all the women out there to sleep with, I don't want to ruin a good friendship.

I ask Cat to assist me on my out of town business meetings, and we have a blast together hitting big cities like Vegas and New York. We're at Roxy's in Manhattan when she meets up with a bouncer. This isn't unusual for Cat—just like me, she's always prowling for a quick hookup. Not wanting to leave the club without her, I wait around until closing, but no Cat. This is Manhattan, New York not Wood River, Illinois, and I start to worry about her. Back at the hotel, I'm mad at myself for letting her go off like that without getting a name, a number...anything. She was pretty hammered early in the evening, long before she met that guy. I brought her here. I should have kept a closer eye on her. What am I going to do if she doesn't make it back to the hotel?

Feeling I shouldn't leave, I wait for her in the hotel room in case she comes back, but I also feel I should be out looking for her. Where, though? Where would I look? How do I go about finding a cute little blonde in Manhattan? I am wide awake at 5 a.m. when Cat rolls in, looking rode hard and put away wet. She smiles and says, "I'm okay!" then falls into bed and instantly passes out. Relieved, I call room service to order breakfast and watch TV while she snores. We laugh about it on the flight back home. It's all in a good night's fun!

My appetite for drugs grows steadily. I need thirty dexedrine a day to keep my energy level up to normal. One day without uppers, and I'd be in bed 24/7, groggy, miserable, jittery, and depressed. I can't live without them. I can't function without them. Since Kevin's arrest, I have found several other dealers to score from. My daily routine is to work a sixteen-hour day, have a couple drinks at a local bar to settle myself, and then go home to attend to my home and my wife. I do this seven days a week. By the time I make it home, there's not much left of me for Ann or my home, and not much time to sleep for that matter, but as long as I have my pills, I'm fine. I'm making it, so don't judge me.

Mikey runs lights for a local band that's gaining popularity in the area. He invites me to come and check it out the following evening at Music Room in Wood River. Of course, I'll go!

After work, I spend a few hours with Cat, stop by Donzo's in Wood River for a couple drinks, and then head down to Music Room. I'm surprised when I walk into a nightclub filled to capacity with highly energized, excited people. The vibe feels great. The dance floor is lined with guys watching, waiting, hoping, anticipating a hookup with any of the girls gyrating to the music in front of the band.

I find a table where I can watch the show, and I order a few drinks and check out the girls on the dance floor. Tonight, I'm more interested in the band than the girls. I'm surprised when I recognize many of the band members. I grew up with these guys. We all went to Roxana High School together.

After the show, they invite me to party with them in the dressing room. Shaking their hands, I congratulate them on a great show and break out an eight ball of coke. Cutting some lines on a mirror, I pass it along, and each of us snort a line as we talk about old times, the band, and my studio.

I tell them about the success of my businesses over the last few years, and then the subject of their band manager comes up. He recently quit, and they're looking for another. I have always had a love for the music business and a desire to work in this field, so when they ask if I'm interested in becoming their manager, I smile and say, "*Yes!* I'm interested."

Most of them already know me. They know I have a small chain of successful video stores and a video production studio. It's apparent that I know how to run a business, and with a manager who owns a video production studio, they will have access to more than any other booking agent around. No other band in this area has the ability to film their very own music videos. My studio also doubles as a photography studio, a recording studio, and a rehearsal hall. Space is not a problem—this studio is huge! With me as their manager, they will have someone with an accomplished background in developing profitable businesses and unlimited access to a photography studio, audio recording studio, video recording studio, and rehearsal hall.

Excited about this new business venture, I look each one in the eye as I shake their hands, sealing the deal. I am the new manager of Rider! High on cocaine, I leave Music Room pumped and so glad to begin shooting more than just weddings and commercials. This is going to be a *blast!*

Still pumped when I get home, I'm reluctant to tell Ann about my new job, so I tell her I'm tired and go straight to bed. Lying in bed, I listen to her talk about something going on Sunday afternoon that we're supposed to attend while my mind spins with a gazillion thoughts of how to bring this band and my studio to its full potential.

I won't make it Sunday, and Ann knows it. She gives up and rolls over. With our backs to each other, I hear her breathing the deep breath of sleep as my mind races with ideas and plans. There's so much to do.

As with all my previous endeavors, I dive into my research and map out a plan. I check out many clubs in the St. Louis area that showcase live bands. I pay attention to the advertising and the way the bands are set up, introduced, and marketed. I note the band's show, the lighting, the quality of sound, the music, the band members' dress, and their overall performance. I pay close attention to all of these different things and how the audience reacts, taking many mental notes.

After a few months of research and rehearsals, I realize that Rider is boring. Musically, they are a great band, but they don't yet have what it takes to create excitement, to stand out during their performance and be remembered after, so I immediately get to work on how we're going to fix this.

I haven't talked with the band about my ideas yet. I'm waiting until after rehearsal when they're worn out, appropriately buzzed, and calm. I listen in awe to the talent before me. Honestly, I'd put our lead singer up against the best in the business. Shutting my eyes as they practice, I roll with the music and envision a great production, a great show. They really are talented. But then I open my eyes and see five awkward high school kids on stage. For this to work, we must create a show, a real live professional wild and crazy show!

There's one guy in the band who's always whining and complaining about something. I feel he's holding us back. I'm relieved when he up and quits because I've had someone in mind to replace him with anyway, a guy named Rusty. Rusty is well-known in the area as an excellent guitarist and showman. He's a few years older than we are, and he used to be part of a successful band good enough to open for some big names at Kiel Auditorium and other St. Louis concert halls. We shop around before approaching him, checking all our options, and then decide he's the one we want.

Rusty agrees to come to one of our rehearsals. We talk, we do a few lines of blow, we play well into the morning hours until the sun comes up, and the deal is made. Rusty is now the lead guitarist for Rider! A few tweaks to their wardrobe and stage performance, and they now look good too. Sitting at the soundboard, I shut my eyes and listen—they're good. Then I open my eyes and watch—they're really good! It's apparent that this band is going places. Rider looks and sounds fantastic.

Time to market this band. We make demos and spend weeks visiting different radio stations, making appointments to talk with their program directors and DJs. Paying for advertising on their station, we talk them into playing our music. If I can sell a thousand-dollar vacuum cleaner to an old lady with no carpet, I can sell this band.

Rider no longer just shows up and plays at local bars. We treat every single show as a rock concert event with advertising, posters, and videos. We build a portable stage complete with ramps, trusses, and scaffolding, everything we need for lights and sound. I lease a forty-foot semi and hire additional roadies to take our show from place to place. Image is everything, and with our spectacular stage setup, we are gaining popularity. I take care of the band and provide whatever they need—equipment, alcohol, speed, and cocaine.

After a few extremely successful performances, club owners give us the green light, providing us free drinks and admission to the strip clubs in Sauget. We're on posters and in the newspapers, so girls recognize us and want to hook up. We party nonstop. I am living the rock star lifestyle and loving every minute of it.

In between shows, rehearsals, and shooting videos, Mineral Springs becomes party central. I'm in close with K-SHE 95, 106.5, and many other St. Louis rock stations. I invite all of them along with DJs from Sauget's well-known strip clubs, PT's and Roxy's. Along the Mississippi River, we party like Studio 54 in New York City from ten at night until early morning.

Those who are still partying when the sun comes up, I hustle out the door around seven. Finding it harder and harder to go home, many times I just don't go home. Rusty and I rent suites at a local hotel to crash in between shows, but it always turns into a party. The chicks love it. People knock on our door at all hours, finding two to three ounces of cocaine spread across our table. Even the hotel's manager and employees regularly frequent our parties.

Life's a big blur, and I roll with it and enjoy the nonstop music, energy, drugs, alcohol, and girls. Cat comes to a show and falls for the lead singer, Ross. Rusty and I, we hang out almost every night at the studio or party at the hotel.

Ann has nothing to do with this lifestyle. We have nothing in common anymore, nothing. I can't talk about my day with her, and I sure ain't going to church with her anytime soon. I have a band to take care of. All my time outside of performances is spent on marketing, planning events and parties, and making sure this band has everything they need—events, unlimited alcohol and drugs, and girls.

Chapter 5
The Band
The Wedding
The Baby!

Rusty has connections in Arizona with a radio station and a recording studio. Last week, he mailed them a few of our most recent demos. Interested in meeting with us, they send two reps to check out Rider's live show in St. Louis. I'm pumped to the max!

In the dressing room before the show, we do a few lines and pop some bennies, whatever the band needs to bring their A game. Rider delivers a fantastic show. The club explodes with fans waving their lighters above their heads, screaming and yelling for more. The atmosphere is tense and crazy. The reps watch it all and are blown away. After the show, we invite the reps to the studio to discuss the band's future. We party until the early morning sun rises over the dissipating fog on the Mississippi River.

Rider rehearses daily, preparing to record an album. We're leaving for Nogales, Arizona in two weeks to record at a studio on the Mexican border, stateside. I find it strange that Mexicans want to invest in an American gringo rock band, but then why not? They're associated with Tel-a-vive network, owned by Warner Brothers. We are their first American rock band, their first American rock project. Until us, they've only worked with American Latino artists. In working with them, we hope to sneak through the back door and avoid the long line at Warner Brother's front door. We are psyched!

I drive to the Mineral Springs studio to finish some last-minute editing before flying to Nogales tomorrow. Working alone tonight, I walk up the steep sidewalk alongside the mall, turn the corner, and walk through the front door, uttering a quick "Hey" to a strangely dressed man sitting at the ice cream parlor. It's quarter to six, so there are still a few people in the mall.

Walking under the mural and turning left toward the studio, my boot heels echo off the hardwood floor. Hearing someone following me, I stop and turn around but see no one. Continuing on down the hall, I unlock the door to the studio, taking a quick look back before securing the door behind me.

I throw my bag on the desk then sit down and get to work editing videos. My desk sits in between the only two doors in my office, both leading to the same hallway., I get lost in my work and lose track of time, spending hours editing to get the perfect cut. Finishing up the video at 3 a.m., I shut down the equipment and pack the videos I'm taking to Arizona in my bag.

Out of the corner of my eye, I see a tall man's figure walk quietly past the door. Glancing to the other door, I see him sneaking past again, and I shout out, "Who's there?"

No answer. The mall closed hours ago, and I made sure to lock myself in. Who is this? How could he have gotten in?

Worried I'm about to be robbed, I glance at my equipment then back to the door. "Is somebody out there?" I shout.

Still no answer, but I can see his shadow moving down the hall. Lowering my tone, I sternly call out, "Come on, man. Who's out there? I'm armed! I'm telling you right now, I'm armed!"

No response, but again he sneaks by the door and heads down the dark hallway. At this hour, whoever it is can't be up to any good.

Trying to keep my eye on both doors, I reach over to the desk drawer and pull out my.38. I raise it to eye level and shout, "I'm telling you, man, I'm armed!"

A shadow moves fast across the door and down the hall. This guy's looking for a place to hide. This dude is definitely up to no good. He speeds past the door on my left, and before he reaches the door on my right, I take aim and pull the trigger, shooting right through the wall behind the desk.

BAM! BAM! BAM! BAM! BAM!

Still holding my gun at eye level, I wait, listening. Everything is silent except the sound of glass hitting the hardwood floor and shattering. Taking one slow step at a time, I walk carefully to the door and peek around the doorframe into the hall. Nothing. I don't know what to do, so I just stand there waiting, listening, and looking up and down the hallway. Nothing. With my gun in hand, I reach for my bag lying on the desk and run like heck out of the mall as fast as I can.

In early morning, the phone rings. It's Tom, the owner of Mineral Springs Mall, and he's clearly upset. "What in the world were you doing here last night, Darwyn?"

Apparently, I shot up the Crystal Gift Boutique.

Agitated, he continues, "Her shop is demolished! You shot right through the wall and destroyed hundreds of dollars of crystal!"

Defending myself, I explain, "Tom, someone was there last night. I was working by myself, and some guy was about to rob me! I'm telling you, someone was in the mall! I'm sorry about the store. Tell them I'll pay for whatever I broke, but I really was scared for my life!" Complete silence, so I say, "Hello?"

Exhaling loudly, he tells me, "You need to come in. We need to talk."

"Can it wait until I get back from Arizona? I'm leaving in a few hours."

"Just make sure you see me as soon as you get back, Darwyn, before you decide to work another all-nighter in my building."

"No problem."

I know what he's going to say, and I don't have time for nonsense. I've heard all the stories from the other shop owners in the building. "This place is haunted with ghosts from the 1920s!"

Blah, blah, blah. Whatever...I have a plane to catch.

After landing in the sweltering heat of Arizona, we arrive at the studio and are told the head honchos in Mexico City want a live performance, so off we go again. Rider rocks Mexico City with a great performance, and we head straight back to Arizona after the show. The same people who own the studio also own a hotel resembling a Motel 6, and they give us free range of the entire top floor. Along with the band, we have a ten-person road crew and everyone's wives and girlfriends. Ann, of course, didn't come with me, but my girlfriend did. We are quite a group!

The same guys who run the studio also own a produce warehouse big enough to convert into a sound stage. I travel with all my equipment, so we record some of our best videos to date and shoot one off to MTV.

I regularly call home to check in with Mom and Sherri just to make sure it's all good while I'm away, answer any questions, and help with any problems, but they got this. They don't need me. Sherri tells me that Ann left, moved in with someone else. I knew she was going to leave sooner or later, but to move in with another guy so soon? Really? Hanging up the phone, I shake my head and remind myself, *Darwyn, you're such a hypocrite.*

The band needs to spend a few more months in Arizona to finish recording, but Sherri is getting married during this time, so I have to return to Illinois for her wedding. I'm in this wedding, and I'm not happy about it. While I was busy starting up the studio and Sherri and Mom had taken over the video stores, guess who was delivering packages to our stores? Dennis! Yes, the jerk jock from school that I had to almost throw down the steps to get him to back off. I knew he was hanging out a little longer than he should talking with Sherri during his deliveries, but I didn't think much of it back then. I mean, she was dating a great guy, and I didn't think Dennis had a chance with a girl like Sherri. She's too good for him.

Sherri is my best friend and always has been. When Mom brought her home from the hospital, I was five. I thought she was mine and took very good care of her. I've always tried to take care of her, but she's all grown now, and I can only do so much. Why would she date a jerk like Dennis? While I was promoting the band, she broke up with her boyfriend, a boyfriend I liked, and Dennis asked her out. I can't believe she said yes. What was she thinking? And *now*, marrying him? Trying to get it out of my head before I hit something, I down a few drinks, pop a couple, and bury myself in work. If I could stop this marriage, I would.

Jet engines fire up, instantly sucking me back into my seat as I sit on a plane bound for St. Louis, heading home for Sherri's wedding. I torture myself with question after question. What does she see in him? How can she be so blind? I also feel guilty that this is supposed to be the happiest day of my sister's life, and I do *not* share her joy. I can't! The closer I get to Illinois, the more I drink, telling myself, *Just one more Jack and water should do the trick.*

The plane touches down in St. Louis on a cool November day. Walking down the ramp and out into the airport, I breathe in moist air. I've only been gone a few months, but it feels like a lifetime.

Ann and I have a house in East Alton on Goulding Street by the railroad tracks. Zach and Annalee rent a little house from Ann's sister a couple blocks down. Their baby was due last week, so I don't know if they'll make the wedding. The reception is just a few blocks away at Lewis and Clark Restaurant on Route 3 next to the levee. That's good because with the amount of alcohol it's going to take to get me through this evening, I shouldn't be driving.

Walking through my front door, I swing it open, bouncing it off the wall. I don't care. I'm drunk, high, and pissed. Looking around my house, it hits me hard, crashing down on me like a weight I cannot bear. I've lost my wife of six years. She's with another man, and my sister is marrying the wrong man. My anxiety skyrockets as I search the kitchen for alcohol.

Mom stops by with my tuxedo, reassuring me and asking me to behave. It'll be okay, she tells me as she smiles, hugs me, straightens my collar, kisses me on the cheek, and then hustles out the door. She has a million things to do—her daughter's getting married this evening. Hanging the baby blue tux on my closet door, I stare at it, loathing it. Shaking my head, I walk to my stash, pop a couple pills, and chase it with some crap Ann left behind. I guzzle it down, whatever it is.

It's time. Sliding into my rented blue tuxedo, I get ready to go to church and act like the good boy I promised Mom I'd be. Tim pulls in the driveway, looking equally blue. Okay, I can do this. I'll do it for Sherri.

No, I can't do this...but I made a promise. I have to keep trying. I have to. Standing with the other groomsmen alongside Tim and Dennis in front of the church, I pretend to support this epitome of a jackass, this ex-high school quarterback that always walked around with his chest puffed out, this mean, vile man who enjoyed making others miserable and my sister's decision to marry him. I seriously cannot stand him!

Everyone stands when the music starts, and I see her, my little sister, walking down the aisle on the arm of our stepfather, and I'm instantly in awe of her elegant beauty, her long, curly blonde hair, her sparkling hazel eyes, her genuine, warm, friendly smile. I've been so busy lately...when did she change from my cute little sister into this beautiful young woman?

Mom looks stunning in the first row as she smiles watching her husband and daughter, a daughter who is a clone of herself, walk the aisle. They all look so happy. I look down, thinking, *Come on, Darwyn, you can do this.* My heart settles a bit, and I can breathe again, but then I look over at Dennis, at the guy we're about to give her to for *life.* He shuffles back and forth a bit and then puffs out his chest, and that's it. I can't take anymore!

Forcing myself to breathe, I stand with every muscle clenched, breaking out into a sweat glaring at him. Visions of beating this guy in the head run through my mind again and again. I stand in excruciating pain, using every ounce of energy I have to restrain myself from shoving him down, smacking his head, asking him how he likes it. I'm scared my little sister is in danger and wondering if he just wants revenge for our past. I'm afraid for her like I was afraid for Mom. I'm worried she's marrying someone like Dad. Beating his head against the altar would feel great right now, and I glare at him, hating him as my blood pressure rises and body parts I can no longer control start to quiver. I should have let him fall down those steps years ago. Why didn't I let him fall?

Listening to them pledge their love and recite those stupid vows makes me wanna puke! How is this happening? I need to stop this, but I made a promise! Standing stiff as a board, I realize it's happening right before my eyes, and I'm doing *nothing!* Anger wells up in me, pumping adrenaline through my body. The time has come. Promise or not, I have to stop this. This is my chance, my moment. This cannot go on one second longer.

Stepping forward, I look over at Sherri. She's smiling, happy, absolutely beautiful. I can't ruin this day for her. Stumbling a little as I pull back my foot, I remain in line waiting, watching. How can she be so gullible? I look over to Mom and Wayne. Mom has tears in her eyes, but she's smiling. Tears of joy for *this?* Wayne keeps giving me an encouraging nod, and I struggle to hang on, trying to get through this.

Sherri and Dennis exchange rings, and I look back at Dennis again, glaring at him, then back at Mom. Breathe, keep breathing! Then the introduction—my little sister is now Mrs. Dennis Rodgers. I am literally going to throw up right here on this altar. Stress? Alcohol? No, it's humiliation. It's the thought that I didn't stop this. It's knowing that I should have, could have, but didn't. Sherri stops to give Mom a rose, and the jerk has the nerve to hug her. My eyes roll, and my hands clench into fists as I fight the urge to slug this guy in the back of the head. I mean, I owe him a few, right? Christmas, New Year's, Easter…there's no way I can do this!

Arriving at the reception, I sit down at the wedding table and take a swig of champagne. Watching my little sister and this guy doing all their wedding stuff makes me seethe, so I hold my glass up in a solo toast, mentally toast to take this guy down, then down what remains in my glass. They both seem so happy, and it infuriates me. I can't watch this. Needing another drink, I push away from the table and walk straight to the bar, ordering a Jack and water. I down it and order another. I will drink this away. I will. After I order another, Mom walks up, and I turn to her and point at Sherri. "How in the world did this happen?" I ask angrily.

Downing my drink, I turn to the bartender before she has time to answer. Rage consumes me as my blood pressure rises. Afraid of losing control, I order yet another, desperately trying to drink away my anger, my disapproval, my resentment for this day and all that it will bring. Ann runs through my head—the idea she's with another man and just moved in with him.

I notice Zach walking toward me with Annalee waddling behind. She hasn't had that baby yet? Annalee stops to talk with someone while Zach tries to talk me down, but he can't. No one can. I order another drink, my goal being to drink to the point that I cannot hit this guy. That's all I'm thinking about doing—hitting him and how good that would feel right now. I'm bent.

I ask Zach if he wants a drink as I reach down in my pocket, pull out a couple white crosses, and chase them with a Jack and water. Zach accepts a drink, turning down the speed. Jack and speed, Jack and speed! I am now amped, mean and ready to confront my new brother-in-law. Mom, Zach, Tim, Wayne, Jack and water…nothing, no one can stop me now!

Turning away from the bar, I bring him into view and stare, envisioning my best approach, how this will start, how this will end. My visions are violent and good. I've been dreaming of this moment. It's time for our little talk, brother-in-law, a talk that isn't going to end well. Time to welcome you to my family. As I walk toward him, he reaches for Sherri's arm, escorting her to the wedding cake table. Stopping, I watch for a brief second then scan the crowd. Sherri is all smiles and gorgeous on her wedding day. Mom stands close by, smiling at them but glancing at me with a worried look. Grandma sits close by, enjoying the moment and completely oblivious to what I have in mind. Wayne is watching me and glancing over at Mom.

Zach and Annalee are on the other side of the room by the exit door. The tension is high. It's now or never.

Jacked up on speed, alcohol, and anger, I walk across the dance floor toward my new brother-in-law. I don't know why, but instead of stopping and confronting him, I walk right past him, past Sherri, Mom, and Wayne, past Tim, past Zach and Annalee and right out the door, not stopping to talk to anyone. I guess more than I want to get a point across to Dennis, I don't want to make a scene and ruin my sister's wedding day.

I am six foot three and dressed in a baby blue tuxedo complete with ruffled shirt and cummerbund. I'm drunk, high, and fuming mad. Looking down at my shiny black size thirteen shoes, I stomp across an abandoned field toward home, a home in which I haven't lived for months, a home that I've shared with my wife of six years who's now living with another man. It's pitch dark as I stumble over thick, overgrown, dead weeds.

The ground vibrates beneath me, and I jolt from the locomotive's air horns screaming out three long, lonely whistles and ending with a quick short one warning of its approach. Looking to my left and judging the distance of its bright light coming around the turn, I run, tripping over the railroad ties, trying to cross the tracks before being separated by this long, lingering freight train. Covered in sandburs, stickers, crushed leaves, and dirt, I make it to the other side in time, feeling the train's massive presence behind me. For some reason, its loud, steady, rhythmic vibe intrigues me.

Reaching home, I slam open my front door. It hits the wall and ricochets back, hitting me. I look around my house, taking inventory of all Ann's left behind. Vases, lamps, pictures, figurines, decorative mirrors…there's too much to list. Picking up a vase we got at our wedding, I toss it up in the air a few times, carefully catching it. Noticing my reflection in a mirror, I hurl the vase as hard as I can, shattering both mirror and vase, shutting my eyes against the fallout. That felt good! Grabbing a lamp, I jerk it out of the wall socket and swing it into our wedding picture. *Wow! That felt great!* Eagerly, I look around for more, smashing and breaking things and tearing down curtains, shades, and blinds. What doesn't come easily, I viciously work at.

I could not accomplish the task of keeping my wife or stopping my sister from marrying that idiot, but I *will* throw this couch out into the front yard! I heave the couch at the front door, watching as it hits the doorframe and bounces back into the living room. Running to the kitchen, I sling everything out of the utility drawer until I find what I'm looking for. There it is, glistening under the kitchen light. Stomping back into the living room, crunching over broken glass and shoving aside anything in my way, I take that shiny hammer to the couch and then throw it again at the front door. Success! Pieces of it now lie in the yard and across the sidewalk. Standing in the doorway, I take a moment to admire my accomplishment then turn back, eyeing the table, chairs, and end tables. I hammer, dismantle, disassemble, demolish, and destroy all of it, bashing it against walls before chucking it out the door.

Flashing red lights blink through the front door as two East Alton cops pull into the driveway. I walk to the door to get a better look. When I see who they are, I immediately turn back to my living room and continue what I started, completely ignoring them. As they walk up the front sidewalk, jumping aside to dodge a chair flying past, I hear one yell, "You settle down or I'm taking you in!"

Stopping dead in my tracks, I shake my head and walk to the door, thinking, *Time to set this guy straight*, I start yelling at him, "I'm inside *my* house breaking *my* stuff, okay? You *cannot* take me to jail for being inside *my* house breaking *my* stuff!" Continuing my rant, I throw a pair of candleholders and a few wall hangings out the door, paying no attention to how close I come to hitting them. "I *do* know the law well enough to know that I can break all the stuff in *my* house if I choose to! I'm not breaking anyone else's stuff! It's *my* stuff! I'll break it if I want!"

Throwing pieces of the coffee table out the door, I tell them, "You guys need to leave! Just go ahead and go!"

They know I'm right, so they turn to leave, and the other officer asks, "Are you going to be okay?"

I know this guy, and he knows me. He knows not to push me, and he knows what he's done. He just doesn't know I know, so I stop what I'm doing and turn to him without saying a word. I point to his car and stare him down thinking to myself, *Of all the people to come and check on me, to try and calm me down, YOU? Really? You tried to mess around with my wife! You're lucky you're not the one lying in the front yard instead of that couch!* I don't break eye contact, glaring at this guy in complete silence until he decides it's best he leave.

Stepping over broken furniture, they make their way to their cars, turn off the flashing lights, and pull away. From the doorway, I look down the road after them. When they're out of sight, I turn back inside, kicking stuff out of my way, and start peeling paneling off the dining room wall. I stumble into the kitchen and try pulling down the cabinets but change my mind, instead kicking in every single kitchen cabinet door and then flinging the cabinet contents over my head.

Highway Joe shows up just in time to see sparks fly as I rip the ceiling fan down in my living room. I like Highway, so I stop and watch as he carefully steps over obstacles and broken glass. With a ceiling fan swinging from my hand, I stand in my demolished home sporting a blue tux now torn and covered in dirt. Blood oozes from a cut on my head and drips onto my shoulder. I look at him innocently. I don't offer my hand as it's a little bloody. With a half-smile on my face, I raise my eyebrows and calmly say, "Hey, Joe. What's up?"

Highway Joe's been a close friend of the family for years. He's more like an uncle to me. He's even worked for me at the video store, but his main job, he's the Madison County Sherriff. I live in Madison County. For being a sheriff, he's kind of a wild and crazy guy. I like Joe. He's a great guy.

Back in high school, Mikey and I were smoking weed and driving around in my van when we noticed those dreaded flashing lights coming up behind us. Scared to death, we pulled over slowly to give ourselves time to hide roach clips and a dime bag under the floor mat. We jumped when we heard a *rap, rap, rap* on the window. I remember smoke billowing out the small crack of my window as I saw Highway Joe's eyes peeking in at me and waving the smoke away. Surprised to see me at the wheel when it cleared, he yelled "Darwyn! What are you doing here? Get *out* of here! *Now! Go!*" He straightened up, waving me on as he kept yelling, "You guys get on home! You get out of here right now!"

Joe's a good friend of mine, has been for years. Looking me up and down and taking in the condition of my clothes, he looks around my house and laughs, telling me, "Dude! Come on, man! You're coming with me."

Staggering a bit, I give him a half-smile and shake my head.

"No. Come on, man," he says. "Let's go."

I'm thinking we're going to the police station, but we walk outside and climb into his bright red '78 Corvette.

Breathing easier in the cool night air, I relax as we drive down the road. I glance at the speedometer and see we're going 110 mph. I look up at the road ahead. "Dude! Is this legal?" I ask.

"Ha! Shut up, and let me drive!"

Laughing with him, I find it ironic I'm with a cop in a Corvette, flying at least sixty miles over the speed limit.

"Where're we going?" I ask, leaning into the sharp turns.

"Don't worry about it."

Highway pulls into BoJacs, a run-down little hole-in-the-wall bar known for the best ham sandwiches in town. It's Zach's uncle's bar. Highway orders a few shots and questions me about what's going on. I vent. He doesn't tell me to calm down or be quiet. He just orders more shots. I tell him everything, going all the way back to high school PE class. He asks, "You want another shot?"

Leaning forward on the table to stabilize myself, trying my best to make my mouth form words correctly, I look over at Highway. "Surrrrrre," I slur, "why not? You do realize I'm drunk, don't you?"

"I do realize that Darwyn, but we're out having a good time, right?"

He orders a couple more shots, and I down them, realizing I've downed every shot while he's been sipping water. I continue my rant about my wife, Dennis, Sherri, high school, the steps, and the wedding, and the more I rant, the more shots he buys. Joe's a good guy.

Early the next morning, the phone rings at Wayne and Rita's house. Rita picks up.

"Rita, it's Joe. He's out cold. I took him to BoJacs for shots. You don't have to worry about him killing himself or anyone else tonight—he's in bed now, passed out cold. No problem. Glad to help. Let me know if you need anything else."

Stretching, I roll over and open my eyes. Where am I? I sit up too fast and immediately lie back down before I puke. Excruciating pain sears through my head, so I do my best to look around without moving. I realize I'm at home in East Alton. How did I get here? Last thing I remember is sitting at BoJacs with Highway Joe. I have a plane to catch, but not for a while. Pulling the covers up to my chin, I slowly roll onto my stomach and fall into a drunken, hungover, comatose sleep.

I wake up feeling like crap and scan the room for a clock, noticing the condition of my house. What happened? Oh boy, it's all coming back. I need to get out of Illinois. I find my watch still intact on the floor in the corner. It's 3 p.m., and my plane leaves at six. Forcing myself out of bed, I pop enough speed to jump-start my body, pack, head to the airport, and fly back to Nogales, hungover as hell.

Ike Kisler, a booking agent, calls to ask if we want to open for a new band whose first hit is currently rising on the charts. The event is in St. Louis. He encourages me, telling me he feels this band is about to take off and it would be a great opportunity for us. I'm skeptical because I've never viewed Rider as being an opener for another band—we are the headliner, the main show.

"Who is it?" I ask.

"They have one hit right now, 'Runaway.' You've probably heard it."

"No. I haven't heard it. Who are they?"

"The band's Bon Jovi."

"No, never heard of them."

"Turn your radio on, dude! You'll hear it. 'Runaway' plays constantly!"

"Okay. What's the gig? What are we talking about?"

"The pay is decent, but the thing is, you have to use their system, okay? You can't bring in your own system. You'll be allowed to use seventeen, maybe eighteen of their hundred par amps, so your light show will be very minimal. You'll have to keep your audio level down to sixty decibels so you're not louder than they'll be when they come out."

I can't agree to this! I say, "Okay, what you're telling me is that we have to suck in order to make this band look good? Right?"

He tries to persuade me. "If the gig in St. Louis works out, we'll take you on tour with us."

"No. We'll pass," I say and hang up the phone. Wow, what a stupid gig. I will not send Rider out on tour to purposely sound crappy just to make another band look good. No way. Who are these guys anyway?

Interested in the album we just cut, Warner Electra Asylum calls wanting to set up a meeting with us in St. Louis to discuss terms. Packing up the crew, we fly back to St. Louis, eager for this meeting. Here's the deal they offer—they'll sign us, but we'll only receive ten percent of the profits. I'm not too thrilled with this offer, but I do some research and find out that Journey only gets seventeen percent, and they're *huge*. So really, for being a new band, ten percent isn't really that bad, plus this is for everyone involved with the band and traveling with the band, not just the band. The more I think about it, it seems like a good deal.

Ready to sign, I approach the band, but I can't get everyone on board. A couple of guys in the band won't sign, thinking they can hold out for more money. The reps are not happy with our decision, and I soon find that no one from any label will talk to me now. Apparently, when a record label offers you a good deal and you turn it down, other labels won't even take the time to look at you. We find ourselves blackballed across the board by the music industry. A *huge* opportunity lost.

We send demos everywhere. MTV airs one of our videos on MTV's Basement Tapes, and HBO plays one on HBO's Video Jukebox, but both of these are self-promotion. No one will even talk with us about a record deal now that we have a reputation for being hard to work with. The band's getting discouraged, and I don't know how to fix this. Continuing to promote them, I beat the streets and sell many records.

Needing a fresh new start, we head to Chicago Paragon Studios to record a new album. While in Chicago, Jon, the keyboard player, tells me that Russ, a PR rep from A&M records, contacted him and wants to meet with us. We find out Russ no longer works for A&M but still has contacts within. Russ has heard our material, and he's interested in taking our music to A&M. Finally!

Super excited about this opportunity, we meet with Russ and are ready to sign when Russ throws in a wrench. Russ will sign Rider, but under one stipulation. He wants my job. He explains to us that in order for Rider to get this record deal, I will have to step down as manager and turn the band over to him.

For the last three years, my number-one goal and only aspiration has been to see Rider succeed. We've had so many opportunities fall through due to bad decisions. I can't risk losing this chance for them. I would rather resign as manager if that's what it takes to see the band succeed. I ask Russ for one thing—I want to remain active with the band in some way. Russ shakes my hand enthusiastically in agreement. Just like that, Rider is offered a record deal with Russ as their new manager. As for me, I haven't yet been told what my new job is.

Back at home, it doesn't take me long to figure out they've weeded me out of the band completely. I am decimated, shattered, and hurt beyond belief. This hits me harder than the split from my wife. I can't imagine a divorce could be any worse than this separation from the band. What do I do now? These are my friends. The band is my life, my job, my way to survive. I helped put this band together. I poured everything I had—physically, mentally, and financially—into this band. I took them from a mere bar band to signing with a record label. All of it—the rock n roll lifestyle, the excitement, action, the pursuit of fame—all of it gone just like that. I'm lost. Completely and totally lost.

I dust myself off and proceed to manage a couple other rock bands, Recker and Gouge, but they're not Rider. I can't shake the feeling that I've lost something great. Hoping the best for Rider, I keep track of them and soon learn that Russ pretty much raped them. With only a verbal promise of a record deal, Russ had each band member sign a contract giving him complete control. The contract stated they are not allowed to play unless Russ is in attendance. If they perform without him, he can legally sue them. They now have to play under his rules, and he refuses to work with them, discuss anything with them, or set up any events. As for their verbal record contract, it's been months since they've played anywhere, and they're still waiting for that record deal to happen. I watch sadly as their future implodes in on them, and again, there's nothing I can do. Rider, a group of talented musicians, my friends, my band slowly dissolves into history.

It's 1985, Ann and I are not yet officially divorced, but we're not married either. It's just a matter of paperwork that I don't have time for. I've moved a few miles north into a doublewide mobile home in

Storyland Park just west of Bethalto where the rent is very cheap. Ann's moved on with her life, and I'm trying to move on with mine.

Every time I hear a Bon Jovi song on the radio, I shake my head, anguished that we're not on tour with them. Turning down that offer haunts me as being one of the dumbest decisions ever made by a band manager. We should have signed for ten percent, and we should have toured with Bon Jovi. Bon Jovi is currently touring with KISS. We should *right now* be touring with KISS. Kiss that one good-bye.

Looking back, I think the problem was that we all lived like rock stars, we partied like rock stars, we really thought we *were* rock stars, but we weren't, not yet. We sure were good together, though. They had talent, and I did a good job promoting them. We had fans, drugs, girls, alcohol, the attention of record labels and the local news, and we just knew we had made it and nothing was going to stop us—nothing. In reality, we did not have a clue how to deal with record companies, and we didn't realize the importance of just getting on stage and going on tour. So many great opportunities were lost, and doors slammed shut just like that—gone, done, finished. Dang, we were close.

Without the band, I have more time than I need, and I find myself falling back into old routines. I have a girlfriend—and have had many—but today is Ann's birthday, so I decide to call her and wish her well, see how she's been. Somewhere in the conversation, I ask her to lunch, and she accepts. We spend the afternoon talking, laughing, and enjoying each other's company like old times, and before I know it, we've decided, maybe, to give our marriage another try. But I have a problem, a *huge* problem—my girlfriend.

I've been trying to cut loose from this girl for a while. Let's just say she's being difficult. I tell her it's over, that she needs to stay away, but she keeps coming back. I tell her I'm getting back together with my wife, and she completely freaks out hollering, yelling, throwing things, and threatening me. I ask her to give back the keys to my trailer, and she refuses, completely flipping her personality now—begging, pleading with me, apologizing and promising to behave, and trying to hug me. I think, *Too late*. I gently push her away, but she won't leave.

Wanting to be with my wife, I sneak calls to Ann asking her to meet me at a hotel so we can spend time together. It's the only way we can see each other until I can permanently shed this crazy girlfriend. Most men having affairs call their girlfriends behind their wife's back to meet privately in hotels. Me? I'm sneaking behind my girlfriend's back to meet my wife in hotels. My girlfriend starts stalking me, constantly showing up at the video stores and following me around. I'm afraid for both Ann and myself, but a few months later, she finally gets the hint and leaves for good. Ann and I spend the next three months together only to find that, like before, this marriage just isn't going to work.

While I'm hanging out with my new girlfriend, Ann calls with some news. She's pregnant, and yes, it's mine. Wow! I did *not* see that coming!

Chapter 6
Alisha
The Coliseum

While setting up the studio for Tuesday night's rehearsal, I notice a cute little blonde walk in with Greg, Recker's sound man. I normally don't check out other guy's women, so I try hard to ignore her, but this one definitely has my attention. Ann's about to have the baby, and after a marginal try on my part, we've been separated for months. I'll be there for Ann, just not as her husband. I will always be there for our baby.

Greg leaves the room, and this cute little blonde introduces herself. We talk until Greg returns. Mikki is easy to talk to, and I enjoy our conversation. After rehearsal, she leaves with Greg, and I don't think much more about her, but then I get a call.

"Hey, I really want to hook up with you."

"What do you mean? Aren't you with Greg?"

"No. Oh no, we're just friends. If you're not interested, that's fine, but if you are, I'd really like to hook up with you."

Intrigued by Mikki's brassy boldness, I quickly respond, "Sounds like fun!"

Not quite sure how to take her or what to expect on our first date, I act a perfect gentleman and plan on dinner at Tony's Steakhouse in Alton. I'm surprised when she kills my plans.

"Let's don't mess with dinner," she says. "Can we get a room?"

Wow! Just wow! Shocked and not knowing her well enough to know if she's kidding or not, I stare at her, trying to read her facial expressions. Yes, she's serious. This gal is no joke. Two weeks later, she moves into my doublewide.

Love, lust…I don't know what we have, and I don't care. This intense new relationship with Mikki motivates me to expedite my divorce with Ann. Our marriage had been toxic for years. Nothing can fix it. It's time to move on.

Ann calls telling me she's at the hospital. I rush to the hospital and run in the front door, looking for the maternity ward. A couple of nurses take me back to wash up and put on scrubs in preparation for the delivery. I walk in to see Ann contracting and am instantly overwhelmed with emotion seeing her on the delivery table in so much pain. For hours, I remain at her side, calmly talking to her, feeding her ice chips, rubbing cramps out of her legs. Finally, baby Alisha enters our world. Within seconds, the doctor places this tiny little girl in my arms, and I am in awe!

Ann's sister Connie films everything. Smiling for the camera, I show off my daughter then look down at Alisha and am mesmerized. She is pink, warm, and wiggly as she turns her head toward me and opens her mouth. She is perfect. My baby daughter, my first child, is absolutely perfect.

Ann and I spend the day talking and laughing. Neither of us can take our eyes off this precious little girl. I stand up to gently hand Alisha to Ann, and I pause, holding her close for just one more second, not wanting to let her go. I forget about everything else. All that matters right now is this baby girl. Ann and I are getting along so well. I stay at the hospital all day and wonder now what? What am I going to do? While Ann sleeps, I check on Alisha in the nursery every few minutes. I just stare at her, my beautiful little girl. I don't want to leave them, but after a day, I need to go home to freshen up and change clothes.

Part of the maternity package at St Joseph's Hospital is a candlelight dinner for two—and a half. Instead of going home, I meet up with Rusty, and we celebrate by toasting the new baby with a gram of coke. The afternoon turns to evening turns to night turns to morning.

Meanwhile across town, waiting on a husband she never really had, Ann, tired of waiting, picks up her knife and cuts into a cold steak as she sits alone in a hospital room at a candlelit table set for two. She slowly chews her steak as a single tear trickles down her cheek. Looking over to the crib as Alisha takes a deep, contented breath, she smiles down at her daughter and says, "It's okay, Alisha. You and me, we're going to be just fine." It's a pivotal moment in Ann's life as courage surges through her, giving her the strength she needs to move on.

I have a lot to work out. I have issues, the band, the new album we're recording, the studio, my soon-to-be ex-wife, my girlfriend, and now my daughter. For the next two days, I drink, do dope, and pop pills excessively. It's how I cope.

I make it back to the hospital in time to drive Ann and Alisha home. Hung over as hell, I pop enough pills to get through the next few hours. The ride is uncomfortably silent, broken only by small coos from Alisha. I don't know how to be a dad, and I'm not changing my lifestyle anytime soon. The band, the studio, Mikki, alcohol, dope, especially dope—it's who I am now.

Through bloodshot eyes, Ann looks at me and asks, "What are we doing, Darwyn? I mean really, *what?* I want—no, I deserve—to know!"

I know she's right, but I have no words for her. We drive home in complete silence, and I drop them off and leave. I know, I'm pathetic. I can't change right now. I can't.

Weeks go by before Ann allows me a day alone with Alisha. I don't argue—she's the mom. Carefully unbuckling her from her car seat, I carry her inside my doublewide and show her to Mikki. I set her down in front of the couch and just stare at her. She's so pure and innocent. Mikki looks down at her just as I get a strong whiff of something nasty. I look up at Mikki. "Whoooooooow!" I exclaim. "What's that?"

"Don't look at me! It's your kid! I don't know how to change one of those things!"

Mikki's not a kid person. She's never been around babies and knows nothing about how to care for one. So with this being my daughter, I attempt to be a good dad and attend to the nasty deed, laughing as Mikki gags and runs out of the trailer. Braving the cold wind, she stands in the front yard smoking a cigarette. Smiling and proud of myself, I make sure Mikki sees me putting that awful diaper in a bag and tying it up to throw away. Holding the swinging bag in front of me, I yell to her, "I did it!" I walk back to the kitchen and push it deep into the trashcan. Phew, that was a bad one.

Having turned my half of the video stores over to Mom, and with Rider out of the picture, my production studio is slowly going belly up. I need a new business and am thinking of opening a nightclub.

It's 1986, and I'm driving south on highway 55 coming home from Springfield when I notice a For Lease sign in the front yard of the historic Coliseum Ballroom in Benld. I've always heard stories about this place. A long time ago when all the neighboring clubs were required to close at one in the morning, everyone would drive out to The Coliseum Ballroom which was allowed to stay open until three. It's been closed for years.

Pulling into the parking lot, I drive to the front door, looking up with admiration at this legendary red brick landmark. Getting out of the van to look around, I get an eerie yet cool vibe as I walk the weed-lined perimeter. Reaching into the console for a pen to write down the phone number, I see an old woman walking across the street toward me. She reminds me of Granny from *The Beverly Hillbillies*—dress, hair, everything. From the middle of the street, she yells, "You looking to do something with this old place?" She's got to be at least eighty.

"Just looking," I yell back as I write down the number.

"This place has some history, that's for sure! My name's Gertrude. What's yours?"

"Darwyn."

I put the pen back, slip the paper into my wallet, and turn to offer my hand. Wow, she has to be at least *ninety*. She gently places her hand in mine, laughing. "Darwyn? Like the man who says we all come from monkeys, huh?"

I smile, finding her humorous. "Except my name is spelled with a Y, not an I."

She snickers. "Like that makes a difference."

Looking over to The Coliseum, she tells me, "My daddy helped build this place. He was shot right outside town there, running moonshine from here. I lived in this town my whole life. I've seen it all. This place looks like crap right now, but back in its day, it had the biggest dance floor from St. Louie to Chicago. That dance floor's least ten thousand square feet." She turns to look up at the building. "They featured the orchestras of Tommy Dorsey, Duke Ellington, Kay Kyser, Count Basie—most all the big bands. Those were the stars of music from the '20s to the '40s. Them were the days, they were. This here Coliseum use ta bring in crowds toppin' three thousand, it did, many of them from St. Louie!"

Pointing south, she looks back at me. "I taught school for forty years and spent an entire quarter teaching about the history of Benld and The Coliseum." She clicks into teacher mode, and I become her student. "When the popularity of the big bands faded, The Coliseum continued to draw crowds from nationally known acts such as The Everly Brothers, Fats Domino, Johnny Rivers, Ray Charles, and Ike and Tina Turner. This here huge gymnasium style building is oddly out of place in this small town of Benld, which is named after the founder Ben L. Dorsey. When The Coliseum opened on Christmas Eve of 1924, it was a hotbed of bootlegging, gambling, and prostitution. Benld's population back then was twice the present-day population of 1,700. Dominic Tarro built this building for a reported $50,000. It opened during the prohibition. That huge dance floor in there is surrounded by seating for 1,500 on the ground floor and an additional 1,500 on the balcony. From the time it opened, the ballroom's popularity and the glamor of big name entertainers was tinged with mystery and violence. Legend has it that Al Capone and other Chicago gangsters frequented here. Tarro was indicted in 1930 for selling illicit liquor and buying corn and sugar for bootleggers."

Leaning back against my van, I cross my legs and listen. She intrigues me.

"Before he was arraigned, he disappeared. His remains were found bound with wire months later along the Sangamon River up north near Springfield. Tarro's widow Marie continued to operate The Coliseum, marrying Jack Irvine in 1944. They kept her going until 1955 when Dominic and Marie's daughter Joyce Tarro took over. Joyce, fearing robbery, always carried a pistol, and sure enough, on February 15, 1976 when she was just fifty-two years old, she was killed during a robbery. She was confronted in the early morning hours while returning home with the previous night's receipts of more than $3,000. Tarro opened fire but was struck by six bullets in a shootout."

This place is perfect! Bending over, I gently shake her tiny hand and say good-bye, thanking her for the lesson. Driving straight to a pay phone, I inquire about the majestic Coliseum Ballroom. By the end of the week, it's mine!

Mikki and I are excited to get the keys and get started. Walking in the front door, we look around in wonder as its history races through our minds. We envision years of laughter, music, and dancing and can't wait to open it for our generation. We have our work cut out for us, though. This place has been empty for years and definitely shows it. It's in such bad shape it'll most likely take months for us to get it ready. We move to Benld to start the long process of cleaning up and restoring this historic club. Unlike Ann who wanted nothing to do with my ventures and was always fearful of the rock 'n' roll lifestyle, Mikki is as excited as I am and is by my side, helping me. Mikki fears nothing and is involved with everything concerning the club. The bands, the people, the excitement, the entire rock scene piques her interest. She is thrilled to death. After having a marriage where I had to hide everything from my wife, it's refreshing to have a partner who's going to work with me, one I can discuss anything with and one who is on board and as excited as I am.

Mikki and I stand in the back of the freshly renovated Coliseum Ballroom as the last coat of paint dries on the huge ten thousand square foot dance floor, captivated by it all. We've worked hard for three long months, and it's done, finished, finally ready to open. Mikey fires up all the lighting, bringing the opera house style stage to life. All three bars, one on each side of the dance floor and one in the balcony, are fully stocked and ready for the Grand Opening Friday night.

For the Grand Opening, I hire a very popular St. Louis heavy metal band I had promoted through my studio. Advertising on the radio, in papers, and on posters and billboards, I treat it as an "event." The night we've been waiting for, working toward for three long months has come, and we're eager and ready, arriving early to check and recheck everything.

The doors open at 7 p.m., and my heart sinks when at 8:30, not a single person besides employees have come through the front doors. The band starts playing at nine in a building designed for three thousand, but there are only ten patrons scattered throughout. I can't believe this! Mikki and I are devastated. Together, we worked so hard for the last three months to accomplish what? Nothing. Just another one of my failed ventures.

Sitting at the bar after closing, going through a few receipts together, Mikki and I drink ourselves stupid. Our only option is to ride out the month as planned until our next lease payment is due, then split.

Not near as excited the next night, we show up at The Coliseum as planned and go through the motions expecting the same results as the night before. But this time, I hear people talking and laughing outside the doors. My breath escapes when I open the doors to see at least two hundred people waiting to get in! Relieved and laughing, I greet them, now excited for the evening's festivities. Enthusiastically, Mikki and I get to work hustling around, making sure it's all good. Two hours later when the band takes the stage, over two thousand people are talking, laughing, dancing, and oh yes, drinking.

In the early morning after the club closes and everyone's gone, Mikki and I sit at the bar, this time excited to go through *many* receipts. We did it! Discovering our Grand Opening was mistakenly advertised for Saturday, not Friday, we realize Friday night's disaster was our own fault. Oops.

Featuring local bands the first three weekends of the month then a national act on the fourth weekend is working great! Every weekend, we pull in more and more people, but I quickly find that being the manager of one of the largest rock clubs in southern Illinois is not easy, especially when I've never even had the experience of tending bar let alone running an entire club. I'm starting to get a little uneasy with the crowd's energy. We have a good number of rowdy locals who work long, hard days all week on the farm, and they're just looking to drink and have some fun on weekends. We also draw an equal number of patrons coming in from the cities with their stunning girlfriends, also looking for a good time away from the norm of the city. I quickly find these two crowds don't mix.

Standing in front of the bar on a sold-out Saturday night, I witness a local accidently spill his drink on one of those high-maintenance city girls. I saw it—it really was an accident. The city boy thinks otherwise and slugs the local who slugs him right back. The girlfriend slugs the local, and the local doesn't hesitate to slug her. As soon as the local boy hits that city girl, Armageddon breaks out! All hell breaks loose as a fifteen-person brawl breaks out with everyone hitting each other, knocking each other down, throwing chairs, throwing people, and breaking tables. I catch a glimpse of someone's fist flying in my direction, so I quickly duck left, swing around on my right heel, and take the punk's leg out from under him while moving toward the bar and away from the center of the mayhem. Not knowing what to do, I watch as this mob wrestles their way toward the door and out into the parking lot. Ten guys are piled up on top of each other, slugging away. I stand watching, realizing just how ill-equipped I am for this.

Mikki's brother Jeff is our doorman. In an attempt to gain control, he starts zapping people with his Taser gun! This apparently ticks some guy off who then throws a beer bottle, cracking Jeff in the head and knocking him down. Out of the corner of my eye, I see Mikki jump on the guy's back and wrap her arm around his throat, slugging the crap out of his face. At this moment, I make a mental note to *never* tick Mikki off.

Pulling out the .38 S&W pistol I have holstered to my back, I raise my hands and fire three shots into the air. Everyone freezes. You can hear a pin drop along with the sirens in the distance getting closer. Everyone runs to their cars, trying to get out of the parking lot before the police arrive. The brawl is over, just like that.

The crowd is still scattering when the police pull in. Reaching behind my back I holster my gun as I walk to the front door and wait for the police. Benld's finest, a four-foot-five-inch police officer who's becoming a Coliseum weekend regular pulls into the parking lot with sirens blaring and lights flashing. He gets out and struts toward me, clearly perturbed. I've nicknamed him "Too Short." Before he reaches me, I smile and yell, "At least this time we didn't need an ambulance!"

He doesn't share my feeling of proficiency. Stopping about five feet in front of me to save his neck from having to look up too far, he angrily asks, "How many times are we going to do this?"

Leaning against the building and lighting a cigarette, I take a long deep draw and ask innocently, "Do what?" Exhaling smoke in his direction I remind him, "We didn't call you. Look around—we handled it."

He responds, "You better get a handle on this because if we get one more call, I'll make sure the city council hears about it!"

"No problem."

He gets in his car and leaves.

Still out of breath, Mikki looks up at me wide-eyed and whispers, "We have to do something or they're going to shut us down."

Following her to the bar, I grab a couple beers and sit down next to her. Handing her one, I chug mine then say, "I know. Hey, I have an idea. It's a little radical, but maybe it'll work."

My cousin is a member of Tonto's motorcycle club, a small-town version of the Hell's Angels. I call him about the problems I'm having at the club. We talk back and forth, and within the week, it's set. The Coliseum now has security. Their job is to watch for and squash any trouble before it starts. It's working great. As soon as a scuffle breaks out, they stop it swiftly and quietly. The word quickly gets around—if you start trouble at The Coliseum, you'll wake up the next morning with something broken, and it won't be your heart. If you get out of line, you'll be wishing you'd just stayed home. As long as you don't cause problems, you can party all you want. Surprisingly, this arrangement is working out better than I expected.

After a few successful months, the president of the Tonto's calls to let me know he's invited some of his biker friends from other clubs to party with us this Saturday night.

"Great! Come on down," I tell him.

I feel obligated to these guys. I mean, it's the least I can do for them. Saturday afternoon, I'm up on a ladder changing the marquee out front when I hear a loud clap of thunder. Confused, I look around at the beautiful, cloudless, sunny day. Unlike a thunderclap, the noise gets louder and louder. I climb down the ladder and look north toward the noise, feeling a little uncomfortable. Then I see a line of motorcycles breaking the horizon. I watch in amazement as a huge caravan—row after row of rumbling, backfiring motorcycles—packs the street. The noise is deafening, and my chest vibrates as, one by one, they drive past me into my parking lot. I stand under the marquee watching as they just keep pulling in, no end in sight.

Not only is Benld a very small town, but about eighty percent of its residents are elderly. The thunderous noise brings everyone out of their homes. Standing out on front porches and lawns in their overalls and flannels, watching this spectacle, they lean on their canes, their mouths hanging open. Some of them are shaking their fists. Being a town with a history of sin and violence going all the way back to the '30s and '40s, they sure are a bunch of stiff necks now. Looking around and analyzing the situation, something crosses my mind—two cops in town? If this gets out of hand, it could get real ugly really fast.

With almost three thousand motorcycles parked in The Coliseum parking lot, we have a packed house, and surprisingly, it's a great evening. The night turns out to be a complete success for the club—but not so much for Benld. The bikers left quite a mess in their wake as they exited town. On my way home, I drive across streets littered with beer cans and bottles. The entire town is trashed—yards and streets are strewn with debris. I've heard reports of several bikers going to the only gas station in town, filling up their tanks, and leaving without paying. They also scared employees and terrorized customers at the Dairy Queen, the only fast food joint in town. Benld's residents have to be furious with me. I'm sure I'll be hearing from them soon.

Weeks pass, and besides casual talk, no one's approached me about last month's Harley invasion. It's all good. We've booked Edgar Winter for our fourth weekend of the month, and I'm excited for Saturday night. By law, you have to be twenty-one to drink in the state of Illinois, but we can still allow eighteen-year-olds into the club to watch the shows. Our system is if you're old enough to drink, the doorman will stamp your hand. No stamp, no alcohol. This way the bartenders can just glance at the customer's hand and know who to serve without having to worry about checking IDs with every order.

I have three bars in this club and at least two thousand people visiting on weekends. It is physically impossible for me to be everywhere making sure all my employees are following rules. Halfway through the performance, Mikki and I take a moment to sit back and enjoy Edgar Winter's "Frankenstein." These are the perks of the job we love so much.

Standing up, I notice a commotion by the front doors. Cops rush in and start handcuffing my bartenders. Too Short slowly struts behind my bar. Reaching up with his stubby little fingers, he rips down my liquor license. Turning proudly and displaying it, he snarls, "You're done!" He looks up at me smiling as he continues, "We have thirteen minors who have signed sworn affidavits that they were served alcohol here tonight."

They set me up! They totally set me up!

Twenty minors sent by the DUI task force were planted in the club tonight for the sole purpose of trying to buy alcohol. Thirteen of them succeeded. It didn't escape my notice that the thirteen who were served were beautiful young ladies who look at least twenty-

85

five. The seven who were not served were dorky guys who looked obviously underage. Nevertheless, I am shut down with legal cause to do so. There is nothing I can do about it.

Waking up the next morning, I pick my pants up off the floor and dig in my pockets. I'm out of pills! Dropping to my knees to search the bottom drawer, I reach deep in the back under some old winter socks, searching for the little wooden box where I stash my coke. *Nothing!* I always keep coke on hand, both to treat the bands and to use when I run out of pills. *Where is it?* I've got nothing. Not a good way to start my morning, especially after the night I had. I can't sleep all day, not today! I need to make calls to cancel upcoming events, I need to search for a job, I need look into moving back, I need to talk to my lawyer about the upcoming legalities of last night. Crap! Crap! *Crap!*

Getting dressed for a trip to Wood River to visit my dealer, I search my closet for a clean shirt. On the top shelf in plain sight, almost as if someone just placed it there, is a Bible. The one Grandma gave me when I was a kid. How is that possible? I haven't seen this Bible in ten years, and I definitely didn't pack it when I moved to this house. I pull it down and take a quick look then toss it back up on the shelf. I'll ask Mikki about it later. First things first, I have got to score some dope. I need a fix, fast.

Pulling out of Benld, I head south on highway 55 for the thirty-minute drive to my dealer's house and ponder my current situation. I also can't stop thinking about that Bible. I know I didn't put it in the closet, and Mikki said she's never seen it before. Someone had to put it there. I mean, it just didn't magically appear after ten years. Cruising past cornfields and cow pastures, I think about Mom and Grandma and how much it would hurt them if they knew only ten percent of the person I've become. An incredible weight crushes me just thinking about them finding out. The idea of hurting either of them is out of the question. They must never know.

With one hundred dollars in my pocket and a drug habit of three hundred a day, what am I going to do? I have to pay Edgar Winter $7,000, but with the cops shutting us down before the night was over, we didn't bring in enough to pay them. After the dealer, I've got to run by Mom's house to borrow money for the band.

I'm broke. I've never been broke before in my life. I've always had an abundant cash flow. Saving and financial planning aren't my strong suits. I've always been comfortable living day to day in a realm of extreme excess, never giving thought it might end. I'm no longer involved with the video stores, my studio and agency are both gone, and now my club is history.

Slowing down to drive through Litchfield, I hit the steering wheel as I realize just what a jam I'm in. The thought of speeding up and running my van into a telephone pole crosses my mind. Then I think of Alisha. She's the one thing that sets everything right in my world. As soon as I score, I'll call Ann and see if I can stop by and see my baby girl.

Chapter 7
1988
TJ
Nikki

With no job, no home, no money, and no idea how to support myself, Mikki and I have no place to go, so we move back into my old room in the basement of Mom's house. What else am I supposed to do? My divorce took over a year to finalize, and one month later, Mikki and I marry on New Year's Eve at a justice of the peace's home with Rusty and his wife standing up for us. Having no cash to keep up my $300-a-day drug habit forces me to cut back on consumption, which means most days I can't even get out of bed. I know I have to do something—there's no way I can continue to live like this. I just don't have a clue what to do. Running up drug debts, I'm bouncing checks all over two counties. My main priority now? Just getting enough money for today's supply.

As I'm paying for a pack of cigarettes at the gas station, I run into TJ, an old friend from high school. He invites me over to get high, telling me he bought Zach's grandpa's old house on Sixth Street in Roxana. Addict rule #1: never pass up free dope!

As I sit down on his living room sofa in a house I've partied in many times, TJ breaks out a giant bag of coke, at least a quarter pound. He scoops out a spoonful, dropping it into a shot glass full of water. He then drops an equal amount of baking soda in the mix, stirring it with a small metal rod and then microwaving it until a teardrop nugget forms on the end of the rod. Loading the nugget in a bong, he draws the first hit and then passes it to me. Lighting the bowl, I take a long deep hit of my first freebased coke and receive an intense and immediate rush.

In contrast to his intimidating six-foot-one-inch frame, TJ is very soft-spoken and laid back with an easygoing disposition. Behind his dark, curly, shoulder-length hair and scraggly mustache, he has one of those faces that no matter what he says or feels, he looks like he's smiling. Still living in Roxana, he hasn't changed a bit since high school. We spend hours getting high, talking, and catching up on each other's lives. When I finish telling him about the arrests and the closing of The Coliseum, TJ starts talking about how he brings in kilos of cocaine from Detroit and could use someone to ride with him. He brings to my attention that with all the people I know that get high, I could move a lot of dope. I'm listening. "Ride with me Darwyn. If you help me sell, you'll have more money than you ever had running that club!"

Only thinking of today, this moment, I tell him, "Right now, I just need some speed, man!" Coke is okay, but it's a short-lived high. I need more.

Smiling, TJ digs in his pocket and pulls out a hundred bucks. He hands it to me, saying, "Pay me back when you can."

I leave immediately, heading straight to my dealer's house.

Mikki quietly listens as I tell her about working with TJ. When I'm done, I can tell she's upset, so I prepare myself for her to read me the riot act. Instead, she blurts out, "I'm pregnant! I think."

Stunned, I ask, "What do you mean, you think?"

"I took a home pregnancy test, and it's positive, but I'm not going to believe it until I hear it from a doctor. If it's true, Darwyn, I'm not ready for this. You and me, we're not ready for a baby! I don't think we'll ever be ready, and now you come home telling me you're going to start dealing *drugs!*"

Mikki looks around at the place we're living in, my high school bedroom. She plops down on the bed. Looking up at me with a troubled face, she asks quietly, "What in the hell are we going to do?"

Pulling her up to me, I hold her close, swaying back and forth. Slowly, reassuringly, I whisper in her ear, "We are going to do whatever we have to do to survive, babe!"

Pushing away, she sits back down and spits out, "You mean whatever we have to do for you to be able to support your habit, Darwyn!"

I set her straight. "Like I said, Mikki, whatever we have to do! Paying for my habit is part of us surviving! You know that! You knew that when we got together! I never hid it from you, Mikki, never! Nothing's changed!"

"Yes, Darwyn! It *has* changed! Back then, you didn't have to deal to pay for your habit!"

The next morning, Mikki drops a urine sample off at the doctor's office. The following day, her doctor's secretary calls to confirm she's pregnant.

Getting ready to drive to Dearborn, MI with TJ, I think about Mikki and our new baby, but then TJ passes over the bong, and it all feels right again. Dearborn's located just outside of Detroit, and TJ tells me this contact deals in millions of dollars' worth of cocaine, so I'm expecting to pull up to some huge, lavish, crazy Scarface kind of house. Instead, we drive down a very modest street and pull up to a very modest house with a chain link fence bordering the edge of the yard. I follow TJ to the front door, stepping over a child's Big Wheel and pushing a ball toward a basketball pole in the driveway.

As I walk in the front door, my sinuses sting from the built-up smell of stale cigarette smoke. Oddly, a woman and three small children are running around in this dingy, crappy, barren home. This house has no furniture whatsoever. There is no couch, no table, no lamps, nothing. The "contact" asks if we want something to drink. We follow him to the kitchen, and he opens his refrigerator and offers us a beer. I notice the only thing in his fridge is one pitcher of iced tea and beer, lots of beer. There are children living in this house, and there is not one single crumb of food in the refrigerator? I feel bad for these kids.

He hands us beers then grabs hold of the fridge and slides it over to expose a secret compartment. Reaching down, he pops open a small door and pulls out three kilos of coke. He hands one to TJ. With a pocketknife, TJ pierces the brick, sticking the knife deep inside, then he pulls it out and carefully licks the knife clean to test the dope's quality. "Excellent!" he proclaims, smiling, and tosses a gym bag full of cash to the contact. On our eight-hour drive back to Roxana, we snort coke until our noses bleed.

TJ was right—in a very short time, I am fat with cash dealing dope for him. Within months, I'm dealing kilos and kilos of cocaine and multiple pounds of marijuana. Most importantly, I no longer have to worry about my daily supply. It doesn't take long before I have established a reputation around town as a high-level drug dealer.

Red, an associate, stops by TJ's to pick up a kilo. He pulls a Ziploc baggie out of his pocket, dumping a small amount of its contents onto a glass coffee table, then looks up at me and says, "Check it out! Just came in from Hawaii."

It looks like shards of broken glass. I watch him chop these crystals into a fine powder, dividing it into three fine lines. He hands me a three-inch straw, and I quickly snort an entire line. Instantaneously, I feel like someone's stabbing me in the eye with an ice pick. Screaming, I grab my face and hold my nose, second-guessing my quick decision. "Oh *man!* What the *hell* is this?"

Red and TJ crack up laughing on the couch, seemingly enjoying my pain. Red says, "Hawaiian Ice. The best crystal meth in the world."

When my pain subsides and I can talk again, I mumble, "Oh man, that was intense."

Fifteen minutes later, with meth rushing through my system, euphoria consumes me. Having taken speed daily for years, meth is similar but *much* more intense. Flying higher than I've ever flown before, I decide I am no longer a speed addict. Wow! Incredible! This stuff is good! I soar for twenty-four straight hours, and from this moment forward, meth is my drug.

Mikki and I are in our new apartment when TJ calls telling me to get ready for another run to Detroit. This time, since we're only picking up one kilo, we fly on a new airline because this airline currently has the laxest security. I don't even need an ID to board. The contact picks us up at the airport in Detroit and takes us back to his dingy, smelly house full of kids, drugs, and beer. This time after the money-dope exchange, I follow TJ to the back bedroom, and we divide the kilo into several small Ziploc baggies and then wrap each bag in plastic wrap. TJ takes off his shirt and pants then duct tapes the wrapped bags of dope sporadically over his body. I do the same. Now this? This is making me a little nervous.

Effortlessly walking through airport security, we board the plane and prepare for takeoff. Feeling completely relaxed as if there isn't $12,000 worth of cocaine strapped to my body, I'm surprised how easy this is. As I'm enjoying our flight back to St. Louis, laughing, talking, and drinking, I suddenly break out in a terrible sweat. My body is reacting to the duct tape and plastic wrap against my skin. Sweat starts dripping, soaking my pants and shirt. Looking down, I become nervous as more noticeable wet splotches appear. I look over at TJ, worried that someone will stop me and question me, which makes me sweat even more. Luckily, unless you're going through customs, it's not required to pass through security getting off a plane. After landing, I quickly walk past airport security, past police, past employees and patrons and go straight outside, leaving the airport without anyone noticing my predicament. Climbing into the car, I breathe deeply and look back at the airport, thinking about what could have happened. Who knew transporting dope through an airport could be this easy?

I arrive home to find Mikki pacing nervously back and forth. She's having contractions. Nicole Bryant, my second daughter, arrives the next morning, and I am again in awe. I hold this sweet little girl and think, *At least I'll be able to be with this one.* Ann and her new guy practically forbid me from seeing Alisha. I leave the hospital and head straight to TJ's to tell him the great news. Passing a bong, we celebrate the birth of my second beautiful daughter.

Over the last several weeks, TJ had become consumed with extreme paranoia. He constantly thinks someone is out to get him and is always fearful of being robbed. I tell him to relax, that it's all good, but my words fall on deaf ears. He's even paranoid about his parents who live a couple blocks away. TJ has two .44 magnum revolvers in cowboy-style holsters hanging on a coat hook by the front door. He now answers the door with his gun drawn, ready to shoot. TJ and I, we work well together—we have for a long time. He tells me what and where to deliver, and I always take care of his business. I make good money working for him, but his paranoia is starting to make me paranoid of *him*.

Hanging out at TJ's and getting high one day, Red suggests, "You know what? We don't have to go to Hawaii to get ice. The chemicals are readily available. If we put in the time and effort to learn, we could make this stuff ourselves."

He's right! After some research, I try several times with no success. Obsessed with figuring this out, I put in long hours in TJ's basement reading manuals, setting up equipment, and trying to cook a good batch of meth. We work at it diligently but just can't get it right.

Refusing to give up after botching batch after batch, I visit a local college medical library and read up on chemistry. I pull every book I can find on pharmaceutical chemicals and write down formulas I think I might need. I don't understand most of what I'm reading, but I stick with it wholeheartedly and quickly educate myself. It's actually starting to make sense. Trial and error, trial and error—Red spends hundreds of dollars funding our experiments as we continue trying to cook the perfect batch. With every failure, I research why it failed and make a new plan. Red purchases whatever I need, believing I will eventually get it right. We learn about phenyl-2-propanone, methylamine, catalyst reductions, and so forth until one night, *SUCCESS!* In just two short months, I figured it out! Red no longer has to go to Hawaii and smuggle back meth. I can make it right here. Ordering big this time, we set up an elaborate meth lab operation in TJ's basement, adding to our already very successful business. We bring in coke from Detroit, pot from Arizona, opium from Indiana, and now offer homemade meth from good ole Roxana.

Months pass, and for all practical purposes, business is going great. TJ stops by our apartment often, always careful not to bring dope anywhere around my family, and Mikki respects him for that. Mikki likes TJ, and TJ is always really cool around Nikki. Even though Mikki never sees it, she knows what I do for a living. She knows where our money comes from. She doesn't like it, but I keep assuring her it's just until I find another way to survive.

Many times, TJ pays me in drugs. He knows I'm not interested in his coke stash. Meth, that's what I want. The high of meth just can't be surpassed. As TJ's paranoia grows, we find it necessary to contract out our collections from those who take their time paying or choose not to pay at all. I soon learn that Red has a bad reputation among drug dealers. He likes to rob them. He often breaks into a drug dealer's home, holds them at gunpoint, and steals their stash! If they aren't home, he'll break in and trash their home until he finds what he came for. Red's a big guy with long, strawberry blonde hair. He's a little crazy — some even consider him brutal. He doesn't have many friends, but I like him, and he likes me. We work well together.

Life is intense. We're moving dope all over the country. Any dope that comes into the area, we have a hand in it. TJ is now basing at least a quarter ounce of coke a day and is becoming more and more paranoid. It's gotten so bad that when I knock on his door, I never know what he's going to do or what state of mind he'll be in. He worries me. I have everything—all my chemicals, formulas, and equipment—in his basement! TJ, my good friend, my business partner, seems to have changed overnight into someone I no longer recognize. I don't know what to do.

Standing outside TJ's door, I knock, but he doesn't answer. I knock harder, louder, but he still won't answer. I know he's in there, and it makes me mad, so I bang as hard as I can on his door yelling, "Hey! It's Darwyn! Open up!"

I can hear him moving around inside, but I can't get him to answer the door. Not knowing what to do, I give up and go home.

As soon as I walk into my apartment, Mikki hands me the phone, "Hey, man! I know it was *you!*"

Completely confused, I ask, "What are you talking about TJ? I was just there, and you wouldn't open the door! Why?"

"I know it was you Darwyn! I was in my bedroom last night, and I watched you crawl through my window! You stole all my dope! I *know* it was *you!*"

Failing to convince TJ that I was not at his house the night before and did not steal his stash, I hang up on him. Somehow in his paranoid mind, he really thinks I came over and stole his dope. Whether someone actually broke into his house and stole his dope, I don't know. I do know it definitely wasn't me, and after a lengthy argument, I don't know what else to say.

Bouncing Nikki on my lap, I think about TJ and his accusations. He's getting so wigged-out that he's doing stupid things now, bringing about unnecessary attention to himself. I'm afraid he's a liability now and a danger to all of us in the business. Most of his contacts have excluded him because of his erratic behavior, dealing only with me now. TJ's pretty far out there and no longer trustworthy. Maybe he blames me because he's jealous since he's no longer needed and feels ostracized. I don't know.

Clearly, TJ has become totally unhinged. He's called me every single day for the last month, threatening me and accusing me of ripping him off. His paranoia is over the top. Mikki, having witnessed many of his threats, is now fearful of him. He stopped by one day while I wasn't here and was acting irrationally toward her and Nikki. He scared them. She's now freaked out and tells me I have to do something. He's made it more than clear he's mad at me. He's gone crazy. We both know he always carries a gun, so now, whenever I leave the apartment, Mikki is so afraid she turns out all the lights and hides with Nikki until I return.

Not only is TJ calling me daily, we see him drive by the apartment and follow us when we leave. For the last few days, he's been tracking us. As a drug user myself, my paranoia has now escalated. It's getting crazy, to the point I can't think clearly. It has to stop, but I don't know how to make it stop.

Our window shatters as a large rock flies through it and lands on the kitchen floor next to my wife and child. Running to grab my gun, I hear TJ screaming, accusing me of stealing from him. Because of his unpredictable behavior, he no longer works with us, so I'm not really sure if he's livid over me taking his place in the business circle or if he's just gone raving mad from his extreme cocaine use. Mikki hides in the bedroom with Nikki, and by the time I run outside, he's gone.

The next day, I'm driving down the road when I look in my rearview mirror and notice TJ is following me again. I pull into a church parking lot, and he pulls in right behind me. I don't want to confront him—I'm trying to lose him. My plan is to pull into this parking lot and quickly exit the other side, hopefully losing him. Then I notice there's no other exit. I have to stop. Frustrated, I take a deep breath, glaring at him as I back up to turn my car around. He pulls in and immediately stops, waiting. On opposite sides of the parking lot, our vehicles facing each other, I stare at him and rev my engine. I've had it. I'm mad! I'm beyond *mad!* This *will* end here and now!

I'm high and wigged-out. Adrenaline races through my veins and takes over my body. My blood's boiling to the point I can no longer take it. I punch the gas pedal to the floor, and the engine vibrates as it roars to life. Cringing from the high-pitched squeal, I can smell rubber burning as the tires spin and slide on the asphalt parking lot. My intention? I am going to ram this guy head on. My car picks up speed as my tires grip the pavement, and he moves toward me with the same intensity. My mind is set. I'm going to do it. I'm not veering off course. This issue with TJ is about to be settled, head on. Gripping the steering wheel, I stay on course, watching as the distance between us vanishes. Then right at the last second, TJ swerves out of the way, screaming at me as we pass by each other's windows. Fishtailing out of the parking lot, I head straight home to tell Mikki what just happened.

"I'm done Mikki! I can't take it anymore! This has to end! *Now!* I don't care how it's going to end, it just has to *end!*"

During my half hour rant, Mikki points out the window, and I turn to see TJ's van driving down the cul-de-sac next to ours. This time, he has a passenger with him. Straining to see who's with him, I watch as he drives to the end of the street and circles, knowing exactly where he's headed next–our street. Looking out the window with my wife and child behind me, sure enough, we watch as he turns onto our road. Not yet settled from the earlier incident, this sends me into a frenzy. I run up the steps and out the door with my sawed-off shotgun.

Mikki cries out, "What are you doing?"

Not thinking, only reacting on overdrive, I walk toward the road, loading my Mossberg. I yell back at her, "This has *got* to end, and it's going to end *right now!*"

Standing in the middle of the street, gun pumped and ready, I drop down on one knee and take aim at TJ's van. Screeching to a halt, TJ throws his van in reverse as I pop off two rounds directly above the van. Daniel is in the passenger seat. I have no beef with him. I watch Daniel flip out as I stay kneeled with my smoking shotgun pointed at their windshield. TJ whips the van around and speeds off as Daniel's bloodcurdling screams fade away.

I can't continue like this. I'm so fed up with this guy following us, threatening us. I watch from the middle of the road until the van is out of sight. Snapping back to reality and realizing the police are most likely on their way, I glance around quickly and then walk back to the apartment.

Holding our crying daughter, Mikki stares at me, horrified. I yell, "We're out of here!"

Bouncing Nikki in her arms, she agrees, pleading, "Let's go! Let's get out of here! Let's move, now!"

"Where?"

"Remember when Rusty said he could get you a job at a recording studio in Phoenix? Let's go!"

"Okay. If that's what you want, let's do it."

I call Rusty and ask, "Is that job offer in Phoenix still available?"

"Absolutely! Come on out. I'll hook you up."

"Great. We're out of here."

Looking around the apartment, we start throwing what we need to pack in the middle of the living room. As I'm packing, I start thinking about our situation, realizing just how dangerous it is. I tell Mikki, "I don't like you being here with the baby. You and Nikki need to stay at your Mom's while I finish packing."

Within minutes, Mikki and the baby are safe at her mom's house, and I'm back at the apartment packing up the small stuff. We decide to leave the furniture and just take what we can quickly carry out the door.

Someone taps at the back door. It's TJ. With the back part of our apartment halfway underground, our windows are high, and I watch TJ's feet as he walks down the hill toward the front of the house. Having already packed the Mossberg in the trunk of my car, I grab a.22 pistol. It's a little bitty thing, almost like a cap gun, but it's all I have right now, and this worries me knowing that TJ always carries his.44. Standing with my back to the wall, holding this little pistol up against my chest, I watch his shadow move again toward the back of my house off the kitchen. When he reaches the back door, I take aim, firing two shots through the door above his head. I watch him run away and can't help but notice how much he's changed in every way—body, mind, and soul. His always smiling face hasn't smiled in months. He looks like a tall bag of bones. TJ used to be my friend, but I don't know who he is now.

Too anxious to pack, I jump in my car and head to the video store to talk to Mom. I need to tell her about my plans to move to Arizona. Just to be safe, I slide my gun into a briefcase, placing it in the front seat beside me. Mom has no idea TJ's been threatening us—how would I explain it? Mom knows I'm messed up, but she has no idea about my lifestyle or what I actually do.

Odies Ice Cream Parlor sits to the left of the video store. With an outside window to order from and outside tables and chairs, Odies has no inside seating. It's packed today, and just as I get out of my car, here comes TJ on foot. I'm drawn to the one stiff arm he holds close to the front of his body as he walks around the corner of Odies toward me. Then I see why—he's holding his.44. There are children lined up at the window of the ice cream parlor, and all the tables are occupied. I open my briefcase, pull out my gun, and quickly draw down on him. We go at each other, both of us pointing our guns. It's a standoff.

Everyone starts screaming, grabbing their children, and running to safety. Some people shove their kids to the ground and cover them with their bodies. Derek sees us from the counter of the video store and immediately calls the police. Mom hears the screams and fearlessly walks right out the front door of the video store, purposely standing directly between TJ and me. She's standing there between our two loaded guns like she's going to stop us with her folded arms and stern motherly look. Panicked, worried, and shaken, I ask, "Mom, what are you doing?"

She's determined to stop this whole thing herself. TJ starts to freak out when he hears her yell for Derek to call the police, but I'm thinking, *Cool, the cops are coming.* Then TJ's dad drives around the corner of the ice cream parlor, and TJ throws his gun in his dad's car. His dad takes off. Now, TJ stands there staring at me, but without a gun. I'm the only one with a gun. Not sure what to do, I quickly lower my gun, look around, and walk inside the video store to the back room. I toss the gun onto an upper shelf.

The cops arrive and ask, "Okay, where's the gun?"

I show them where it is and give it to them. I'm the one being arrested, cuffed, and escorted out the door. I notice TJ in the parking lot. He yells, "Hey, Darwyn! All I want to do is talk to you, man!"

"You lying son of a bitch! Just go! Get out of my face, dude, seriously!"

I go to jail, and TJ does not. I explain my situation to the cops, and one of them tells me, "If I had TJ coming after me with a gun, I'd carry a gun, too, and if I had the opportunity to take him out, I would."

They pretend to be cool about it, but I know they would like nothing more than for TJ and me to just kill each other. They know me from the video store and know I come from a good family. They're all aware of my situation, much more than Mom is. They know I've gone rotten, made bad decisions, and am still making bad decisions, and they know exactly what I do for a living. I call my lawyer, who calls the DA for me, telling him, "Hey look, Darwyn's on his way out of town. He's getting ready to move. This feud between these two's been boiling for a while. If he promises to get out of town immediately, will you drop the charges?"

They agree to drop all charges as long as I leave town immediately. As soon as the Wood River police release me, I pick up my family, but I have one more stop before Phoenix. I have to stop in and say good-bye to Grandma.

Chapter 8
1989
Phoenix
Chris

Grandma seems relieved when I tell her we're moving to Arizona. This surprises me. Apparently, she knows more than I realize.

Mikki, Nikki, and I head west with only what we quickly threw in the car. We have no idea what life will be like in Arizona, but we know it'll be better without TJ and his.44. I'm done dealing drugs and look forward to working in the recording industry again.

Completely strung out from stress along with going through withdrawals, I keep telling myself this is my chance for a fresh start. I'm going to quit getting high, and with my new job, I won't have to sell drugs anymore. It's time to live a clean life. During the two-day drive to Arizona, I reassure Mikki, promising these things to her repeatedly. I also make this promise to myself. Deep down inside, part of me just laughs.

Rusty and his wife Diane have already secured an apartment for us in the same complex in which they live. The doors on all three floors of this apartment complex face each other around a center courtyard filled with beautiful palm trees and flowering cacti. Feeling hopeful about our new life across the country, I pay our deposit at the front office and immediately unpack the car. Ten minutes later, we're completely moved in. Having fled Illinois so quickly, we left everything behind—our furniture, beds, appliances, and most of Nikki's toys.

Shopping at local garage sales the following day, we find lawn furniture and furnish our apartment as cheaply as possible. I spend the evening scrubbing used chairs and a table along with hooking up an old black and white TV. Without a proper antenna, I attach a clothes hanger to the back of the TV, allowing some reception. It's snowy, but we can make out a few stations.

Excited to start my new job, I ride with Rusty to Pantheon Studio and am impressed at how nice of a studio it is. Located in Scottsdale, Arizona, it looks like a little adobe house sitting out in the middle of the desert, but inside, it's been completely converted into a recording studio. Rusty's worked here for a while, playing background guitar on different tracks for albums. I start training for assistant sound director for a new project starting soon. The studio just finished a Waylon Jennings project, and I am stoked to the max when I learn that Willie Nelson's project is next.

It doesn't take long for me to realize everyone working at Pantheon is spun. Not cocaine spun but speed spun, meth spun. It takes a tweeker to spot a tweeker. I notice one of the sound guys working on a track when I leave work at five. I come back at eight the next morning, and there he is, in the exact same spot and same clothes, having worked all day and all night—and still working. He hasn't moved from his seat. His eyes are wide as silver dollars, and he's sweating profusely as he remains completely focused on the audio console connected through a patchbay to the racks of gear.

The writing's on the wall, and I'm thinking, *Oh, brother! Here we go again. I've jumped out of the frying pan into the fire!* I don't ask and don't use, but it's not long before I'm offered.

"Ya man. If you want to get high, dude, there's plenty of stuff around. No problem."

I'm thinking, *No problem? Yeah man, this just might be a problem!*

The temptation's too great, and I justify it by telling myself I'll only do a bump or two, just enough to really get into the recording sessions bringing my A game. I assure the worried voice within that I will *not* go back to it full blown, just use while working at the studio. Seven days later, I'm using every day.

Five weeks later, on Monday morning, I'm high and driving to work. Rusty and I pull into the studio driveway wondering where everyone is. The studio is completely locked up with no one in sight. We head to a pay phone and make a few calls trying to figure out what's going on. Unbelievable! The IRS had been investigating Willie Nelson, and this investigation trickled down to the studio. The government came in and closed it down, taking everything in it. One day I'm training, working, making money, and getting ready to mix for Willie Nelson, and the next day it's gone, over, history. Done, just like that.

Totally bummed about losing my job and missing the opportunity to work with Willie Nelson, I find myself jobless and moneyless again with a wife, a baby, and no way to score dope. Being new to Arizona with no family around to fall back on, I'm clueless about what to do. I feel overwhelmed and pressured with my back up against a wall.

Adrian and Linda live in the apartment next to us. Adrian is a very cut and cocky dude, a bona fide male Chippendale dancer with a long, curly mullet and impressive clothes. Everyone can hear him coming and going as his silver-tipped cowboy boots click loudly across the catwalk floor. He looks like a cop with his openly holstered gun slung across his shoulder. His wife Linda is a tall knockout. She looks like Cindy Crawford and is absolutely stunning.

Mikki tells Linda about the studio closing, and they offer me a job. Adrian and Linda own a security system company that installs alarms in homes and businesses. I am their new field representative. Not long after my employment with Security One, Mikki informs me she's pregnant with our second child, my third. Linda tells us she's also pregnant and due only a couple weeks after Mikki.

After I've been working the floor at Security One for a few months, Adrian calls me to his office and says, "Hey, dude. You get high?"

Laughing, I think, *Are you kidding me!* I nod my head, and he pulls out a huge bag of meth from the bottom drawer of his desk. He dips in, scooping out a heaping spoonful, and he hands it to me, saying, "Here you go!"

I take the entire spoonful of dope and drop it all under my tongue. He looks at me, amazed. "I've never seen anyone do dope like that! That's crazy! You're crazy!"

As the meth dissolves, calming me, I mumble, "You have no idea."

Months fly by as I work for Security One. Adrian keeps me high, but nothing is for free. After he deducts my meth bill, there's not enough left to pay the rent. Even though I don't make enough to live on, at least I have dope.

I'm frustrated when Security One closes its doors the same month my son Christopher is due. They didn't close because they weren't doing a good business. Security One closed because of poor management. We had a good business selling and installing alarm systems, but it's no surprise—tweekers can't manage their pants zippers let alone run a business. Mikki is about to have my third child, I need dope, and I'm out of work again.

Adrian and Linda pack up and move to a new home in Alta Mesa. I have to score some dope, and yes, I know I need to support my family, too. I want to support them, but as always, dope comes first. Fortunately, Adrian and Linda offer to let us stay with them until I find another job.

Financially, the only thing I have right now is a maxed-out credit card to a gas station chain. Jacked up on meth, I stay up for days and finally come up with a plan. For all purchases over $50.00, the sales clerk phones the credit card office for approval. If there's a problem, they confiscate the card. If I keep my credit card purchases under $50.00, they never call for verification. So I drive from gas station to gas station and purchase two cartons of cigarettes on credit from each of the one hundred stores, being careful never to go over $50.00. Within the week, I've purchased two hundred cases of cigarettes that I turn around and sell at area bars in Scottsdale and Tempe, offering fifty percent off. The bar owners jump on the deal, glad to stock their cigarette machines with discounted cigarettes. In a few short weeks,

I've made a couple thousand dollars with much less risk than selling drugs. I'm trying to stay away from that game. I really am.

Knowing I can't run this scam long—and I don't want to anyway—I fill out applications and send out resumes daily searching for a job. A good solid prospect comes along offering $300.00 a day, but it's not scheduled to start for another week. I had previously worked on a job for Digital's business seminar with this same studio, and they want me to start a production video for Ford.

Mikki is due in a few weeks, and we plan on going back to Illinois for the birth. She wants to be with family, but I need to work on the Ford production. I'm trying to be a responsible father—I need to work, but I also don't want to miss my son's birth. I send Mikki back to Illinois with Nikki so I can stay and finish the video, get my money, and fly back in time for Chris's birth. That's the plan.

Adrian and I are flying high, and Linda is so jealous. She's pregnant, so she can't do drugs, but she wants to, really bad. She loves meth, but she's responsible enough not to use while pregnant, so she's really moody right now. I'm laughing as she's griping at us when the phone rings. It's Grandma calling from Illinois telling me that Mikki is on her way to the hospital! *Noooo!*

Grandma's news feels like a punch in the stomach. I'm supposed to be there! Flipping out, I pace back and forth, feeling horrible and not knowing what to do. She's not due for ten more days. My wife's in labor, my son will arrive soon, and I'm supposed to be there, but no way can I get there in time.

I arrive in Illinois three days later. Mikki and Chris are already home from the hospital. Mikki is rightfully a little angry with me for missing Chris's birth, but no angrier than I am with myself.

High and hung over, I walk remorsefully into my in-law's home. I hear Nikki scream, "Daddy!" As she runs up to me with her arms held high, I am struck at how much she looks like me. I pick her up, kissing her cheek, and she giggles. Then with a more serious look than a two-year-old should have, she points at her mom as she walks into the room holding Chris and cries, "Take him back! No want baby. Take him back!"

I laugh at her as I feel her pain. For two years, she has been the center of her mother's attention, and she does not like this new addition to our family, not at all. Kissing her again, I set her down, eager to hold my newborn son.

By the look on my wife's face, I can tell she's still angry at me, but at this moment, I can only think about this precious new life, my first son, Christopher Bryant. Taking him from Mikki, I sit down on the couch and just stare at him. He's mine. Wow! I have three kids now and not a dime to my name.

When we left Arizona, we were living in someone else's home, so we really have no place to go back to and no money to travel with a family of four. Being stuck in Illinois living with Mikki's parents clearly isn't working. I need to make money fast, at least enough to get us back to Arizona.

At the corner store, I run into Highway Joe and ask about TJ. He tells me TJ's in jail, has been for three months, and won't be out for another six months. Relieved I don't have to worry about him right now, I still need to lay low and not draw attention to myself. I've only been gone a year, not near enough time for the heat to cool down.

Mikki's friend Belinda offers to let us stay with her, so we move about fifteen miles south of Wood River to Granite City. It's close to family yet far enough away for me to stay out of sight. While we're hanging out with Belinda one night, a friend of hers stops by. He reminds me of Kenny Rogers—gray hair, beard, warm and friendly-looking with a cowboy hat and vest. He talks with a deep southern drawl, and I catch myself snickering when Belinda introduces him as Cowboy, but he has dope, so I overlook his stupid nickname.

Mikki is shocked when she realizes Cowboy has stopped by to deliver a bag of dope to Belinda. We had no idea Belinda used. As the exchange goes down, I look over at Mikki as she sits on the couch feeding the baby. She shakes her head, saying ever so quietly under her breath, "Here we go again." She follows this with a big sigh. I have to admit, this exchange amuses me. I also find it strange how this stuff keeps following me around.

Cowboy is an old timer full of interesting stories. He tells me he's one of the major drug dealers in Granite City. I explain to him what brought me to this point in my life, and when he realizes I know how to make the very drug he loves and sells, his interest in me is piqued. Offering to get me high, he makes an offer I can't refuse. Disgusted, Mikki stands and hustles to the back bedroom with Nikki and Chris.

Cowboy and I get high as I listen to his offer. "I will buy everything you need if you'll cook for me. I'll also pay all living expenses for you and your family."

I willingly accept his offer, and Mikki is right, here we go again. I'm back to work doing the only thing I know how to do that'll bring in enough money to buy dope and support my family. I'm back in business!

Chapter 9
Belleville, IL
Second Move to Phoenix

Cowboy rents a two-bedroom apartment in Belleville big enough for the four of us. I jump right in, preparing to cook my first batch of dope, but I find the chemicals much harder to obtain this time. Needing an appropriate reason to order these chemicals, I create a bogus company, Biochemical Research and Analysis Lab. I have all my orders shipped to a rented mail-drop box I use as my new business address. I also rent a storage facility across town in which to stash all the chemicals and equipment, keeping it far away from Mikki and the kids. This is also where I set up my cooking site. Cowboy funds everything.

Per policy, before chemicals can be distributed, the chemical companies are required to call and question about how all chemical orders are to be utilized. I script a convincing line of bull, and it works. Most of the chemicals needed to cook dope have multiple uses, so I just need to know which formula to propose and make sure the combinations I order don't have anything to do with manufacturing an illegal substance. Speaking confidently and professionally, I list each chemical, giving them a complete synthesis. To throw off suspicion, I order from two different companies and request many other chemicals a research lab would need. Ordering five random chemicals I don't need for every chemical I do need in seven separate shipments for each batch of meth keeps me far under the DEA's radar.

With a few profitable batches already under my belt, I am going to cook my final batch of meth tonight. I promised Mikki I'd stop after I'd made enough cash to get us back to Arizona. I pull into the storage compound, eager to cook this last batch, rid the storage facility of all evidence, and move back to Phoenix. The owner walks out of her office straight toward me with both arms waving me to stop. I always enjoy talking with her, so I pull over short of my unit to get out and visit and let her know I won't be renting next month. Walking toward her, I ask how she's doing, but mid-sentence she interrupts nervously and says, "I'm doing fine, but you're not going to be doing too good!"

Completely confused, I ask, "Why's that?"

"I have to tell you something. I'm telling you this, but you didn't hear it from me. Got it?" she says, anxiously looking around. She looks back at me with a worried look on her face, "The DEA was here this morning. They were at your unit. They didn't have a warrant, so I wouldn't let them search your area, but they had drug-sniffing dogs out here, and they want me to call them as soon as you arrive. You listening?"

Pointing north, she informs me, "They're in a hotel right up the road, but you know what? I lost my boy to those jerks last year, and they can kiss my butt!"

Fully alarmed, I run back to my car, yelling over my shoulder, "Thanks for telling me!"

"I don't know what you're doing," she shouts, "and I don't want to know, but you need to get out of here right now!"

The drive home feels like an eternity. I force myself to stay under the speed limit while my brain scrambles for a plan. Running in the front door, I shout, "We have to leave, *now!*"

Without question, Mikki starts throwing our most important belongings in the middle of the living room floor as I run out the door to get a U-Haul and boxes. Ninety minutes later, the four of us are on our way to Arizona with only what we could quickly toss into the back of a pull-along trailer, again leaving all our big stuff behind.

Pulling a U-Haul trailer behind our old 1970 Ford E-150 van and traveling with a three-year-old and a one-year-old does not make for an enjoyable trip. Chris gets motion sickness and has thrown up in almost every town we've driven through, starting in Belleville. How can one little baby produce so much vomit? This poor little guy is sicker than a dog, but we can't stop, We have to get far away from Illinois as fast as we can.

Desperate to vanish without a trace, we pull into a drugstore and purchase a supply of paper towels, baby wipes, and garbage bags. I notice a box of bleach blond hair dye and throw it on the counter with the rest. We pay cash and are back on the road in minutes.

Driving through Oklahoma, I spot a phone booth alongside a gas station. I really like our landlord and pull over to call and let her know we've moved. Lighting up a cigarette, I deposit a few dimes and dial her number, explaining I relocated for a new job. Clearly annoyed, she says, "Well yeah, I kind of figured out you left. Who's going to pay for the damages?"

Confused, I ask her, "What are you talking about?"

"At four this morning, the DEA along with about thirty cops kicked in the door and ransacked the apartment!"

An icy chill runs up my spine as I realize they missed us by only a few hours. I apologize to her, hang up the phone, and turn to Mikki. "Well, I can't go by Darwyn anymore. Apparently, I'm wanted."

Inhaling a long, deep drag, I stare back down the highway, wondering just how close behind us they might be. Flicking my cigarette in the rocks, I walk back to the van "I have to change my name," I explain to Mikki. "They kicked in our door and obviously have a warrant for my arrest, a warrant for Darwyn Bryant."

Opening the van door, I look in the back seat at Nikki and Chris. They're so young, so innocent. Shaking my head, I climb in and fire up the engine. Glancing down the highway again, I remind Mikki as I pull out, "You cannot call me Darwyn anymore."

Mikki doesn't look at me, doesn't say a word as we drive westward in complete, awkward silence. Chris throws up again and cries as Nikki screams her disgust. Mikki climbs in the back to clean it up and tries to calm them down. Staring straight down the road, my mind's in a whirlwind as I try to figure all this out.

A few months ago, I purchased a book from an underground publishing company on how to create a new identity. This company specializes in books on how to pretty much do anything illegal—lock picking, growing pot, bomb making, and even committing the perfect murder. Mikki and I decide that from now on, I will be Michael Briant, a much more common name than Darwyn Bryant.

Eighteen hundred miles later, we pull into a motel in Flagstaff, Arizona. It's only a couple hours from our destination of Phoenix, but I'm exhausted. I cannot drive one more mile. Chris sleeps without throwing up for the first time in two days, allowing us all to get some rest. One night's sleep does not even come close to taking away the stress in my life right now.

Within minutes of beginning the descent out of the Flagstaff Mountains and heading down toward Phoenix, Chris starts crying, gags, and throws up. Mikki climbs in the back as I take it easy, tapping the brakes and keeping it slow around the turns on the steep grades. Everything from the last few years rolls through my mind, suffocating me. I can't take it! I cannot take any more! I'm so freaking tired of my life, but I see no other way! I don't know what to do. I don't know how to fix this. I'm wanted by the feds! From now on, I'll have to live my life on the run or go to prison…or die. It scares me how much this last scenario is starting to become my most preferred scenario. Do I really want to die? *No!* I just don't know how to fix this. I keep trying to analyze what went wrong. When did all this start? How did I get here? By trying my hardest to do what's best for my family. I don't know where to go, what to do, or how to fix this. I just don't. My mind races day and night, producing nothing useful.

I glance at Mikki who's staring out the window with an frown etched on her face. It's been years since I've seen her smile, seen her happy, and I wonder what she's thinking right now. We don't talk much about our life or our future anymore. Yes, she's voiced her disapproval at times, but mostly she just rolls with the punches. What can she be thinking now that I've gotten us into this mess?

In the rearview mirror, I look at my two children who depend on me. I look back over at Mikki and wonder why she stays with me. She's done nothing. She could walk away from all of this. It's me they're looking for, not her. Is she thinking the same?

Suddenly, alarmed by a loud horrible grind when I push on the brake pedal, the van picks up speed. I scream, "What the heck! *The brakes have gone out!*"

I'm taking twenty-mile-per-hour turns at forty-five miles per hour, and I can feel the sway and tug of the trailer pulling at the back of my van. Mikki quickly unbuckles and reaches back to tighten the kid's seat belts. Buckling up again, she puts her feet on the dash, preparing for impact. With my heart pounding, I grip the steering wheel and downshift, trying my hardest to stay on my side of the road as I skid around steep turns, scared I'll jackknife the trailer into oncoming traffic. I don't think the transmission can hold out much longer. It whines loudly, slowing us to a more manageable speed.

Luckily, we're close to the bottom of the mountain, so once the road levels out, I easily bring the van and trailer to a crawl and stop at the first service station for repairs. Throwing the van in park, I turn off the engine and just sit for a moment, catching my breath and thinking about what could have happened.

Mikki and I take the kids to eat while they evaluate the van's damage.

"You're lucky," the mechanic tells us. "The pads wore down so far that it popped the plug out of the master cylinder. You're all lucky to be alive."

Three hours later, just when Chris is starting to feel better, we're back on the road again. Poor little guy.

Mikki calls Linda as soon as we arrive in Phoenix. She tells Mikki that Adrian left her right after their baby was born, and she invites us to stay with her until we find a place of our own. Adrian leaving is no surprise as they've always had an on-again, off-again relationship.

Following the instructions in my book of frauds to a T, I establish a new identity. The first step is to create a falsified birth certificate. Usually the hardest part of creating a fake birth certificate is to duplicate the county seal embossed on the document, but coincidentally, before I left Illinois, I had wandered into a local park-and-swap flea market and found an old county notary seal. It cost all of three dollars. Money well spent.

I copy my original birth certificate and white out all the info that needs to be changed. Having also purchased a 1960 typewriter from a flea market, I use it to type in my new name. I also change my parents' names and the town in which I was born. I make a copy of this doctored certificate so the whited-out areas aren't so noticeable. Taking my three-dollar county seal, I emboss this document, making it look legitimate.

Now, a thirty-year-old document doesn't look this new. To quickly age it, I lay this forged document on a cookie sheet and pour a very thin layer of coffee over the entire certificate then bake it at a low temperature until the coffee evaporates. It works! It now has an authentic aged patina, but it still doesn't look handled. To give it that worn look, I dust it with cigarette ashes, carefully rubbing them in. I fold and refold it many times in a tri-fold to give it that handled, worn look. It's finished, and it does indeed look official. Walking into the local DMV, I walk out with a brand-new license under my new name, Michael Briant.

We find an apartment in Mesa and move in under Michael's name. This place is a dive, but right now, it's the only place I can find that won't run a credit check. With a move across country, a fresh start, a new name, and new hair color, my goal right now is to find legitimate work. Well, as legitimate as possible for only being able to work for cash.

I start working for a carpet cleaning company, and Mikki finds a job as a telemarketer. On the surface, it seems to be working, but in reality, I'm busting my butt cleaning carpets fifteen to sixteen hours a day and making very little money, just enough to survive. I switch to another carpet cleaning company that offers to pay more, but my daily drug habit still use up three-fourths of my pay. Scoring dope in Phoenix is as easy as buying cigarettes, and I simply cannot survive a sixteen-hour workday without the help of meth.

Sitting on the couch, I pull out my stash before heading to work. The kids are still in bed sleeping as I scoop my last bit of dope on a spoon. I hear the morning news anchor report of an epidemic that has gripped the city. "Phoenix has been declared the meth capital of the country!" He has my attention,

Lifting my spoon to face level, I stare at it a moment then deposit all of it under my tongue, mumbling, "Lucky me" as the meth dissolves, giving me what I need to make it through just one more day.

I adjust the water temperature in the shower, and Mikki sticks her head in the bathroom. "You're showering again?" she asks.

"Yes, Mikki. Again!" I say roughly and close the bathroom door. Phoenix's one hundred and ten degree heat combined with meth means I sweat like a pig. Taking three showers a day is not unreasonable.

Getting undressed, I look in the mirror and think, *Oh, man! What have I become?* I look like walking death. My shoulder-length, bleached hair contrasts against my complexion, now dark from the Arizona sun. Due to lack of appetite, my skin stretches tightly over bones with no meat and no fat in between. My gray-blue eyes stare out from two hollow sockets. My six-foot-four-inch frame weighs 160 pounds soaking wet. But do you know what really disgusts me when I look in the mirror? Knowing what I've become inside. There is nothing short of hurting my kids that I won't do to get the money I need to score drugs. Nothing. My moral compass shut down long ago, and every shred of decency and self-respect I used to have is now gone.

Cold water washes over my body as I stand in the shower, and remorse fills my heart and consumes my mind. I'm overcome with guilt for what I've done to Mom and Wayne, Grandma, Sherri, Tim, Mikki, Nikki, Chris, Ann, and Alisha and realize that any hope of being a respected son, grandson, brother, husband, or father to any of them in any way is gone, gone forever.

After busting my butt daily for fifteen hours making peanuts while they bank off my sweat, I'm done. I can't do this anymore. Having learned the trade and knowing I can make a heck of a lot more money cleaning carpets on my own, I deliberately walk into the company office when no one is there to steal their customer ledger. It's a list of all their potential customers and all their upcoming jobs. It's a gold mine! Later that night, I break into a local equipment supply store and steal everything I need to go out on my own. The next day, I open my very own carpet cleaning company. I now make a decent living working an eight-hour day. Business is going well as the weeks fly by.

Hearing a knock at the door, I answer it without first checking the peephole. *Holy crap!* Shocked to see two cops staring back at me, I mentally ream myself for being so stupid. Questions swirl through my mind. Do they know who I really am? Are they here to arrest me? For drugs? Drug trafficking? Fraud? Burglary?'

I try my best to keep cool, remain calm, and act normal as they explain that a customer of mine reported all her jewelry missing after she hired me to clean her carpets. Ironically, I had nothing to do with this theft. The police ask to see my business license and insurance information—I have none to give them. Since they have no evidence I took her jewelry, they can't charge me for theft, but they do report me for operating a business without a license. Just like that, my carpet cleaning business is done and Michael Briant has had a run-in with the law. Dang!

Late at night, I sit thinking about what I'm going to do now. I need dope, so I call Richard, someone I met in the carpet cleaning business. His contact usually has pretty good stuff. He tells me his dealer, Sonny, is super paranoid. I think, *Rightfully so as you just blurted out his name!* You are never supposed to speak your dealer's name. Never. That's Tweeker Etiquette 101. He should know this. He tells me he can score, but he needs a ride to Sonny's place, and I think, *Wow! Rule number two! Never take anyone to your dealer's house!* But I need dope, so I'm glad to drive Richard to Sonny's apartment to get what I need.

On the way over, Richard very seriously tells me how everything with Sonny is cloak-and-dagger. "No one gets in his door without knowing the code," he says.

It takes everything I have to keep from laughing at his melodramatic performance, but I continue listening with raised eyebrows.

"I have to knock a certain knock, a code to gain entrance. Sonny's extremely sketchy, very paranoid and doesn't want to meet anyone new."

This guy is way too serious!

"He's connected with the Hell's Angels and the Aryan Brotherhood."

You would have thought he was taking me to meet Sammy the Bull or something. Rolling my eyes, I think, *Oh, brother. What an idiot!* I just want some dope. That's all.

Richard tells me to stay in the car as we pull into an apartment complex. I've decided if I ever deal again, there is *no way* I will ever sell to Richard. He's an idiot, the type who'll get you busted in a New York minute. "No problem," I tell him as he walks away.

Immediately coming back, he sticks his head in the car window, "Sonny says to go ahead and bring you inside. He doesn't think it's cool leaving you in the car. It looks too suspicious."

Just wanting to get my dope and leave, I exit the car, mumbling, "No joke."

A tiny red-headed firecracker covered in tattoos from her neck to her toes and wearing short shorts and a halter top opens the door after the "secret" knock. In a very mousy, squeaky, annoying voice, she tells us to have a seat. *Only in Phoenix,* I think as I look around at this apartment, feeling like I've walked into the jungles of Jumanji.

I'm in awe that a place like this could actually exist inside an apartment and amazed at the gigantic plants everywhere and the mounted animals hanging from the ceiling intertwined with jungle vines and leaves. I follow the sound of rushing water, and there it is, a waterfall in his apartment! Who has a waterfall in their apartment?

Tina, the gal who opened the door, starts to say something but is interrupted by thunderous footsteps that grow louder with every approaching step. A silhouette appears down the hall, taking up the entire doorway. Sonny is probably six foot two but appears much bigger—he's humongous! His long, curly black hair swings around his burly biker torso as he thumps toward us. He stares a hole in me, and a deep baritone bellows through his Fu Manchu mustache. "Who the heck are *you?*"

Saying nothing, I return his glare with a slight nod. We size each other up as he throws a bag of dope out on the table. Pulling out a chair on the opposite side, he sits down, staring at me the entire time. I tell him, "I've been buying your stuff for weeks through Richard." I look over to Richard then back to Sonny. "Not bad," I tell him.

Cocking his head to one side, Sonny says, "Not bad? What exactly do you mean, not bad?"

I'm straight with him. "Well, it might be panther piss, but it's not prop dope."

Panther piss is a term meth cooks use for dope synthesized using anhydrous ammonia. It has the pungent smell of cat urine. Prop dope is a term used for dope derived from phenyl-2-propanone, the latter being the most desirable but almost impossible to find. It's the original meth synthesis formulated by Hitler's chemist to fuel the Third Reich. With dozens of concoctions out there, the most common right now is the Red, White, and Black strain, getting its name from the three main ingredients, pseudoephedrine, red phosphorus, and black iodine. It may be cheap and easy to make, but it's not near as good as the other stuff.

Sonny gruffly asks if I have a knife. Leaning back to straighten my leg, I pull out a pocketknife. As I flip it around to hand it to him, he roars at me. *"That? You call that a knife? That ain't no knife!"* Standing up, he pulls a fourteen-inch bowie knife from behind his back, yelling, "Now *this* is a *freaking knife!"* He swiftly sticks the tip of the blade into the tabletop next to my fingers.

Jumping back, I laugh at his cheesy impersonation of Crocodile Dundee and decide that I like this guy.

Then Sonny asks in a more normal tone, "So you know about cooking dope, do ya?"

"What makes you think that?"

"Oh, come on man! Nobody knows about different types of dope unless they're a cook." He leans forward, glaring at me. "Unless you're a cop! You a *cop*?"

Glaring right back, I take the bag of dope on the table and dip out a half gram. Tossing it under my tongue, I lean toward him and mumble, "Would a cop do that?"

Eyes wide, he looks at me, amazed, "Man, you're one crazy dude!"

"You're not the first one to tell me that."

Richard speaks up, "I gotta go, man! My ole lady's waiting on me."

Sonny stares at me as he tells Richard, "Go ahead and go. I'll take your friend home."

As soon as Richard's out the door, Sonny asks, "So what's your story, and what are you doing hanging out with someone like Richard?"

"I was going to ask you the same thing."

"I inherited him from a buddy of mine. Richard's his nephew. That's how I got him. You?"

"I just need some dope, man. Having just moved back to Phoenix, I don't want to draw attention to myself after all the crap I left behind in Illinois. I haven't bothered to get very well connected yet."

Sonny and I get high and talk for hours. I feel I can trust this guy, so I tell him everything from fleeing Illinois to changing my name. Intrigued with the story of my fake birth certificate and new driver's license, he tells me about some people he wants me to meet. "Come on. Let's take a ride, then I'll drop you off at your place."

Three miles from Sonny's home, we pull into an auto body shop at 11:30 p.m. The shop is closed at this hour, but I notice lights on inside as I follow Sonny to the back service door. Listening to him lightly rap a Morse code type knock on the door, I shake my head and chuckle under my breath. These guys and their secret codes. The door swings open, and I'm not laughing anymore!

Staring down the barrel of a MAC 10 machine pistol pointed right at my head, I think, *Nope, this is no longer funny.* Afraid to move, I stand waiting for Sonny's next move. The guy with the gun looks from me to Sonny then barks at me, "Get in here!"

Sonny calmly walks in and turns to me. "Don't worry," he says. "He greets everyone like this."

Once we're inside, the guy with the gun hollers at Sonny *"What do you think you're doing bringing someone over here without talking to me first?"* Actually, he hollers this more as a statement than a question.

Sonny tries to placate him, "Relax, Butch. I paged you, but you never called back. Believe me, you want to know this guy."

Sonny introduces me to Butch, and Butch lowers his pistol. Still clearly annoyed, he asks, "Okay, tell me exactly why I want to know this guy?"

Sonny asks Butch, "Is Larry here? He needs to hear this, too."

Larry walks into the room. He's shirtless and has a shaved head. He's completely covered in tattoos—two SS bolts protrude from his neck, and Aryan Brotherhood is tattooed in an old English font across his chest. Realizing these guys are the real deal, I say nothing as Sonny tells my story. They're especially interested in my fake ID and how I obtained it. Both of them look over my Arizona driver's license, and Larry holds it up. "And this, this is not you?" he asks.

"Nope." I don't understand why he cares.

Butch hands me back my ID. "We need some IDs. How much for this?"

I'd never thought about making IDs for someone else or how much I'd charge, so off the top of my head, I tell him, "Well, I can forge the documents you need, but you'll have to take them to the DMV and have IDs made."

"No problem. How much?"

"$500 a pop," I tell them, not having any idea if I'm anywhere in the ballpark.

"We need twelve."

"Okay. I need their ages and ethnicity."

"Ethna-what?" Butch asks, confused.

"Their race. I need to know if they're black, white, Mexican. You know, their ethnicity." I realize these guys are as dumb as they are scary.

Larry asks, "By the end of the week?"

With confidence, I tell him, "You got it."

He motions toward the doorway, signaling it's time for me to leave. On my way to the door, he authoritatively informs me of one more thing. "Oh! By the way, *you* don't be cooking any dope in this town unless you run it through us. You hear me?"

I simply nod as I stare straight ahead and walk out, glad to exit this auto shop.

On the drive home, Sonny explains, "These guys are Aryan Brotherhood. They deal with the Mexican Mafia, smuggling dope and illegal immigrants from Mexico."

"The Aryan Brotherhood is dealing with the Mexican Mafia? Isn't that a conflict of interest? What happened to all the 'white power' stuff and sticking with your own kind?"

With a smart-aleck tone, Sonny explains, "They're not swapping spit with each other! Business is business, and these guys are all about business. They need IDs to ensure their runners and mules safe passage."

"Yeah, I kinda picked up on that."

Glad for the opportunity to make quick cash, I deliver twelve impressive documents in only four days for an easy $6,000. It doesn't take long before I'm making documents for half the underground in Phoenix. I'm relieved to be making just as good money as I was cooking dope without nearly the risk or hassle.

Reading further into my wicked book of fraud, I decide to put another scam into play. First, I need a few IDs of my own and a valid checking account number. With Mikki now married to a wanted man, she can no longer use her ID—she'll be traced. Because of this, I had kept a $58.00 paycheck of hers from an old job. It just wasn't enough money to risk cashing. I purchase a bundle of security paper, the same type banks use for printing checks and find an old CheckMaster check writer at a local pawnshop. The CheckMaster embosses the amount of the check onto the paper just like banks and large companies do.

I find a twenty-four-hour self-serve copy center and carefully white out all the handwritten info on Mikki's old paycheck. Running it through the copy machine on security paper with the handwritten information now gone, in minutes I have in my possession dozens of blank company checks. Next, I run all the checks through a perforation machine so that each check has an authentic-looking perforated edge. I quickly scoop up my fresh blank checks, hide them in my van, and drive home.

While Mikki and the kids are sound asleep, I sit at the kitchen table until early morning, running each check through the check writer for different amounts—$611.12, $1189.14, $323.43, $619.16, and so on.

Armed with a fake ID—not the Michael Briant one I use daily but one I made just for this venture—I shop at the one hundred and thirty-eight grocery stores in the Valley, cashing a check in each one. Using the exact same lines over and over, I become more confident with every delivery.

Standing at the customer service desk, I throw out my best smile and say, "Excuse me. I'm on my way home from work, and my wife asked if I'd pick up a few things. I just got paid but haven't had a chance to cash my check yet. If I buy a few groceries, could you cash my paycheck?"

They always respond with, "Let me see the check and your ID please."

Pulling out my wallet, I say, "No problem" as I hand them a check along with my ID.

Today I'm William Lee Madison. Giving the ID a quick look over, the man in customer service initials the corner and hands it back, saying, "Here you go, Mr. Madison. Take it through checkout whenever you're ready. Thank you for shopping with us."

"Thank you," I say sincerely as I turn away.

With an approved check in my wallet, I leisurely walk the grocery aisles, throwing a few items in my cart. Making small talk with the cashier, I pay with a fake paycheck written out for hundreds. The cashier accepts my check and without hesitation counts out hundreds in change, handing it to me with a smile. I thank them and leave with a sack full of groceries and a pocket full of cash. Immediately, I drive to the next store to repeat the process all over again until all my checks are cashed.

Sonny, my partner in crime, is getting a kick out of watching me do my thing. He drops me off at the front door then waits in the parking lot with the car running just in case something goes wrong and I have to make a quick exit. With over one hundred checks, I hit almost every store in the next few days, profiting hundreds of dollars in groceries and over $36,000.00 in cash. This fraud proves to be extremely profitable. Come on now, I'm not cooking dope!

Deciding to step up my game, I buy a legitimate cashier's check from the bank and use the same process I did with the company check. Sonny and I drive around looking for expensive items—a guitar at a music shop, an engagement ring at a jewelry store, or an expensive set of tires and wheels at a pro auto parts place. Pretending to be highly interested but unsure of an actual purchase, I let the salesman work hard at selling their product then ask for an exact total including tax. Telling them I need to go to the bank to get money, I return an hour later with a cashier's check made out for the exact amount. I successfully purchase many items this way. Because it's a cashier's check, they never ask for an ID. This is just too easy.

Having acquired plenty of cash in the last few days, I decide to pace myself and let things cool off. Within the next few weeks, there'll be close to $50,000 coming up missing in the metro Phoenix area and some pretty hacked-off store merchants.

Mikki walks by as I'm counting out thousands of dollars in cash at the kitchen table. Pulling out a chair, she sits across from me and scans the piles of stacked ten, twenty, fifty, and hundred-dollar bills that I've lined up in neat rows. She looks at me with concern and asks, "Does it ever bother you? What you're doing to others? Do you feel even a little bit guilty? Dealing drugs is one thing, but being a thief, that's another."

I finish counting another stack of fifties, placing it perfectly in line with the others. Reaching under the table into a garbage bag, I grab another handful of bills to count. Glancing up at her, I smile and proudly state, "I'd rather think of myself as a scam artist."

"Whatever, Darwyn, you're still a thief!"

Her words sting, and with a quick sweep of my arm I knock all the neat stacks of cash back into the garbage bag, shove it in the attic, and walk out the door. "I'll be at Sonny's."

It's all I can say right now.

Turning on the police scanner as soon as I start my van is a tool of the trade. It's always good to know what they're up to. Halfway to Sonny's place, the scanner catches my attention when I hear, "Subject is pulling out of his apartment complex driving a dark green 1978 Torino. 10-4."

I think, *Huh? Sonny drives a dark green Torino. I wonder what year it is.*

Another voice comes in, "Subject has long, dark, curly hair and a Fu Manchu mustache."

That's Sonny, all right. They're following him!

Speeding in hopes of reaching him and somehow warning him, I hit the normal four o'clock bumper to bumper traffic with still a few miles between us. Inching along, listening to the scanner, I know they're still following him, but I can't figure out what their plans are or why they want him. If I find him, I don't have a clue what my plan is, either. I just know I have to try to do something.

Sighting an alleyway to my right, I turn in, hoping to reach the next block quickly, but I run into a gridlock there as well. The scanner comes to life. "He just pulled into Gold's Pawnshop. Keep all marked vehicles away. Repeat, keep all marked vehicles away! We'll take him down when he exits. 10-4."

Oh man! They're going to bust him! With a few blocks to go, I take the shoulder quickly, getting around traffic, and see two unmarked police cars pulled off on the side of the road. I can always spot them by the license plates and two to three short antennas on the trunk. Trying my best to slide back into traffic unnoticed, I inch past them. I listen to the scanner but hear nothing about a white van running along the shoulder. Phew!

At the next intersection, the pawnshop comes into view, and sure enough, there's Sonny's car without a cop in sight. The scanner calls out, "Everyone sit tight! The K-9 unit's on the way."

I pull slowly into the parking lot, knowing cops are watching me at this very minute. My heart pounds, and sweat pours down my back as I look around. They're out there right now, sitting tight and watching, ready to make a bust.

Exiting my van, I stroll nonchalantly into the pawnshop, acting as if I don't know what's about to go down. Operating on pure adrenaline, I force myself to remain calm as I spot Sonny with his back to me, examining something on an upper shelf. Acting interested in a JVC receiver within reach, I stop parallel to him and whisper just loud enough for him to hear, "Don't look at me, Sonny. Trust me, don't look at me and don't say a word—just listen!"

Sonny continues to look at the item on the shelf as I continue to show interest in the receiver. "Cops are outside, man," I tell him. "They're waiting on you. I heard it on the scanner. They plan on taking you down when you leave. Nod if you understand."

Keeping Sonny in my peripheral vision, I watch him nod slowly.

With his body turned so no one can see, Sonny pulls a bag of dope from his pocket and shoves it down the neck of a hair dryer on a lower shelf. I whisper, "Good luck, bro."

I've done what I can for Sonny and am ready to put as much distance between the pawnshop and myself as I can without alarming the cops. The street is still congested, and I slowly pull out, inch my way through traffic, and head straight to a pay phone. I need to tell Tina the cops probably have Sonny by now.

Later that evening, I run by Sonny's apartment and knock the secret knock. "What the heck was that all about?" I ask, glad to see him answer the door.

"Someone tried to get me busted! I'm not sure exactly who, but I have an idea. The cops were confident I had dope on me and totally confused when they didn't find any. Someone had to have told them I just scored. That's the only reason they would've been so sure." Sonny asks, "How the heck did you do that, man? How'd you know?"

"I told you, man. I heard it on the scanner." Laughing, I continue, "They described your car, and when they said Fu Manchu mustache, I knew it was you, man! I was only a few miles away but almost didn't make it in time."

Looking at me appreciatively, he says, "Man, that was freaking amazing, brother! Really, I've never had anyone stick their neck out for me like that before. Thank you!"

As he shakes my hand, I smile and remind him, "Hey, I kinda need ya, bro. Don't worry about it."

"Oh crap!" he yells "Let's go! We got to get to that hair dryer at the pawnshop before someone else does!"

Twenty minutes later, back at Sonny's, I watch him extract the bag of dope from his newly purchased used hair dryer. He looks at me and speaks in a serious voice. "It's time I pay someone a visit. I've figured out who's behind this."

Sonny tells me about a guy named Danny who's been trying to get him out of the way for some time now—not as a rival drug dealer but because of Tina, his girlfriend. "Danny's been trying to get in Tina's pants for months," he tells me.

I think to myself, *Really?* but I'm not about to challenge his suspicion.

Forty-eight hours later, Danny is reported missing. Months pass, and no one ever sees or hears from Danny again.

Chapter 10
Barry
Randy
Sonny

Sonny and I are hanging out in his living room when we hear a coded knock on the front door. I roll my eyes as Sonny says, "I know you think it's cheesy, but it works."

I don't say a word. He looks through the peephole before releasing the lock and opens the door for someone I've never seen before. I eye him, thinking the only thing that stands out about the guy is the fact that nothing stands out about the guy. I find him strange, and not strange because he looks normal but strange because he doesn't look normal for our crowd. He reminds me of a schoolteacher. I stand up and shake his hand. Sonny introduces him as Barry.

Barry wastes no time getting right down to business, telling Sonny he's going to cook dope in his garage and needs someone to move it for him. Sonny tells him, "If it's good and the price is right, I can move whatever you bring me."

They strike up a deal.,

Barry leaves and I look over at Sonny and mutter, "Strange dude."

Sonny strokes his Fu Manchu in deep thought then snaps back, saying, "Yeah, real strange dude. Let's see what he comes up with, though. In the meantime, don't let him know anything about your hustle. I don't know if we can trust him yet. We need to tread lightly with this guy."

Two days later, Barry calls wanting Sonny and I to stop by his house and check out the batch of dope they just cooked. Driving into a gated community in East Mesa, we pull up to a typical stucco home decorated with brick and stone. Upon walking through his front door, my nose is assaulted with the distinct caustic odor of cooked meth. I watch several tweekers run around as if they're busy doing something important, but in reality, they're just spinning in circles, accomplishing nothing. Barry's girlfriend Karin sits on the sofa with a huge bowl of meth, smoking from a large glass pipe. Randy, a sketchy dude, just seems to be in everyone's way. I've met him before, and it's very apparent he has some major issues, probably from being spun way too long.

Barry calls from the kitchen. "In here!" he says as he scrapes a batch of freshly cooked dope off a Pyrex tray onto the kitchen counter to cool. He's as calm as if he was cooling off freshly baked cookies. He looks toward the garage door. "Carl's in the garage finishing another batch," he says.

The garage door opens, and in walks a middle-aged balding man carrying a tray of dope. A red haze trails him—red phosphorus, the telltale sign of a poorly ventilated meth lab.

As he waddles in, I scrutinize his extremely swollen ankles which are exposed below a pair of filthy cargo shorts. Swollen extremities are evidence of extended chemical exposure, common with long-term meth cooks.

"Here you go!" he says through a toothless grin as he sets the tray down. Barry tells Sonny, "Okay, this should give us a solid pound. Time to start bagging it up."

Barry yells toward the living room, *"Karin! Get in here and get to work!"* He looks at us. "Come on, let's go get some fresh air out back."

Sonny and I follow him outside into a backyard full of rocks and cacti with one lone tree all surrounded by a six-foot fence. As we sit down around the fire pit, Barry pulls out a glass pipe and pocket torch. I watch him fire up a bowl of dope. He takes a slow deep hit, passes it along, and exhales. "I think ole Randy's in some deep trouble!" he says. "Word is, 'The Five' are looking for him, and he needs to leave before they trace him back here."

I ask, "Who are The Five?"

"They're a group of five crooked cops for hire. They take care of business for the Aryan Brotherhood and the Hell's Angels."

"What in the hell did Randy do?"

Barry shakes his head. "Dunno. I just know I wouldn't wanna be him right now."

Scoring an ounce of dope from Barry, we walk back through the house and out the front door. Sitting in the passenger seat, I light a cigarette and stare at the house. "Let's go." I tell Sonny. "This place creeps me out!"

"Me too," he says gruffly. "Let's get out of here!"

I go back to Sonny's place and spend the night, which isn't uncommon since we stay up for days without sleep. At eight in the morning, someone lightly knocks the secret code on Sonny's front door. Peeking through the peephole, Sonny opens the door for Barry. "What's up?" he asks.

Obviously shaken, Barry enters and paces back and forth. "They killed him!" he says.

Ducking around a vine, Barry stops in front of Sonny. He looks scared. *"They killed Randy!* He was found at two o'clock this morning a mile from my house. He was lying in the middle of the intersection, naked. He'd been run over multiple times. This wasn't an accident! Do you know what this means? It means they were watching him at my house! It means they followed him from my house! They had to've!"

Barry looks nervously at me then back to Sonny, shaking his head. He starts pacing again. "I'm shutting down shop for a while. I don't know what he did, and I don't want to know, but now I'm on their radar! I can't take any chances!"

Sonny shoots me a look like I'm crazy when I fail to engage my brain before I open my mouth and invite Barry to stay with us until he finds another place. As Sonny's eyebrows rise, I realize just how dangerous this offer is. I hold my breath as I wait for Barry's answer.

"Nah, that's alright, but hey, thanks anyway."

Taking a deep breath, Sonny shakes his head, shutting the door behind Barry. I say, "I've been in Mesa way too long. It's time to move to Scottsdale."

Back home, I yell to my wife. "Mikki! We need to leave. Now!"

Mikki starts tossing things in boxes as I search for a new place to live. Moving often is how I survive. It's how I avoid getting busted. We never stay in one place longer than a couple months, always moving under a new identity. Today, I'm Haley G. K. Jacobs.

Money isn't an object at this moment so we can live pretty much wherever we want for the next few months. I find a nice little apartment in an affluent neighborhood in Scottsdale on the top floor of a three-story complex. Off the living room balcony is a great view of Ventura Drive and an upscale business complex full of fine dining, expensive boutiques, and business offices.

By one in the morning, Mikki and the kids are sound asleep in our new home. I decide to slip out the back door and take a walk around the neighborhood as most tweekers do. I have no place in particular to go, and no real reason to be out walking other than that tweekers can't sleep, so we walk or drive through the night while normal people are fast asleep, holding true to the reputation of us as "creatures of the night."

I stroll through the apartment complex then cross the street, thinking maybe I'll get lucky and find an unlocked Mercedes or something. Checking the few remaining cars in the lot to no avail, I head back home, cutting through the back alley behind the business offices, when an open dumpster catches my eye. Veering over to peek inside, I spot a perfectly good briefcase lying right on top. As I reach in to take the case, I also notice a cardboard box full of papers printed with a realtor's heading and logo.

Visible condensation escapes my mouth under the dim streetlight in the midnight hours of this cold desert alley. I hold a briefcase in one hand and a stack of papers in my other hand, and my brain races with a million thoughts of what I can do as I realize just what I've found.

Having grabbed the briefcase and the entire box of papers, I quietly slip in my back door, trying not to wake anyone. Quietly sitting at the kitchen table, I flip through the many documents in complete awe, not believing my good fortune. I glance toward the hallway. Mikki cannot see this. In my hands, I have close to one hundred credit applications from individuals applying for loans to buy real estate—I'm talking million dollar homes! I have each of their entire portfolios complete with names, addresses, social security numbers, birthdates, previous addresses, employment histories, bank account information, and even mother's maiden names! Someone from the realtor's office just dumped all these intact credit reports into the dumpster, and now they're mine! I have everything I need to easily create many more highly profitable identities.

The counterfeit check game has pretty much run its course, so without hesitation, I get right to work, excited about my new hustle. This scheme is going to take a little more structure and time, but it'll be worth it. I use information from five of the applications to make birth certificates, productively employing the leftover coffee in my cup.

Keeping track of applications utilized, not wanting to be caught accidently using them again once they've been flagged, I organize everything in my newly acquired briefcase.

I spend the day renting a different mailbox for each identity and visit the surrounding DMVs in the area, securing five new elite identities. Along the way, I pick up as many credit card applications as I can find in the Valley.

Late at night, I fill out multiple credit card applications for each new identity using the rented mailboxes as my home address. The cool thing about a rented mailbox versus a post office box is the mailbox looks like a regular address. No one knows by looking at it that it's not a home address, which is imperative for this scam.

After a week, I drive to my five mailboxes to find each one filled with approved credit cards, all with limits as high as $10,000. Armed with numerous IDs and credit cards, Sonny and I go on a shopping spree to buy expensive jewelry, guns and anything else we can turn around quickly. Within a month, we acquire over $180,000 in merchandise.

Since I can only use these cards for thirty days because once they're flagged, they're no longer safe, I come up with a plan to maximize each card before the risk of getting caught increases.

Shopping at the jewelry store in one of the many local malls, I browse for an anniversary gift for my wife—that's what I tell the clerk who excitedly shows me some expensive pieces.

Most of the jewelry stores give instant credit with a matching ID and credit card, which I have tucked away in my back pocket. It's a gold card, which is even better as it symbolizes wealth and excellent credit. The clerk displays some of their most elegant and expensive pieces, and I take my time choosing just the right one for the occasion. Asking for instant credit, I'm approved within minutes and leave with my big-ticket item.

In a few days when the credit card bill is delivered to my rented mailbox, I print a cashier's check for the exact amount and stop by the store to pay it off in full, clearing my balance down to zero. Smiling, I thank them and leave, immediately driving to the same store in a different location to start the process all over again. Depending on how fast they send the bill out, I can max out one credit card multiple times, acquiring $40,000 to $80,000 from one card in a month. After the thirty days is up, I discard the matching ID and credit card and move on to the next one, always a step ahead.

Don't get me wrong, I do keep some things for my wife. I take care of Mikki and make sure she receives some pretty nice pieces for all my efforts.

Because I have to move my family often, these credit cards come in handy for renting some really nice places to live. I also drive the best cars I can find. I'm driving a Lexus now. I've had it for almost a month, so it's time to drop it off before the bill doesn't get paid, therefore red flagging a fraudulent card that will inevitably place this car on a hot list, but I'll do it tomorrow. Right now, I need to get some smokes and stop by Sonny's for a little dope.

Driving south on Hayden toward Tempe, I look in my rearview mirror and notice a pair of headlights closing in behind me. This idiot is riding my bumper, and I can't figure out why he doesn't just go around. Punching the gas pedal to the floor, I watch him in my rearview mirror and wonder just what this guy's up to. It's ten at night with no traffic in sight, so I gun the Lexus, and it lunges forward, quickly accelerating to seventy-five miles per hour, but this joker stays right on me. Leaning with the car through sharp, evasive turns at high speeds and loudly screeching the tires, I quickly straighten out the wheel. I check my rearview mirror to see if I've lost him. Nope! He is stuck to me like glue! Now, if he were a cop, he'd have turned on his lights by now.

Thinking about what happened to Randy, I start to worry, so I reach under my seat to retrieve my Tech 9. *Dang!* Suddenly realizing I gave that gun to Sonny to sell, I slap around under the seat hoping to find something, anything. Nothing! Coming up on a shopping center, I sit up straight, place both hands on the steering wheel, and cut a sharp left, causing sparks to fly from under the bottom of the Lexus as I bounce over the median into the parking lot. I weave through parked cars, trying to lose this guy and exit the other side, and out of nowhere a black sedan cuts me off dead. Screeching to a halt, a red mustang, the car that's been riding me, slides in, blocking me from behind. I'm trapped.

The drivers of both cars jump out, yelling, *"Police! Don't move!"* They walk toward me with guns pointed at my head. Crap! Cops! I don't move. The cop from the sedan yells, "Take your hands off the wheel!" and the cop from the mustang opens my door and throws me to the ground, cuffing my hands behind my back.

I hear the faint sound of sirens getting progressively louder, and then a squad car pulls up, and off I go to the Scottsdale Police Station.

Sitting in the back of the squad car, I try to come up with a plan before we reach the station. If I just knew what name, what crime… I'm clueless as to which of the hundreds of crimes I've committed under various names I'm currently being arrested for. I don't speak a word. My mind spins ideas around as the voice within me warns, *Be ready! Be smart! Think fast!*

I'm handcuffed to a table in the interrogation room. A detective resembling Ernie from *My Three Sons* walks toward me. This is the most unintimidating cop I have ever seen, and he actually smiles as he introduces himself as Detective Arnold. He asks, "Okay, we know you're using a fraudulent credit card, so therefore we know your name isn't Mikhail. What's your name, and where'd you get the card?"

And there it is! That's *exactly* what I was waiting for! Mikhail Cole is the identity I used to rent the Lexus, so they know nothing about me. They don't know who I am or what I do. Without even knowing it, this cop just gave me my ticket out of here.

I give Arnold my best upset and apologetic act. "Oh man! I can't believe I was so stupid! I'm Michael Briant. I lost my job cleaning carpets, and I'm having a hard time finding work. I got a wife and two kids to feed. It's been rough!"

Detective Arnold swings a chair around, straddling it backward with his arms propped up on the back and asks, "Who made this ID?"

I shamefully proclaim, "I met some guy with ties to an outfit in California. He told me I could make some easy cash. He said all I have to do is take a credit card and ID they gave me and do a little shopping with it. They told me I'd get a good return after they sold the items I bought. Just now I was taking that Lexus to their designated drop off."

With no time to plan, I come up with this ruse as I speak. I'm good at it. I show no hesitation or even the slightest hint of deception. I've got this cop's attention and continue. "They're a pretty big operation from what I can tell."

Hoping he takes the bait, I look at him with concern, waiting for his response. "Michael, you have one way out of this. Do you want to help yourself?"

Bingo! Holding back a smile, I force my face to display innocence. "Yes! How?"

I stare him right in the eyes as I blink back bogus tears, thinking to myself, *These cops are so predictable. Dang, I'm good.*

Ernie goes on to explain, "We need you to wear a wire and get a new ID and credit card from them. Call them and tell them the one you had got burned and you had to ditch it and need another." He looks at me with genuine concern. "Are you willing to do this, Michael?"

Not wanting to react too fast and possibly make him suspicious, I ask, "So how is this going to help me?"

Looking me straight in the eyes, he explains, "You help us nail these guys, and we'll make sure you walk. We ran your name, Michael. You're as clean as a whistle. You've never even had a parking ticket."

Quickly changing my laugh into a cough, I gain composure, donning a straight face. "Okay. I'll do it. I'll never find work if I have something like this on my record. Thank you. Thank you so much! I appreciate you giving me this chance. Hey man, I won't let you down!"

Ernie stands up to release my handcuffs then shakes my hand. Just like that, I'm walking out the front door with instructions to stay by my phone, and they'll contact me tomorrow. Wow! Hahaha. Come on now, this is funny.

Standing on the sidewalk in front of the police department, I stop and light a cigarette, inhaling deeply as I look around for a pay phone to call for a ride. Detective Arnold walks out the front door and looks at me, "You need a ride? Come on. I'll give you a ride home."

He walks past me, smiling and waving me to follow. Thinking this guy is way too nice for a cop, I shake my head as I drop my cigarette and step on it then follow him to his car. I really don't want him to know where I live, but he has my address, so it really doesn't matter. If I don't accept, it'll throw up a red flag.

Walking away from his car at the apartment complex, I look back at him and wave, mentally encouraging him, *Go on. Just leave. Hurry.* Out loud, I say, "Thank you! I'll wait for your call!"

Detective Arnold drives away. Walking in my front door, I shout, "Mikki! We have to leave, *now!*"

From a hotel twenty miles down the road, I call Sonny's house, but there's no answer. That's not uncommon. He seldom answers his phone. I need him to help me figure out a plan. Hoping he's home, I leave Mikki and the kids at the hotel and drive to his house. I have to talk to someone, and I can't talk to Mikki about this—she doesn't even know about this last scam. She understands I use fake IDs, but she has no idea how I get them or how I use them.

Rounding the corner to Sonny's apartment, I immediately pull over when I see police cars. Sirens are blaring, an ambulance waits, rescue trucks are lined up. All their lights are flashing, and just as I come to a stop, a Medivac helicopter takes flight. *Now what?*

Visibly shaken, Sonny's wife stands outside the complex, crying as she talks with a cop. I want to run to her and find out what's going on, but it's too dangerous. There are too many cops here right now. What if someone recognizes me?

The cop she's talking to walks away to speak with another cop, and Tina looks my way and holds up a finger as if saying, "Wait a minute." Dying to know what's going on, I stay out of sight and wait until the rescue vehicles drive away. When the last cop is gone, Tina walks over and leans inside the passenger window. Still crying, she wipes tears from her eyes and stutters, "He shot him!"

"Who? The *cops*? The cops shot him?"

"No. Not the cops. Roy. Roy shot him!"

I have no idea who Roy is, so I ask about Sonny, "How is he? I mean, is he going to be okay?"

In a broken voice, Tina tries to explain through uncontrolled breaths. "He was shot in the leg, and the blood, the blood just keeps *gushing*!" With her hand, she blots under her eyes and nose, wiping it on her shorts, "They think it hit an artery. That's why there's so much blood. They're flying him to Good Samaritan Hospital. Can you take me to him?"

She's broken. I can't refuse, so I tell her, "Sure, I'll take you! I just can't go in or stick around. I can't be seen by any cops right now." Reaching across the seat to open her door, I tell her, "Come on. Get in here. Let's go."

On the drive to Good Samaritan, I explain my situation to Tina. As I pull up to the front doors, I say, "Page me as soon as you know something, will ya?"

"I will. Thanks, Michael."

As she walks in the front door of the hospital, I slowly pull away, hoping that Sonny is going to be okay. Man, what a night!

The cops now know my face and are most likely looking for me, my best friend and main contact is in the hospital fighting for his life, I have no job, no place to live, no means to feed my wife and children, and no family to turn to. I have to cool it on the fraud game for a while, or I'll get caught. What am I going to do? I have to make money! I have to buy dope!

Falling back into the only thing I know how to do that will bring me quick cash and dope, I contact Barry and Carl. Barry offers to let Mikki, the kids, and I crash at his place while I come up with a new game plan. Meanwhile, Carl and I find a secluded place outside of the Valley where it's not so risky to set up a lab. Together we cook a few batches of dope, enough to hold me over for a while.

I impress Carl with my level of knowledge in cooking meth, showing him a way to increase his yield by thirty percent. This means thirty percent more profit. That's huge! What I don't like is we're not cooking the good stuff. I need pharmaceutical grade chemicals for that, so for right now, this pseudoephedrine crap will just have to do.

A little after ten, I bag the last of the meth we just finished drying. In Barry's truck, I head to Crazy Horse Saloon on the north side of town with a quarter pound to deliver to some bikers. I decide to take a shortcut across the Indian Reservation, straight into Scottsdale. I'm extra careful to use my turn signals and drive the speed limit and am heading north on Scottsdale Road when a car pulls up beside me. Instantaneously, another car comes in tight behind me with another swerving in front, tapping his brakes. I know immediately what's going on. This is a felony stop. After boxing me in, they all stop at the same time, leaving me nowhere to go.

Before I can blink an eye, twelve officers circle the truck, all with guns drawn. Moving slowly, I look down to see a perfect pattern of laser dots across my chest. I hear, *"Don't move! Get out of the car!"*

I'm thinking, *God, help me out here! Do you want me to freeze? Or do you want me to get out of the car?* Putting my hands high in the air, I decide to wait for their next move.

An officer approaches, opens my door, and pulls me out, slamming my face down on the pavement and cuffing my hands behind my back. I briefly wonder just where Mr. Nice Guy Ernie is. These guys seem to be enjoying the rough stuff a little too much.

I'm hauled straight to Maricopa County Jail and charged with possession of a controlled substance under the name of Michael Briant along with a few charges pending in Scottsdale. I fight back a smile. *Ha, this is good. Really, it is. They have no idea who I am.*

Seven in the morning rolls around, and I'm taken in front of a judge who sets bail at $5,000. I call Barry as soon as they allow and tell him, "Barry, you need to get me out of here! I have a cashier's check. Mikki can show you where my stuff is. Here's what you're gonna do!"

Two hours later, I stroll out the front door of the county jail, stopping to tap down a box of cigarettes as I look around. I light one up just as Barry pulls up to give me a ride. I walk to the car smiling. Barry did exactly what I needed him to do. He made a cashier's check out for $5,000, and the clerk didn't even bat an eye. She just took it and called for my release. Now I really do have to get out of town. Tonight, before they figure out I just scammed them.

I glance back before getting in the car. *Now that they have my fingerprints*, I think, *it's only a matter of time before they make the connection between Michael Briant and Darwyn Bryant.*

I walk into my apartment and shout, "We have to leave, *now!*"

Mikki rolls her eyes and starts packing.

Chapter 11
Laughlin: 1993

Two hundred thirty-five miles northwest of Phoenix, I cross over the Colorado River from Bullhead City, Arizona into Laughlin, Nevada. Since I cannot risk being seen in the Valley of the Sun, Laughlin feels like a good place to keep a low profile and hide out for a while. It's far enough away to be safe yet close enough to my contacts. I cannot survive in Phoenix without my contacts.

Big name casinos line Laughlin's main street, the same found in Vegas but without the chaos a multitude of people bring. Unlike Vegas, Laughlin is clean, nice, and almost peaceful with the majority of its occupants being retirees. I drive around, scoping out the surrounding area. I have never seen so many tiny old people in one place in my life. Laughing, I tell Mikki, "I'm definitely going to stand out with my tall frame and long blond hair!"

Pulling into the first gas station I see, I call Tina to check on Sonny. "He's home now, and man, is he ever on the war path!"

Smiling, I listen to Tina, glad to know he's recovering. Then her voice turns serious. "Detective Morgan stopped by the hospital questioning Sonny about you, Michael. Sonny answered honestly, telling him he has no idea where you are. They're looking for you, Michael. Sonny says to be careful, so be careful, will ya?"

"Thanks, Tina, I will. Tell him we'll touch base as soon as I get settled."

Stepping away from the phone booth, I take a long, deep drag and look around, wondering how far behind they might be. Reality weighs heavy on me. They're searching for me. I'm on the run. A little voice inside keeps reminding me I'll be on the run from now until I'm either caught or dead. I see no other alternative, but in the meantime, I'll give them a run for their money! Flicking my burning cigarette butt into the rock garden alongside the booth, I climb back in the car and drive away.

Downtown Laughlin sits low in a valley right on the Colorado River. Driving up a steep road toward apartment-lined bluffs gives me the illusion of driving up a mountainside, but it's merely a river bluff. I find a nice little apartment complex with a paved two-lane road connecting it to town. Pulling into the parking lot close to the office, Mikki and I get out and immediately light cigarettes. Sidestream smoke gently drifts out over the bluffs as we stand along the steep edge overlooking the city.

"Wow! Amazing view!" I say.

Mikki nurses her cigarette with a solemn face, not speaking a word.

Who am I kidding? We can't enjoy this. This is just temporary, just a place to hole up until I walk in the door again and tell her to pack up the kids.

Shaking my thoughts away, I walk back to the car and reach under Nikki's seat to pull out my briefcase. I need a new identity to secure this apartment. It's necessary to use someone's actual identity to get an apartment because they require proof of previous addresses along with a good credit rating in order to obtain a decent place to live. False identities don't offer that kind of security. Nikki, now five, and Chris, three, are eager to get out and play. Flipping through my collection of IDs and ignoring their pleas, I pull out a driver's license with multiple matching credit cards, replacing the ones in my wallet with them. Tilting my head side to side, I crack my neck and slide the wallet into my back pocket, preparing myself to become Nicolas Sheridan Kennedy. Nicolas is number thirteen of the seventy-three identities at my disposal. Just like that, an aerospace engineer from Redding, California walks through the apartment office doors with a big smile, offering a handshake as he introduces himself as Nic Kennedy. Twelve hours later, we're eating pizza in front of the TV in our new living room.

Not yet wanting to play the fraud game in Laughlin, I immediately set up to cook dope. I'm almost broke—I have to do something. A large-scale operation is out of the question in this small apartment, so I stay busy cooking small amounts.

I'm careful not to let anyone know my whereabouts and have told two people where I live only because I need them. One of them delivers my chemicals, and the other one's my runner. This keeps me out of sight. Jon Davis, my runner and friend from Sunny Slope, has always proved reliable. His job is to take the finished product to Phoenix for distribution and bring back my money. That's it. That's all he has to do.

Nikki stands in front of the TV flipping through stations looking for cartoons when I catch a glimpse of a news report. Grabbing the control from her, I flip back to the station reporting on someone being released from a Scottsdale jail using a counterfeit cashier's check for bail. Oh man, someone's gonna get in trouble for that! The journalist goes on to report that the Scottsdale Police Department has fueled a massive hunt covering most of the southern parts of the state. Forced to stay out of the area and out of sight as it's way too hot for me, I feel somewhat safe here in Laughlin. I knew the police were going to be fuming when they put it all together and figured out I eluded their capture again, slipping right out from under their nose. With a slight smirk, I hand Nikki the control and walk down the hallway to the back bedroom to finish a batch I have cooking.

Nikki and Chris play in the living room as I dry a batch of meth in an acetone bath on the other side of the apartment. I push away thoughts of how dangerous this is. I know if something goes wrong, the entire apartment will go up like a tinderbox, but I'm confident of my skills as a cook. I need meth, and I need money. The risks addicts take are foreign to those who have never suffered this affliction. Now risks taken by an addict with skills...let's just say it's what keeps thousands of detectives and agents employed.

Davis drives up to Laughlin for the two quarter-pound bags I have ready for distribution. We talk and drink Cokes at the kitchen table until it's time for him to leave. He packs the bags deep in his backpack and throws it over his shoulder. Stepping outside and lighting smokes, we scan our surroundings while walking toward his car. Davis turns the ignition, but it sputters and dies. Realizing it's not going to start after a few more tries, I dig in my pocket and give him the keys to my brand-new black Jeep Wrangler, compliments of Nic Kennedy's perfect credit rating. We have to get this stuff back to Phoenix. I watch as he pulls out of the parking lot and heads down toward Laughlin. For some reason, something doesn't feel quite right.

Twenty-four hours later, no Davis. Wanting my money, I wait anxiously, wondering where he is. I have a gut feeling something's gone terribly wrong. Finally, his wife calls from Phoenix in tears, "The California State Police have Jon! They picked him up in Needles a few hours ago!"

That's the route I told him to take!

She continues, "He was driving with his brights on, and a cop going the opposite way flashed him. He couldn't find them quick enough to dim them, so the cop turned around and pulled him over."

Dang! *Dang!* It's always the stupidest little things that get people busted.

The Jeep was purchased with a fraudulent card. Therefore, it shows up on a hotlist. I carry a sawed-off shotgun on a rack above the visor, and unfortunately for Davis, they find it along with some fake credit cards and a little dope he kept after the drop. He was lucky, though—he'd already made the drop—but not so lucky for me because they confiscated all my money. So Davis is arrested for possession of a stolen vehicle, fraudulent credit cards, a sawed-off shotgun, and dope. Not good for a black man in the southwest.

Mikki is listening to my one-sided conversation, and as I hang up the phone, we know exactly what has to be done. Everyone in this game knows. When someone gets popped committing crimes for you, their number-one ticket out of jail is to roll on the next person up. That would be me. No words are spoken as I place the phone on its hook and look in Mikki's eyes. She nervously shakes her head and walks away, wasting no time in starting to pack. I join her.

An hour of nonstop hustling flies by, and the apartment's almost packed. I search for a cigarette but find none. Still racking my brain for an exit strategy, I need to come up with a plan, but all I can think about is lighting up a smoke. *Dang!* I always run out at the most inopportune time. "Mikki! I'm going to run down to the gas station and grab some smokes. You need anything? I'll be right back."

"*No!*" she yells from the kid's room. "Don't go! Not now! We can get them on our way out!"

I walk out the door, pretending not to hear her.

The police now have my Jeep, so I climb into our large, old, junker, piece-of-crap car and fire it up. Rumbling down the road toward town, I miss my Jeep but pacify myself by deciding what type of luxury car I'll pick out tomorrow with my new identity.

I ask the clerk for a couple packs of Camels and walk outside, tapping a box down. Glancing around, I stop and light one up, wondering just how close behind me they are. No one seems to care I'm here, so I throw the smokes through the window onto the passenger seat and drive back up the road toward the apartment.

Coming up over a hill on the main drag, I notice a black Jeep Wrangler sitting off the side of the road. Leaning forward, I stare as I drive by, wondering if it's mine. Nope, Not my Jeep but the Nevada highway patrol Jeep! Instantly looking down at my speedometer reading—fifty-five—I look back up just in time to catch a forty-five mile per hour speed limit sign fly by with a sign below it reading, "Strictly Enforced." Looking in my rearview mirror, I think, *No, no, no!* as I take my foot off the gas pedal and watch the black Jeep pull out so fast its tires spin, flinging gravel behind. Lights start flashing, and the siren wails, and I think to myself, *Oh boy, here we go again.*

Wondering if this is a routine traffic stop or did Davis tell them everything about me, it crosses my mind to make a run for it, but I can't leave Mikki and the kids to fend for themselves. Pulling over to the side of the road, I decide to take my chances, reassuring myself that I can always bolt if things get hairy. I mean, he's only one cop.

Watching him pull in behind me, I take a deep breath and prepare myself to go into my fake persona of Nic Kennedy. Viewing him in the rearview mirror as he exits the Jeep, I have a bad feeling about this guy. Instantly picking up on his haughty demeanor, I watch him strut toward my window. He has a fresh flat top military haircut, a perfect handlebar mustache, and is wearing army fatigues. A cop in army fatigues…this can't be good.

He asks for my ID, so I hand him Nic's. Seconds feel like hours as I think of Mikki back at the apartment, probably done packing by now and wondering where I am.

In my rearview mirror, I watch him talk on a hand radio, and when he exits his Jeep, I switch to my side mirror as he walks toward me holding Nic's ID. I quickly notice his other hand holds the top of a holstered gun as if ready to draw. My confidence is shaken, but I try to remain cool and throw him a nonchalant, "So…what's up?"

Obviously suspicious, he growls, *"Get out of the car!"*

Millions of thoughts race through my head, but first and foremost, I sure wish I had listened to Mikki. Sweating profusely, I start to lose my cool and can't seem to pull myself together. I know I'm acting sketchy, and in trying my hardest not to, my anxiety skyrockets, and I can't help but wonder if he's on to me. I stare at him through my open car window, trying to figure out if this guy knows who I am and wondering if I'm about to go to jail.

Feeling off my game, I struggle to control my nerves, and army guy picks up my scent, giving him probable cause to open my door and pull me out of the car. One side of my brain is screaming at me to stop being so obvious while the other side won't stop lecturing me for being so stupid, and as hard as I try, I can't keep it together. My confidence as a skilled con man bottoms out, and this cop's all over it. I need a few minutes to think, to plan. Come on, Darwyn, *think!*

By now, Mikki is probably looking out the window knowing something's up and wondering what she should do. She was so nervous and ready to get out of town. She warned me not to leave. Why didn't I listen? If I don't show up real soon, she is going to be freaking out! The other side of my brain screams, *These thoughts won't get you home to her! Come on now, think!*

While my brain fights with itself, Mr. Fatigues starts throwing question after question at me. "What are you doing? Where are you going? What's your real name?"

Acting stunned, I answer the best I can. "What are you talking about? I'm Nic Kennedy, just like it says!"

I can tell he's not buying it even though he's holding a real driver's license issued by the state of Arizona.

Without breaking eye contact, he walks right up to my face and spits out, "Well, what the heck are you doing in Laughlin, Nevada if you work in Redding, California and have an Arizona driver's license? Explain that!"

"I'm in town looking for a job at the casino."

With a smart-aleck tone, he asks, "Now why would an aerospace engineer from Redding, California want a job at a casino in Laughlin, Nevada? Talk!"

Since we haven't discussed my job as an aerospace engineer, he did indeed call in this license. Wishing I'd rehearsed this identity better, I stare at this guy and realize I've gotten sloppy. The one thing that has allowed me to elude capture thus far has been my meticulous attention to detail. I can see in this cop's face that things aren't adding up, and this crushes my confidence even more.

Trying to regain a cool composure with a little sarcastic humor backfires on me, and the next thing I know, Fatigues slams me down over the hood of the car. The palm of his hand shoves my cheek against the hot car while he holds me in a full armlock behind my back. I don't want to fight him, but all of a sudden I find myself in a scuffle as I push back against his hand just enough to stop the side of my face from searing against the scorching hood. I struggle to lift my face, but otherwise, I allow him to hold me down.

He uses his body weight to secure me against the car, and I gag from the smell of his soured milk breath as he spits in my ear as he says, "I *hate* it when punks like you lie to police! You tell me the truth right now, or I'll break your legs!"

My mind screams, *Get a grip or you're not going to get out of this!* I take a deep breath and yell at the top of my lungs, "I am telling you the truth, man! I don't know what your problem is! You ran my ID! It's clean! You know it, and I know it! You have no right to do this! I told you, I lost my job in California, and that's why I'm down here looking for a job! I'm just trying to make my way! The only thing I'm guilty of is going ten miles an hour over the speed limit, so give me a ticket or put me in jail!"

I impress myself with my display of acting livid and think I hid my fear pretty well, but again it backfires. I can't catch a break with this guy. He cuffs me up and hauls me off to jail.

I'm not yet sure how much they know about me, so I stick with my story of being Nic Kennedy and answer as few questions as I can get away with. Waiting in a cell at a little holding jail in Laughlin, a substation of Cook County, I sit wondering if this is it, if this is my end. They're holding me because they don't believe I am who I say I am, but they can't prove I'm not. A glimmer of hope surges through me when they take me back for fingerprints. It'll take them four or five days to get the results back, and they can't hold me for probable cause over twenty-four hours. This is my ticket out.

Sparing Mikki and the kids a frightening scene of armed police bursting through their front door, I refrain from giving them our apartment number. Sitting in the cell waiting, I now have plenty of time to think and make a plan. Relieved when my bond is set, I think to myself, *Well that's no big deal.*

When allowed my phone call, I tell Mikki, "Call the bail bondsman. My bond is $200." Hiding a snicker behind a cough, I continue, "Get it to the bondsman, and I'll be released. They have me for speeding and possible deception, but they can't prove deception, so speeding is the only solid charge."

Mikki, understanding the urgency, immediately packs the kids into a taxi, and in a few hours, I calmly stroll out the front door of the police station, stopping to light a cigarette and look around. Mikki reaches across the seat, opens the passenger door of our just released clunker, and encourages me to hurry and get in. When the kids see me, they yell, "*Daddy!*"

I climb in, smiling, and wink at Mikki. Turning away, she ignores me as she drives back to the apartment. Too late now to rent a U-Haul, we put the kids to bed and hole up in the apartment for a long, stressful night, knowing it's only a matter of time before they figure out what just happened.

With packed boxes stacked across the living room, Mikki and I stake out the road leading down the hill toward town, questioning every move, every sound, every car light. Incessantly watching, we whisper, "Who's that? What was that?" Our minds are in a complete state of paranoia making sleep impossible while our kids sleep soundly in the back bedroom.

As always, I'm higher than a kite. Now, in survival mode, my mind and my body are racing in overdrive, figuring, planning, organizing, moving boxes to best get them out in the morning then moving them to yet a better position, and running to the window at every noise.

Finally, the sun breaks over the Colorado River, and I am out the door, crossing the bridge to Bullhead City. As soon as the doors open at the dealer, I pick out a new car and rent a U-Haul trailer under a new name. By ten in the morning, all the boxes are packed, the kids are buckled in their seats, and Mikki and I are headed across the river, out of Nevada and back into Arizona, on the run with no place to go. I can't believe I now feel safer in Arizona than Nevada when just a few days ago, it was the opposite.

Mikki doesn't do drugs, so she is wiped out from all that's happened in the last twenty-four hours. Since we have no place to go, we decide not to drive but stay at a hotel in Bullhead City. We need time to think, get some rest, put a game plan together, and figure things out.

Mikki digs through the U-Haul for clothes, toys, and snacks while I hook up the police scanner in our hotel room. Searching different frequencies, I stop when I hear them call out the name of the street of the apartment we just left. Mikki walks in with a couple bags, setting them on the floor for the kids as I motion for her to join me. The kids pull toys out of the bags as Mikki and I listen to MAGNET, the local drug enforcement agency, and the Cook County police call out the name of our apartment complex. Moments later, they call out the exact number of our apartment, 4A. We listen through radio static as a police dispatcher makes the call to kick in our front door. Mikki and I look at each other, completely aware it's only been a little over an hour since we left. Clearly disappointed, the detectives find an abandoned apartment occupied only by the large pieces of furniture we left behind. Again, we're gone only moments before the raid!

No longer feeling safe so close to the raid, it's urgent we get further away. I dial Adrian's number, who is currently back with Linda after one of their many breakups, and explain our situation to him. They invite us to stay with them in North Ridge, California right outside of Los Angeles. We check out of the hotel and head south down through Lake Havasu and Quartzite, cutting over on highway 10 into Blythe, California. By the time we reach Blythe, we are so freaking tired we cannot go one more mile. Blythe, being such a small town, has only a little shack of a hotel, but I figure we can't be choosy right now and pull in to spend the night. Since I'm not in Arizona or Nevada, I feel somewhat safe here. Mikki calls Linda to let her know we'll be there in the morning. I haven't slept in a week, and as soon as my head hits the pillow, I am out cold.

Lighting a cigarette upon waking, I turn on the morning news and immediately nudge Mikki. She has *got* to see this! No way! Mikki sleepily rolls over then tunes into the screen, quickly sitting up in disbelief. Lighting a cigarette, she watches the news footage in shock. This can't be happening!

North Ridge and a big part of Eastern Los Angeles just got slammed with an earthquake. Total pandemonium. Everyone is going crazy. We try call after call but can't get hold of Adrian and Linda to see if they're okay, if they're alive. Remaining holed up in this shanty hotel, we continue to call while watching news footage after news footage all day long and into evening when finally Adrian calls telling us that their apartment building split in half, but the three of them are alive and unharmed. Needless to say, we won't be going to North Ridge.

I'm hiding out in this little hotel with all my stuff packed in a U-Haul parked just outside the window, and I have no idea where to go. I decide to head north, back up to Lake Havasu. When I drove through on the way down, it reminded me of a retirement community, very peaceful, very quiet. It is definitely not a place anyone would look for criminal activity.

When we enter the city again, I tell Mikki as if we're normal parents, "What a perfect place to raise a family!"

Her unresponsiveness reminds me how ridiculous my statement is. Glancing in the rearview mirror at Nikki and Chris in the back seat, I shake my head and chuckle out loud at the idea that I, Darwyn Bryant, could *ever* settle somewhere long enough to raise a family. My chuckles quickly turn into hysterical laughter, and Mikki stares at me solemnly and asks, "What in the world is so funny?"

Overwrought with emotion that I usually numb with meth, my hysterical laughter turns to gut-wrenching sobs. I choke out, "Me? Raise a family?"

It's clear I'll never have a chance to raise my kids. I blew that opportunity a long time ago. As I weep, Mikki turns away from me and stares out the passenger window. Besides answering the kids, we don't talk the rest of the night. I know what she's thinking. The same thing I am. We both understand that eventually this is going to end, and it isn't going to end amicably.

I find a place I'm interested in and pull over to do a bump, collect myself, and retire Nicolas Sheridan Kennedy to the "used" side of my identity folder. Pulling out a new ID and credit cards, I walk through the office doors with a big smile and throw out my hand, introducing myself as Carson Finch. I have no problem securing a place to live. Needing to lay low until things cool down, we decide not to contact anyone, not even our parents. I have plenty of cash to get us through a couple months along with many other identities. I feel safe here even though I'm back in Arizona. Mikki and I discuss moving to Idaho or maybe Florida, anywhere away from the southwest or the Midwest. I have some connections on the east coast that I haven't told Mikki about yet. I'll fill her in when the time comes.

Chapter 12
Lake Havasu
December 1993

With Nevada's Cook County police department aggressively hunting me, I now feel safer back in Arizona. It's been months since I've lived in Arizona, so their search for me should have cooled by now. As we move into our new home, Mikki and I worry about Adrian and Linda, wondering if they've found a place to stay. We discuss inviting them to stay with us for a while but then ask ourselves, "If you're in a pot of boiling water, is it wise to invite friends to join in a precarious bath?" We agree to catch up with them later.

Lake Havasu sits along a mountainside where the Colorado River divides California and Arizona. Opposite the river on the other side of town, the mountainside is steep with no roads or highways leading in or out of town. Because of this white rock mountain, there is only one way in and one way out via Highway 93 running north and south. There are many side roads and back streets in town, but they all eventually dead-end in cul-de-sacs leading right back to Highway 93. It's such a small, isolated little town far away from everything. I feel safe hiding out here and plan on staying a while until things cool down.

We move into a very nice duplex in a great neighborhood with an elementary school at the end of the block. Nikki will soon be six and should have started school last August. We are now in a situation where we no longer have two little babies that we can just up and move at a moment's notice, but by enrolling Nikki in school, it opens up another opportunity for something to go wrong, adding a whole new level of stress.

Even I understand the importance of my daughter attending school, so hand in hand, I walk Nikki to the end of the block and enroll her in kindergarten. She is thrilled to death! I find I am, too, but I struggle with happiness in sharing her excitement and fear of what this might open up for me. For the first time in my life, I feel somewhat like a normal father registering my daughter for school and meeting her teacher, but I find myself constantly scanning, looking, and planning an exit strategy just in case I'm recognized.

Nikki easily makes many new friends, and I smile as I watch her, thinking to myself, *So this is what being a real parent is like, what normal people feel like, what normal people do.* Up to this point, nothing in our life has been normal.

I have a new morning routine. I'm always the first one up, if I go to bed at all. Chris wakes up and slowly wanders in, wanting to just sit on the floor with his truck and watch cartoons. When Nikki wakes up, she yells, "Daddy!" as she runs across the living room and jumps into my arms for some big hugs. No matter where Chris sits to watch his cartoons, Nikki alters her path to kick him as she runs to me, whispering in my ear as she points at her little brother, "I don't like him, Daddy." He just wants to sit in front of the TV and watch cartoons, but she can't pass him by without inflicting a little pain, a big sister's love. I feel so bad for Chris.

After breakfast, Nikki and I walk to school, enjoying the perfect morning weather. At the corner of the schoolyard, I stop and watch her take off, running across the grass on her little chicken legs to meet her friend. She gives her little friend a big hug, and they walk off holding hands. Nikki, she has my heart. She is so much a part of me in every single way, shape, and form.

Weeks fly by, and spring is right around the corner. I wake up Saturday morning feeling lousy and drag myself out of bed. When my foot hits the floor, pain shoots up my leg. I look down and yell, "Mikki! Come look at this!"

During the night, my calf turned beet red, is hot as hell, and is swollen to twice its normal size. Mikki walks in and looks down at my leg. "What in the world did you do?" she asks.

"Nothing! I don't know, but it hurts like crazy!"

Mikki advises me, "You better get that checked out. It's probably a spider bite."

"Yeah, maybe."

Mikki watches me struggle to slide my shorts on and stoops down in front of my swollen leg. "Here, let me help you. Come on. I'll drive."

She hustles the kids to the car, and off we all go to an urgent care center in town.

After a brief examination, the doctor orders blood work. This should be interesting. Looking perplexed when he enters the room with my results, he informs me, "You have a severe case of cellulitis."

Looking down at my painful leg, I ask, "Okay. What's that?"

"Cellulitis is common with potentially serious bacterial skin infections. In extreme cases like yours, left untreated, it can rapidly spread throughout the body and become life-threatening."

Mikki and I look at each other and then back to the doctor. He says, "I'm going to put you on a strong antibiotic regimen. You need to stay off your feet for at least five days."

I glance at Mikki then look down at my leg, thinking, *Yeah, right.*

The doctor stares at me with a questioning look for a moment and then looks at Mikki. He observes each of the kids and walks out the door. I think he suspects I need a lot more than antibiotics. I mean, he just read my blood work, and I'm guessing he most likely detected illegal toxins in my system. I leave the urgent care center with a prescription in hand, feeling that his perplexed look can be attributed more to what he found in my system than to my cellulitis.

After filling my prescription, I go home with every intention to rest as much as I can in the hope this heals quickly. My siesta lasts about forty-five minutes, and I can't take it any longer. Getting up, I head out the door, but *wow* does my leg hurt! Pushing the pain out of my mind, I drive to the gas station for a pack of smokes.

Besides my throbbing leg, things are good right now. We live in a nice place in a good neighborhood, and my daughter is in a great school. We love it here, but reality weighs heavy on me as always. Using my real name living in the real world, I could never afford to live like this, to maintain this lifestyle, to survive in this neighborhood.

I haven't cooked dope or pulled off any fraudulent schemes in months, allowing us to momentarily relax a little and behave like a somewhat normal family. It won't last long, though, because money is starting to run low, forcing me to make plans to procure more. I absolutely hate the thought of spoiling the life we have here, but I'm going to have to make another check run or cook some dope to afford to stay. We have to eat and pay the rent, and when I don't make dope, I'm forced to buy it.

To keep my family in this false sense of normalcy, I'm going to have to do what I do best, print and cash fraudulent checks or cook another batch of dope. I decide to do both and do it big this time. Man, I love living here and don't want to spoil it, but what other choice do I have? I figure if I cook enough at one time to hold us over for several years, it will give me time to figure out how to get back to the normal world and hopefully get out of this crappy life forever. That's my plan now. Go big and never do this again!

It's been a while since I've "worked," and I no longer have the comfort of my contacts in Phoenix close by to help. I'm inspecting the garage, planning the best place to set up a lab, when Nikki excitedly reminds me it's time to walk her to school. I hobble into the bedroom to grab a shirt. Lying in the drawer on top of my shirts is a Bible. Feeling a little queasy, I hold onto the chest of drawers for support, thinking, *No way!* Wondering where it came from, I pick up the Bible to see if it's the same one Grandma gave me. It couldn't possibly be the same one. I mean, I've moved a dozen times since the last time I saw it.

Feeling as if I'm in an episode of *The Twilight Zone*, I carefully unzip and open the Bible to the first page. There it is, Grandma's inscription. Unbelievable!

Nikki runs into the bedroom, pleading with me to hurry, so I carefully place the Bible back in the drawer. Taking Nikki's hand, I walk past Mikki toward the front door and ask, "Hey Mik, did you put that Bible in my drawer?"

Looking at me as if I have a third eye, Mikki answers with attitude, "Bible? What are you talking about?"

"Never mind."

Nikki holds tight to my hand as she skips down the sidewalk, keeping up with my long, slow stride. My Nikki, she makes me smile.

Walking back alone, I climb into the car and take a drive around town. Lake Havasu's big claim to fame is its London Bridge. They have an actual bridge from London that has been erected over the Colorado River. It was dismantled in London, brought here to Lake Havasu, and reassembled.

I stop at a Circle K for gas and smokes, and some kid hands me a flyer announcing a youth church rally on the riverfront. "Come on down if you can make it! It's a great time!" he says.

I take the flyer and read, *A Special Invite from Youth Pastor Ward Cusic.* It's complete with time and location. I nod at the kid and throw it in the back seat.

Driving away I think, *God? I haven't thought about God in years. Why would I? I'm sure he's given up on me. Why is God even on my mind? This is stupid, Darwyn, stop it!* I know God doesn't care about me anymore, and I have other things I need to think about like feeding my family and scoring some dope. I push God out of my thoughts and get back to concentrating on my plan.

Thinking it's probably still too risky right now, I decide against printing checks, so I get busy preparing to cook dope. My available resources look good for cooking a large batch. My huge garage has a ventilation system completely separate from the house along with its own running water. I can make this work!

I contact Barry, and he tells me Carl, his cook, died a few weeks ago from organ failure due to extreme chemical exposure, so he's looking for a new source. Sonny wants in also. I tell them about the secluded place I've moved to. "I can set up shop here, but it'll have to be a one or two shot deal. We have to go big and make it count. Let's do two cooks, five pounds each. That should bring in around $300,000 for only a few days' work. If I do this, can you guys move that much for me?"

"No worries!" they say, excited that I'm back in the game.

Sonny makes it a point to tell me that he no longer trusts Barry and won't come around if Barry's here. I tell him, "Well, this is the last time I'll be cooking with Barry. This is it for me. After this, I'm done. I'm taking Mikki and the kids and moving back east.

"Sure, you are."

"I'm serious, dude! This is it!"

First on my list, I need chemicals and equipment. As I left everything I had back in Laughlin, I have to start from the beginning, ordering my supplies all over again. I want to make the good dope, no bunk junk, but I can't make prop right now—the chemicals are just too hard to get. I can still make a really good ephedrine hybrid. I need pharmaceutical grade chemicals to make it, though—none of that pseudoephedrine extracted from pills. The only way to get these chemicals is to do the same thing I did in Belleville. My mistake in Belleville was I stayed in one place way too long, ordering over and over and having it delivered to the exact same address. I won't do that again. This time will be different. My plan is to order everything I need at one time but from several different companies. I'll have the supplies delivered to many locations miles away from each other and arrange their pickups. I plan to make a very good, very large batch, large enough to sustain me a long time, and then I'll shut it all down and find another way to survive.

I create another biochemical research and analysis lab, this time under the name Quantum Research. This allows me access to top grade pharmaceutical chemicals. This time, I prepare a synthesis on professional paper with the company name on the letterhead and list the chemicals ordered and the uses of each. I order all the chemicals I need along with many chemicals I don't and organize the deliveries to different locations. It's a little time consuming but easy to do. No one checks to see if these analysis labs exist, if it's legit, or if there's even a building at the address where it's being shipped. As far as I know, there are no investigations, no follow-ups once the chemicals are shipped, nothing. It's unbelievably easy.

My main delivery address at Mail Boxes 'n' More is in Quartzite, about fifty miles south of Lake Havasu. Since this is the only mail drop within fifty miles that will accept large packages, I have the smaller packages delivered elsewhere. Mail Boxes 'n' More is located in a small, nondescript, L-shaped strip mall right in the middle of town. Not a lot happens in Quartzsite. They have a national rock show every year where they show quartz rocks and sell them, and that's about it. That's all they're known for—quartz rocks.

I didn't pay much attention to the surrounding businesses in the small strip mall, but I did notice a laundromat and an unmarked building on the other side. This is the only mailbox rental that will accept large shipments, and I feel comfortable that it's in a small town like Quartzsite. These shipments don't come in normal brown boxes. They come in huge crates with large red warning labels on the side that say "Lithium Aluminum Hydride, DANGER! EXPLOSIVES! HANDLE WITH CARE!" Being shipped to such a small town, they are much less likely to be noticed.

With the project in motion, packages start arriving at the various mailboxes, and I coordinate with people to have them picked up and delivered to me. I struggle with my decision to cook again, but thinking about the $300,000 I will profit keeps me moving forward as planned. One more cook, and I'm done with this forever.

Remembering I need a five-gallon triple neck flask large enough for a five-pound yield, I order it to be delivered to Quartzite. Sitting back in my chair and rubbing my forehead, I realize I still haven't addressed my main problem. With this large of a cook, what am I going to do about the smell? Cooking quality meth puts out a horrible stench that will span blocks. I decide on a cold cook method meaning instead of using high heat for a short time, I'll use low heat for a longer time, similar to a slow cooker. This method will minimize the risk of explosion, but it still doesn't address the smell.

My leg's getting worse, but I can't rest until this is done. Looking into our sewer system, I discover that we are not on city sewer but a septic system, which means we have a huge tank buried out in the backyard collecting everything. If I run a hose from the top of the flask down the drain, it should push the smelly vapors into the septic tank. At the same time, I can run another hose from the water faucet into the same drain to ensure these smelly vapors are forced all the way into the tank. As long as I treat the septic tank with an enzyme to break down the odor, it should keep the gasses from building up, thereby destroying the odor and minimizing the chance of explosion. With a good sound plan, I immediately get started setting up the lab complete with my invention of a water trap drainage system.

I test it out on a small amount to see if it works. It does! All the pungent odors are successfully pushed down into the septic tank and buried safely underground. Even while standing in the garage, I cannot smell a thing. I'm ready to cook the big one!

163

I rid the garage of all evidence after my dry run just in case. I install a dead bolt from the kitchen to the garage to make sure my kids do not have any access whatsoever to this lab until the job is finished and the garage is completely scrubbed clean.

In the rafters of the garage, I've already stored L-ephedrine and anhydrous ammonia. I call Barry to tell him the last shipment has been verified. "There'll be two packages. Pick them up on your way in, and let's get this over with."

Barry pulls into the driveway with the packages in the bed of his truck. Karin jumps out and walks to the front door as Barry backs out and drives away. Karin tells us he ran to the gas station for smokes and will be back in five minutes.

Five minutes turn to one hour, and no Barry. I've stood looking out the window for over an hour now and have a gut feeling something's gone terribly wrong. I can't wait any longer, so I walk out the door, telling Mikki and Karin, "I'm going to look for Barry. Something's not right."

Turning on the police scanner, I back out of the driveway and head south on Nacoma toward Highway 93. Unlike Phoenix with its roads laid out in an easy to follow, perfectly straight grid running north and south, east and west with very few curves, Lake Havasu's roads are like a bowl of spaghetti—twisting, squirrely, curvy roads running in any and all directions with no rhyme or reason.

As I'm wondering where I should look for Barry, I notice headlights coming up on me from behind immediately followed by the police scanner calling out, "South on Nacoma."

Okay, I'm going south on Nacoma. I turn right on Little Chief, and the scanner calls out, "Right on Little Chief."

Crap! They're following me!

Turning onto Highway 93, I remain cool, drive the speed limit, and try to figure out my next move. Knowing most of these streets end in cul-de-sacs but many do connect like a maze, I turn right on McCullouch looking for a side street to turn on, thinking if I can get out of their line of sight for just one second, I can lose them.

They remain about three car lengths behind me, calling out my every move. It's apparent they have no idea I'm listening, that I know they're behind me. I make a right off McCullouch into a residential subdivision full of tract homes, side-by-side duplicates all in a row. I'm fighting a fever, and my leg has swollen to the size of a watermelon from my knee to my ankle. The pain is unbearable. Reluctantly, I reach the understanding that my only chance of escape is to ditch this van and run on foot, but with this leg, *how?*

Not knowing what happened to Barry and worried about Mikki and the kids, I have to get back to the house, but I can't let this guy follow me back. I have to lose him. I'm about three miles from home, and I continue to drive slowly, following all the rules and knowing they're going to swoop in on me soon. I have to do something fast.

The road starts to wind and curve through the subdivision, so as soon as I no longer see headlights in my rearview mirror, I make my move. Pain sears up my leg as I press the gas pedal to the floor, speeding, winding, turning, and skidding around corners, putting as much distance between us as fast as I can. I'm flying like a bullet at sixty-five to seventy-five miles an hour in a fifteen-mile-per-hour zone, cringing at every curve because I'm worried I'm going to flip the van. Then I see it! Ahead of me on the left is a house with a wide-open garage, and not one single light is turned on! Screeching through a left turn, I pull in, hitting the brakes as I kill the engine and lights while sinking low in my seat—just in time to look in my rearview mirror and see a police car zoom past. Taking a moment to catch my breath and touch my leg, I wait and watch as they zoom past the opposite way. I'm being hunted as I sit in this stranger's garage, saying a prayer that these people are not home and won't be home anytime soon. Twenty long minutes pass.

I recently purchased a new cell phone that allows me to make calls from anywhere. It's too big to carry on me, so I keep it in the glove compartment of the van. Still sitting low in the van, I dial Mikki to warn her of what's going on, and she doesn't believe me. "Oh, come on now, Darwyn, you're just being paranoid. You're always thinking you're being followed, and now with the fever, it's just making it worse. Come on home."

"*No*, Mikki! This is *not* just paranoia! *I am being followed!* Has Barry come back yet?"

"No, he hasn't."

"Well, Mikki, he's not coming back! I'm sure they got him! That's the only reason they'd be following me right now."

She asks, "Where are you?"

"About three miles away. I'm trying to get home, but I can't get back out on the road with this van. They're looking for it. They're looking for me!"

Mikki's still not convinced, so I hang up and shove the phone in my pocket. Deserting the van in this stranger's garage, I take off on foot. Traveling through backyards to keep from being noticed, I'm forced to jump six-foot cinderblock fences one after another. I have to get back to Mikki and the kids. The pain in my leg is beyond unbearable. Stopping to catch my breath, I reach for the cell phone to call Mikki, and it's gone! *No!* Leaning forward with my hands on my thighs, I look around, completely disoriented from all the twisty, winding roads.

My leg is on fire, and my head pounds with fever as I look around to get my bearings on the shortest route home. The mountain is east. I need to go north, so I take off running making sure to keep the mountainside on my right. After jumping the backyard fences of house after house after house, I've riled up every dog in the area. They're agitated, growling, barking, and howling, all warning me to stay out of their yards and doing their best to alert their owners.

Sprinting, jumping, climbing, and hurdling fence after fence, I gasp for air, dragging my throbbing watermelon leg with me. Pain shoots into my hip with every step, but I continue on, telling myself just one more fence and trying my best to come down on my good leg. I land in a backyard face to face with a snarling dog as big as a Rottweiler. Running as fast as I can across the yard before he chews my butt, I hurdle over another fence and land on my side right in a patch of paddle cacti.

My skin and clothes now pierced with cactus needles, I quickly jump up and take off for the next fence, splashing down into the shallow end of a swimming pool. Soaking wet, I push through the water as fast as I can. Back porch lights pop on as the owners check to see what fell in their pool. Fence after fence, and finally I see my street.

Leaning against my neighbor's fence, which is caddy-corner across the street, I catch my breath and look to the left at my front yard. Further to the left, I notice four white vans in the school parking lot. I drop to the ground and watch men dressed in black emerge from the vans. They suit themselves up and adjust their guns. I cannot let them come in on Mikki and the kids without being there. I *have* to get in the house before they do.

Crawling across the neighbor's yard toward home, I try to stay out of sight. In a split second, without warning like out of a space movie, my entire home is engulfed in a blazing light shinning down from above. This huge beam of light has lit up the entire area, blinding me. I freeze and wait, listening, but hear no sounds. Then over my heavy breathing, I can hear the rhythmic sound of propellers cutting through the air above my head. Moving slowly, I look up and see some kind of helicopter, a stealth helicopter like those used by the military. As I lay on my belly looking at my illuminated house, my only thought is, *Oh man!* In a split second, the light's gone!

Immediately, I crawl across the street through my yard and up to the door, softly banging and quietly yelling, "*Mikki! Quick! Let me in!*"

Mikki casually opens the door and asks, "So what's going on?"

Quickly pushing past her, I shut and lock the door behind me and walk to the window to peek out, warning the both of them, "We're about to get raided! They're in the school parking lot all suited up! This is it, Mikki! They're coming down on us!"

I'm standing in the living room soaking wet and covered in dirt and cactus needles, nervous and jittery, and she asks, "Are you sure?"

I tell her about being followed, hopping fences, avoiding dogs, battling cacti, falling in a swimming pool, and then about the men in the school parking lot and about the stealth helicopter with the beam of light.

She still doesn't believe me. "How in the world would they know we're here?"

"I'm not joking, Mikki!"

I fail to get across to her what's about to happen, what's about to go down, and she's startled when sees them, shadows outside our window, bodies moving around the outside of the house. Karin immediately curls up in a ball on the sofa and starts whimpering, asking over and over, "Where's Barry?"

"I'm sure they've got him," I tell her. "I have no idea what's happened to him, but unless he somehow got away, I'm sure they've got him."

I limp out to the garage and take a quick inventory of what I actually have, quickly flushing the dope from my stash down the toilet. All that's in my garage now are a few chemicals. The rest are with Barry. I'm not concerned about my house. It's clean as far as dope, although they will find a small arsenal.

Hyped up on adrenaline, a voice inside commands me to quickly flush the chemicals I've stored down the drain, ridding my garage of everything. Without these chemicals, they've got nothing on me as far as dope. A quieter, smarter voice warns me that if I flush this mixture of chemicals down into the septic tank, blending them together, it would undoubtedly create combustion. We'd be sitting on a powder keg. It might work, but it might be suicide. Something inside me clicks, and I instantly relax as I come to the conclusion they're here, they're coming in, we have nowhere to go, this is it, we're done.

A strange calm floods over me as I turn and walk back into the living room. Mikki stares at me, struggling not to cry. I know the end's drawing near, and I'm oddly relieved. I am so ready for all of this to be over, and well, it's about to be over. Taking Mikki's hand, I lead her to the bedroom and lie down with her, knowing this is probably going to be the last time we ever lie next to each other. Completely exhausted, I hold her close and pass out cold.

BANG! BANG! BANG!

"Mrs. Bryant! Open the door! It's the police! Open up, Mrs. Bryant! We're coming in!"

I roll over and look at the time, 7 a.m. Mikki slowly gets out of bed and walks down the hall to check on the kids. I roll back over and pull the covers up to my chin, thinking if they want me, they're going to have to come and get me out of bed. Shutting my eyes, I try to quiet the voices within.

BANG! BANG! BANG!

"Mrs. Bryant! Open the door! We know you're in there!"

Mikki slowly walks to the front door and unlocks it. Four officers with guns drawn rush in. I can see them from the open door of my bedroom, so I turn on my back and put my hands behind my head to settle in and watch the show. They obviously have no idea I'm here. Mikki walks over to the couch and sits next to Karin. I hear the police questioning them, but neither Mikki nor Karin answer.

Lying in bed, I watch as an officer backs down the hallway toward me. I shake my head. *What idiots!* I think. *If I had a gun, if I was that type of person, I could take him out right now.* It's like watching the keystone cops. I watch them open the door to Nikki and Chris's room, calling in for a couple of women cops to better handle the situation. Mikki and Karin remain quiet on the couch.

Startled, a cop finally spots me lying in bed and yells out, *"Freeze!"*

Instantaneously, all the cops in the house raise their guns again, covering Mikki, Karin, and me. I say quietly, "I'm not going anywhere, man. I'm here."

The lead detective, an Irish-looking guy with curly red hair, comes in and asks sternly, "What's your name?!"

Taking a deep, weary breath, I tell him, "Come on, man. You know who I am or you wouldn't be here."

He yells, *"Get up!"*

I whip the covers down and get up, struggling to stand on my dark red, grossly swollen leg. Surprised when he sees my leg the officer asks, "What happened to you?"

Not believing he really cares, I say, "The doctor said it's cellulitis."

I stand before the officers, waiting for them to grab me, throw me to the ground, force my hands behind my back with their knees pushing on my neck while handcuffing me, but surprisingly, they allow me to simply turn around as they handcuff my hands behind my back.

They escort me into the living room where Karin, Mikki, and the kids are huddled on the couch crying, and someone says, "Take him on to the police station."

I ask, "What about them?" looking over to Mikki and the kids.

"We're not done with them yet."

With my hands cuffed behind my back and an officer on each side, I'm taken out the front door into the bright Arizona sun. I look around, surprised to see police cars lining the street as far as the eye can see with a helicopter overhead and some sort of military vehicle in my driveway alongside a hazmat truck. Men are busy putting on their hazmat suits, getting ready to clean up a meth lab that doesn't exist. I'm escorted toward a waiting police car with an armed officer standing by. Just as I climb into the backseat and the door slams shut, an assortment of cops, agents, ATF, DEA, MAGNET, and county and state police all start high-fiving each other. I watch their reaction for a moment then tell the driver, "They act like a bunch of high school football players who just won a game."

He responds, "Better! They just caught one of Arizona's Top Ten Most Wanted!"

I stare out the car window as we back up through the crowd and drive away. Millions of thoughts race through my head, and I flinch when the officer strikes up a conversation. Having found my small arsenal in the house, he now realizes that I could have easily shot him when he was in the hallway backing up toward me. He thanks me for being so cooperative. I tell him the truth, "I may be a lot of things, but that's not me. I'm tired. I'm done. I knew you were out there and I was just lying down waiting for your next move."

He responds, "We had no idea you were even in the house. We thought you were long gone. The last time we saw you, you were in a vehicle turning off McCullough. We thought you had gotten away. We waited all night for you to come home and then figured you ran, so we decided to come in and arrest your wife."

Alarmed, I look at him. "Are you going to arrest Mikki?!"

He responds as if I should know. "Yeah, we're going to arrest her."

Surprised, I ask, "What are you charging her with?"

Matter-of-factly he informs me, "The exact same crimes we're charging you with. She lives there, too."

At the police station, they immediately take me back to start proceedings, verbally listing my charges:

1) Manufacturing methamphetamine

2) Possession of dangerous chemicals

3) Fraudulent schemes (they found my identity folder, twenty-seven Arizona-issued driver's licenses, all with my picture, and matching credit cards)

4) Weapons charge

5) Counterfeiting charge (they found the equipment I use to make counterfeit checks, birth certificates, etc.)

6) Multiple fraud charges

Noticing a security mirror in the upper corner of the room, I'm again stunned when I see my reflection. In my mind, I keep thinking I still look like what I looked like years ago, but now staring at my reflection, I can't believe what I see. I look harrowing, like something out of a horror film. At six foot four, I'm skinny as a rail. My bleach blonde hair is long, down past my shoulders. I have a red bandana tied around my head and a feather dangling from my earring. I step closer, looking deep into my eyes, and I see evil, someone without a soul, and I have to look away. They snap my picture and moments later hand me my jail ID card. I'm speechless. I look at this photo and think, *No, that can't be me,* but it is.

I've been arrested many times but never processed. This is my first time actually being processed into a jail. I'm sitting and waiting for an interrogation or something, and I see them bring in Mikki and Karin. Wondering where my kids are, I jump up, freaking out and yelling at Mikki, "Where's the kids? Where's the kids?"

She cries out, shaking her head, "I don't know! They took them. The state's got them doing something...I don't know!"

A detective speaks up, "They're on their way to foster care until you can make arrangements for a family member to pick them up."

Mikki and I scream, freaking out that Nikki and Chris are in foster care. The thought of them in the hands of complete strangers blows our minds.

Mikki and I are sitting in the interrogation room with a detective. He questions us, trying to get information. We don't answer, but I have a question for him, "If I talk to you, how is that going to help me in any way, shape, or form?"

He stands up, saying angrily, "Well, it won't help you because you're done," and he walks out.

A few minutes later, another cop walks in and sits down across from us. He says, "You don't remember me, do you?"

I look him up and down and answer honestly, "No."

Mikki shakes her head.

He introduces himself and tells me he's with the DEA. "I've been following you since Belleville, Illinois. I've been tracking you two ever since, and I've finally got you."

I stare at the floor. It's been four years since we've lived in Belleville. *Great, you got me,* I think. He goes on to explain that he works out of the St. Louis, Missouri office just across the river from Belleville. He smiles as he continues, "It's taken me a long time to find you!"

Shaking his head, he explains that his office in STL is in the same building that housed the chemical company I was ordering from. They're required to report any and all chemicals ordered that could be used in the manufacturing of anything related to drugs.

It hits me—the two are co-partnered! I sit up and listen as he goes on to tell me that the Quartzite mailbox was housed next to a substation for the US Marshalls office. I had no idea. I thought I was smarter than them, throwing them off by ordering random chemicals, but they knew all along. They knew exactly what I was doing! Staring down at the floor, I shake my head. I can't believe it. This entire time, the US Marshalls were following me, documenting all of my activities, and keeping me under surveillance. Unbelievable!

I look back up at him when he asks about my elaborate meth lab. He asks where I've hid all the dope. I simply and honestly reply, "I don't have no dope."

I can see the irritation in his face as he realizes they messed up. They thought I had already cooked dope and the lab was up and running, but I hadn't started yet. If they had waited just a few more hours, they would have caught me cooking ten pounds of dope. They jumped the gun and are aggravated because they can't find one single grain of dope in my van, in my house, or on me.

Because they don't find dope, the DEA chooses not to prosecute. It's not worth their time. If they had found dope, I would have been turned over to the feds by now for prosecution. The fact that I have absolutely no dope makes their case against me very weak. All they have on me is possession of chemicals, and not even all the chemicals needed to make dope were found in one place so that can't even be argued. The fact that the remaining chemicals were with Barry doesn't matter—they have to be all in one place to make a manufacturing charge stick. None of this really matters as far as getting out of jail anytime soon. This is just one of many charges pending against me. Three other counties are looking for me, and soon, it'll all come out.

The DEA leaves disappointed, and Lake Havasu's detectives come back in to question me. They encourage me to talk, saying that I can help myself by giving them information. I tell them, "But I'm the head of the operation, and everyone works for me. Even if I'm willing, I have no one to turn in."

Wanting me to give them the names of my crew they warn me, "You're going to be gone the rest of your life, but if you cooperate, your wife doesn't have to be."

Mikki quickly speaks up, "Keep your mouth shut!"

I look at her as tears roll down her cheeks. That's all she says. She tells me to keep my mouth shut. I look back to the detective, and I keep my mouth shut. We both go to jail.

Mikki is keeping her wits about her better than I am. She's sent to the female holding cell next to mine, the male holding cell. These holding cells temporarily house us while they prepare a bed in a more permanent place called "the pod." Each holding cell has a few toilets out in the open for about twenty people. You know you're in jail when a dude walks up, drops his drawers, and takes a crap right in front of you. This is the first time I have ever witnessed anything like that before in my life. I tell myself to get used to it. Someone seasoned, who's spent time in jail, they know the routine. If you gotta go, you gotta go—they don't think anything about it. Having never been "in" before, I find it quite disturbing.

Glancing around the cell, I notice Barry passed out on a bench. I haven't seen him since he left the house. I wake him up and ask him what happened. He tells me that when he pulled into the gas station, they swooped in on him. They told him they followed him from Quartzite to Lake Havasu in a single engine Cessna. They showed him photos they took of him picking up packages from the mailbox. They asked him who lived in my house and questioned him about me. They showed him pictures of me and asked, "Is this Darwyn Bryant?" to which he answered, "No, that's not Darwyn Bryant, that's Michael."

Barry had no idea I was using a fake name and swore up and down to the officer that I really was Michael. I had never told him my real name. Up to this point, nobody in Arizona knew me as Darwyn. The cops, as I encountered them over the last few years, didn't know who I was either until after they released me. They knew there was a Darwyn Bryant who was wanted, but they never figured out I was Darwyn until I was long gone.

I'm escorted out of the holding cell to make my phone call and dread the thought of having to explain all this to Mom. I dial her number, and Wayne answers, telling me she's not home. I explain my predicament to my stepdad, and he listens quietly. When I'm finished, he responds in a low voice, "Oh no! Your mom doesn't know yet, huh?"

"No, she doesn't. I don't know what my bond is or bail or anything. I'll call when I know."

The next day, we all go in front of a judge. Barry's bond is $10,000. Mikki's bond is $10,000. I have a $25,000 bond in Coconino County, a $25,000 bond in Pima County, a $50,000 bond in Maricopa County, and a $100,000 cash only bond in Mohave County. Now, the problem with a cash only bond is there will be no ten percent down and no putting up property. They want $100,000 cash for my release and nothing else.

Barry calls his parents who live about 120 miles away. They arrange his bond and try to get all his proceedings moved to a closer precinct. Mikki calls her mom and dad and makes arrangements for them to pick up Nikki and Chris.

The longer my name circulates through the system, the more charges come in, meaning more bonds and more money required for my release. They have it arranged so that even if I do make bail in one county, the other counties are set to raise my bond. By the time I call Mom, I have to tell her it's near impossible for me to get out of jail.

Chapter 13
Mohave County Jail
Prison
March 1994- 1996

Barry and I spend the night in the holding cell, and in early morning, Barry's dad pays his bail, securing his release. I watch him leave and sit back down to wait—that's pretty much all there is to do now, wait and sleep.

I strike up a conversation with a "regular," questioning him about this place. He tells me there are four pods, Pod A, B, C and D. Directly below these pods are identical pods housing the women. Each pod has one hundred bunks, meaning this jail is capable of housing up to eight hundred people. Each pod has a day room with fifteen cells along the side, two beds in each cell. An upper tier has an additional fifteen cells with two bunk beds per cell, same size area with four beds instead of two off a balcony overlooking the day room. There are an additional five bunk beds out in the day room along the wall. This is where they place the extras until a cell opens up.

In late afternoon, I'm told to step out of the holding cell and turn around with my hands behind my back. Just like when they transported me across the street for my bail hearing, I'm handcuffed so tight my hands swell and sting. Instructed to follow an officer, I walk through the sally port doors toward Pod D, followed by an armed guard. I walk down the sandy-colored hallway and through the door, and my body tenses when the loud clunk of metal hits concrete as the door slides shut behind me with such finality. I take two steps and wait for the door behind me to be secured before the door in front electronically opens. We repeat this process a few times before reaching the pod. The unfamiliar sound of the heavy metal doors slamming against concrete echoes in my head as I walk through the final door into D-pod.

In a quick glance, I notice this door is the only way in and out. There are no windows, no other exit doors. The officer frees my wrists and gives me a property bag. I squeeze my hands into fists then stretch my fingers open, causing extreme pain as the blood flows back to my stinging palms.

Looking straight ahead as I walk toward my bunk, I take in everything with my peripheral vision. There are tables and stools out in the large room, all bolted to the concrete floor. Men move around freely, some at tables playing cards and others working out doing pushups or jogging. Everyone is dressed in bright orange scrubs.

I expect trouble. I've heard stories about problems upon entry to jails and prisons. New inmates are challenged to see what they're about, see where they stand.

I'm assigned to a top bunk along the wall in the day room, a normal procedure for newcomers. I am beyond tired and just want to sleep. Twenty-four hours without dope, and I am crashing hard. I stretch my sheet out on the bunk, lie down, and pass out cold.

I awaken, vaguely hearing someone call out for breakfast, but I can't even open my eyes let alone get up, so I roll over and black out.

"Hey, bro! Your ole lady wants to talk to you."

What the—? My head is buried in a pillow. I try to regain consciousness but then assume I must be dreaming. They can't be talking to me. Ignoring my dream, I stir a little, not even opening my eyes, and travel back to my comfortable unconscious state.

Louder this time, I hear someone say, "Dude! She keeps calling for you!"

I just want to sleep, but then he gets my attention. "You're Bryant, right?"

Rubbing my face, I lift my head, opening one eye to look at him. Who is he and what does he want? Throwing my head back down and covering my eyes from the painful lights, I ask, "What are you talking about, man?"

He replies, "She's on the toilet phone."

Shading my eyes, I lift my head, confused. "The *what?*" Still groggy, I sit up, look around, and ask, "How long have I been out?"

With a slight snicker, he replies, "You came in two days ago, bro!"

"Man! Really? I gotta pee!"

His eyes widen, and he smiles, saying, "Well, come on! You can pee while you talk to your ole lady!"

Rubbing my eyes, I run my fingers across the top of my head, pushing back my hair as I mumble, "You're not kidding, are you?"

He waves me to follow. "No! Come on, bro. Follow me."

I slowly climb down from the top bunk, favoring my leg, but man, I need to get to that bathroom quick. Every muscle in my body is stiff and sore from crashing for two full days. Limping along, I follow him to his cell, noticing the toilet located within an arm's reach in between two bunks. A sink is mounted directly over the toilet, and a small metal slab is directly above it to use as a mirror, but it doesn't reflect very well.

I stand over the toilet to do my business, and when I'm done, the guy walks in and points to an air vent behind the toilet. He says it's connected to the vents in the women's pod below and tells me if I place my ear on the vent, I'll be able to hear the women below. I'm not quite sure if I'm about to be hazed or if I can trust this guy, so I give him a look, and he backs away, telling me again to place my mouth close to the vent and call her name.

When he's at a safe distance, I place my ear to the vent and smile looking back at him, because yes, I can hear women talking! He encourages me, "Well, go ahead! Call out her name! If she's not there, someone will go get her!"

Feeling ridiculous, I place my mouth as close to the vent as is sanitary and call out, "Hey, Mikki!" as I look back at the guy.

Mikki yells back, "I'm here!"

Forgetting my surroundings as soon as I hear Mikki's voice, I tell her, "Mik, I'm so sorry."

After a long pause, she replies with a coldness in her voice I've never heard from her before, "It's kinda late for that, don't you think?"

I assure her, "We're going to get you out of here so you can get the kids! There's no way I'll be getting out, but we can get the money for your bond. It's not that much!"

We talk for a while, and when it's time to go, I tell her with sincerity, "It's so good to hear your voice, Mikki."

"Yours too."

"Good night."

"G'night."

Feeling miserable, I head straight back to my bunk. As soon as my head hits the pillow, I am out cold.

Twelve hours later, I wake long enough to eat chow during slop call. Immediately afterward, I collapse back in bed, falling fast asleep.

It's day five without dope. I haven't gone this long without dope in eighteen years. Miserable, depressed, exhausted, I just want to die. Man, I need some dope, but I need a cigarette even more.

After ten days in jail, Mikki is released on her own recognizance at her first court hearing. Her father flew in last week to get Nikki and Chris out of foster care. They plan to fly back to Illinois together.

Tobacco is prohibited in county jail, but occasionally I get a whiff of cigarette smoke. I notice men slipping into one of the cells, and a moment later, a cloud of smoke drifts out. Don tells me the women are allowed to leave jail during the day to cook and do laundry. When they come back in for the night, they smuggle in tobacco, weed, and other contraband. "Okay, great!" I say. "But we never see the women. How do we get stuff from them?"

"Fishing!" he replies. "Come on, I'll show you."

I sit on the side of the bunk in his cell as he demonstrates and explains. "We pull threads off our bedding and tie them together to make a thirty-foot long line."

Then he pulls out from under his bunk a long line of thread, showing me a comb tied to the end. "Then we take the line and tie the end to a plastic comb."

I watch, completely baffled.

"With the comb tied to one end, we correspond a flush with the women below."

He yells down to the women to see if anyone's there. They are there, so he continues explaining, "If we flush at the exact same time, the water pushes the line down into their toilet."

I watch as he organizes a simultaneous flush with the women below and then continues explaining to me. "Don't let go, just hold onto your end of the line while they tie a sealed baggie with your stuff to the other end. They'll tell you when they're done, and then you just pull it back up through the toilet."

He stands by the toilet holding his end of thread, keeping his ear close to the vent. We talk a little, and then he slowly pulls on the string, and sure enough, he pulls up a plastic baggie with ten cigarettes, rolling papers, three joints, and a lighter!

Unfreakingbelievable!

Now with fishing as my new favorite sport, I immediately check my bedding, pulling off all loose threads—or anything that looks like it could possibly become loose—to start the process of making my very own fishing line. Cigarettes and the occasional joint are great to get, but what I want, what I need is speed. Fishing daily, I ask the women to send up speed, but apparently no one can score any.

Treating cigarettes like a joint, I take a few drags then put it out and hide it in a safe place so I can light up later. Roy mentions he knows how to make alcohol. The next morning, I follow him in the breakfast line to watch him make what he calls Jailhouse Hooch. He eats everything on his tray except for a few small items—fruit, fruit juice, a packet of sugar, and a small corner of toast (yeast). He takes it to his cell, and I watch as he mixes it all in a rinsed-out shampoo bottle, throwing it under his bunk. He explains it takes one week to ferment; when the bottle bloats out like a balloon, it's ready to drink. I wash my hair with a lot of shampoo, ready to try this out. Now granted, I've heard some guys have thrown up after drinking this.

A week later, I open the bloated bottle and drink, getting a pretty good buzz on, then extreme nausea. Nope. Not for me.

Day by day, I'm starting to feel normal again, which is kind of a high all its own. I can't even remember the last time I've gone this long without drugs in my system, and it feels weird but good.

With my arrest all over the news and in the papers, I find I've earned a higher status in jail, not with the guards but with the other cellies. I am treated with the utmost respect, and I soon learn this is clearly my number one commodity. Without respect, I have nothing, literally nothing. Life is much easier with respect. For instance, whoever is fishing for goods always shares with me. I'm never left out. When the library cart comes around, I get first pick of the books. These acts may seem small and meaningless, but when you're in jail, they are some very nice perks.

Two of the guards treat me like everyone else, but the rest of them have a grudge against me. Many of the guards are county cops, so upon my entry, they already had a preconceived impression of me. It doesn't matter how I act in jail, they despise me and cuff me so tight my hands swell. For ten days, I went without a toothbrush and toothpaste even though I asked for them daily. They kept telling me they were out, but they had enough for every single person coming in after me. I watch others fill out the forms necessary to request a phone call, receiving permission within an hour. With me, it takes days for my telephone papers to be approved. When I have visitors, I sit in a cubicle and look through a window at my visitor. A guard stands directly behind me, and verbal communication is through a phone. It is impossible to have any type of physical contact with my visitors. Therefore, there is no possible way for an inmate and a visitor to pass anything back and forth. Yet every single time I have a visitor, they insist on a strip search just to humiliate me. Every single time, I am taken into the back room and told to remove all my clothes for a quick cavity search. Only then am I allowed to dress pick up a phone behind a glass window to talk with my lawyer or my mom. I don't expect the guards to be respectful of me, but they push me to my limit trying to get me to act out. There are days I am close to breaking, but I'm smart enough to stop, realizing that's what they want. They want me to lose control so they can add another charge against me. I won't let them have that. I won't.

I've carried a police scanner since I started this business, and many times I have listened to them as they arrested someone else thinking it was me. I have to admit I enjoyed that. It frustrates them that when they finally did arrest me, they jumped the gun and couldn't even charge me with a little bit of dope. This has aggravated them beyond belief, and now I'm paying for it. I admit I do gloat over the fact that after chasing me for years, when they did catch me, they blew it by just a few hours, eliminating any chance they had to charge me for manufacturing—even though we all know I was.

I'm being transported from Mohave County Jail back to Lake Havasu to face a misdemeanor charge in a little superior court. We begin the normal routine of preparing for transport with waist, ankle, and wrist shackles and, as always, my hands are instantly blue, swollen, and throbbing before I even leave the building. Lake Havasu is about an hour's drive—that's a long time to be cuffed this tightly. Numbness should come soon. Please come soon.

There are two of us traveling this morning, the cop and me. He leads me to the back of a police van, and surprisingly, before he climbs in the driver's seat, he removes *all* my shackles! I am *so* relieved and surprised as this is one of the guards who makes jail time absolutely miserable for me.

I look out the window, viewing a world I haven't seen in weeks— plants, people, stores, birds, and sunshine. The sun feels good on my skin as I rub my tingling hands together, trying to wake them up. An hour flies by, and the guard pulls up to the front of the courthouse about thirty feet from the front doors.

Lake Havasu's courthouse sits in town surrounded by roads all lined with businesses and stores. I'm looking around, taking everything in, when the driver—also a police officer, and my guard—climbs out of the van and opens the back door where I'm sitting. He doesn't look at me, doesn't say a word to me, doesn't even gesture with his hands. He just turns toward the courthouse and walks inside without me! Just like that, I'm sitting unshackled in the back of a police van with the door swung wide open. I'm not quite sure what to do, so I stay seated and wait. After a few minutes, I lean forward to look around. I don't know what's going on, but something doesn't feel right. Then it hits me. They're setting me up! They want me to bolt so they can get me with another charge or put a bullet in me. Caught or die runs through my head, and I'm not ready to die, so I lean back against the seat and stare straight ahead as my mind processes all of this.

The officer's already inside, so even if I get out to walk into the courthouse to find him, they can say that I tried to escape, and no telling what will happen in that case, so I remain in the back of the police van and stare out the window. The longer I sit, the madder I get. This little Arizona town, they want the prestige of being the big guys who get me. I'm a big deal to them. If this had happened in Phoenix, it wouldn't have been that big of a deal. I won't let them have their day. Ten long minutes pass before the officer comes back out. He cuffs me extra tight this time and angrily escorts me into the courthouse. He's angry, and so am I! I fight off the feeling the best I can because there's nothing I can do about it at this point, and if I act out, he wins!

I stand before the judge for my bond reduction hearing cuffed so tight I'm beyond pain. Thank God, my hands are starting to go numb. My glimmer of hope to be leaving soon disintegrates as my public defender asks for a bond reduction. The prosecutor jumps up, yelling, "Your Honor! You cannot let this man out of jail! It took the police years to catch him. If he is granted bail, he will just create another identity and disappear. We will never find him again. Mr. Bryant is a one-man crime wave. He simply cannot be released!"

With a slight shrug, I look at the prosecutor, thinking, *I have to admit he has a point.* My bonds remain the same.

Days, weeks, and months roll by ever so slowly as my attorney desperately works on a plea deal trying to shorten the twenty-five-year sentence hanging over my head.

Smokes, food, and phone calls and letters from Mikki, Mom, and Grandma are now the highlights of my days. Everyone I love lives hundreds of miles away in Illinois. Mikki and the kids are still with her parents.

The jail is no longer prolonging my phone call approval papers, and I'm allowed fifteen minutes three to four times a week. I've talked to Grandma more since I've been in jail than in the last ten years combined. The food here is no better than a nasty TV dinner, and when I hang up the phone with Grandma, I walk back to my cell missing the times I sat in her kitchen before church eating wonderful homemade biscuits and gravy. I like being drug-free with a clear mind, but now I struggle daily with guilt and shame, two emotions that eluded me under the influence of meth. All those Sunday mornings I turned Grandma down while passed out in a drunken stupor... I'd give anything right now to have one of them back, to sit at Grandma's kitchen table in a house filled with love, sizzling bacon, and fried eggs, all for me. What have I done?

Monday through Saturday, I wait anxiously for the mail to be delivered. On schedule, I walk to the north side of D-pod and wait in line with a group of other hopeful men eager to get their mail. I'm always relieved when I see Mikki's handwriting on one of my envelopes. Strolling back to my bunk, I open her letters and read about the outside world, about all the things I'm missing with Nikki and Chris, and about her continued love for me that I desperately crave right now. I keep her letters in my property bag under my bunk and pull them out to read many times over late at night when I miss her most.

During my last phone call with Mikki, we discussed her and the kids moving back to Arizona so we can be closer to each other. I know the best thing for her right now would be to stay with her parents, but I can't wait any longer to see her and the kids, so yes, I tell her it's a good idea. Even though all our visits will be on a phone looking through a glass window, I will at least get to see them.

Two weeks pass, and I wait anxiously for Mikki to come visit. She calls and tells me they moved in with Carol. "Carol?" I say. "Your sleazy friend Carol? Mik, that wasn't the plan! Carol lives in Phoenix! That's two hundred miles away! Why would you do that?"

One week, two weeks, three weeks slowly drag by. Mikki and the kids have not visited once. I see them no more than when they lived in Illinois. Questioning her about this last-minute decision does no good—her answers make no sense to me.

Days, weeks pass without a visit from Mikki. Every single day, I go through the procedure to place a call to her, but she hasn't answered any of my calls for the last two weeks. Was I too rough on her? Did I not make myself clear? Why won't she answer the phone? None of this makes sense. I have talked to my wife every single day for the last seven years, and now nothing. Why won't she talk to me? I won't give up. What else do I have to do?

Two more weeks drag along. I call Mikki multiple times a day, but she still won't answer. Routinely, I walk to the north side of D-pod and wait for my mail. I hesitantly accept it from the guard each time only to be disappointed over and over—no envelopes with her handwriting. I have no idea what has happened to my family. Are my children okay? Is Mikki okay? Are they alive? What is going on? Where are they? Why doesn't anyone answer the phone? Why is she doing this? Why won't she contact me?

I shake it off. *It's cool*, I tell myself. *I can do this.* I walk back with a lump in my throat, waiting for another day to pass. Deep down inside, I know something is terribly wrong. I just don't know what or why. I have no idea what's happened to my family and no way to find out.

A few more weeks come and go with no word from my wife. I have tried daily to locate her, but I can't. All I can do from jail is make a phone call, and that's it. It's not enough. I spend my days filling out paperwork each time I try to call her, dialing her number, and listening to the phone ring only to hang up and start the process all over again. I sit in jail waiting, worrying, imagining every possible dreadful scenario. It's eating me up, and I try to shake these thoughts from my mind, but within seconds they resurface—again and again through my every waking moment. Yes, I've called other people I'm approved to call, but it doesn't matter. No one will give me any information about Mikki or my children. I'm losing it. God help me, I'm losing it!

Six excruciating weeks pass, and *finally* Carol picks up on the other end. I know Carol doesn't like me, and that's okay because I don't like her, either. Carol takes great delight in divulging that Mikki has met someone else. Emphasizing just how much she really likes this new guy, she goes on to say Mik and the kids have already moved in with him. In a straightforward voice, she tells me, "Mikki had no way to support herself, and she's got two kids. What else was she supposed to do?"

I slowly hang up the phone and just stand there. I don't know what to do. My head spins as I feel myself spiraling down a deep dark hole. Staring at the phone in complete shock, I force oxygen in and out of my lungs. I turn around slowly and quietly walk back to my bunk. The pain I feel right now is unbearable! Never have I felt pain like this before. Never have I felt such abandonment.

I sit on the edge of my bunk, staring straight ahead. I can't move. I'm trying to control my breathing, but the pain's intolerable. Dizzy and nauseous, I hear the 9 p.m. lockup buzzer sound, immediately followed by the shuffle of men's feet as they quickly file into their cellblocks for the night. All of it sounds a million miles away as I continue down the rabbit's hole.

I've been in jail so long I'm down in one of the choice cells off the day room that I share with Chuck. The steel doors grind closed and the locks click as I sit frozen on the edge of my cot late into the night.

I have kept every single one of Mikki's letters from the last five months. Reaching under my bunk, I pull out my property bag and hold one of her letters. Feeling along the wrinkled envelope with my fingertips, I remove the letter and start to read, but now her words are daggers in my heart. It's bull crap! All lies! Remembering what her letters once meant to me, I carefully slide it back into its envelope.

I need a bump! If I just had some dope, I wouldn't feel, wouldn't hurt, wouldn't care. Feeling *sucks!* I have to stop this pain. Never before have I experienced this level of hurt. Somehow, some way, I will make it stop!

I place her letters back in my box, and there it is—my razor is lying right next to her letters. I didn't even have to look for it. It's just there, conveniently right there. It happens suddenly. A decision has been made. I don't quite understand who made it, but I blindly follow its will.

Easily breaking the plastic open, I remove the razor blade inside. Knowing what the result will be, I sit down on the toilet and slash open my wrist, thinking, *This will end my pain.*

Blood oozes from the open wound as I repeat the action on the other wrist. It's done. No turning back now. I shut my eyes and lean back to wait for my demise. Moments pass, and I look down at my wrists. I realize that at this rate of blood loss, I'll heal before I bleed out, so I pick up the razor again and slash the heck out of both my wrists.

After multiple slashes, I haven't yet cut deep enough to reach my main artery. As I'm working at this, I think, *Who knew the human body was so resilient?* I soon realize how difficult this task is without the proper instruments, but that doesn't stop me. I am now more determined than ever to succeed, and I continue working at it, cutting again and again, digging deeper and deeper, but I still can't reach that artery. Stopping for a moment, I realize there's no pain. This is good.

Relentlessly, feverishly, I work at it, trying to finish what I've started, but all I've managed to do is make a complete mess of my wrists and everything within close range. Bright red blood flows out of the wounds, streaming down both my arms, dripping off my elbows, running down my legs, pooling on the floor around my feet. When I switch the razor from one hand to the other, blood spatters on my shirt, across the bed, on the wall. Some of it hits Chuck as he sleeps. I still can't get more than a slow, steady stream, and at this pace, it will be hours before I lose enough blood. Chuck awakens to find me sitting on the toilet with a razor in my hand and blood everywhere.

He jumps up and yells, *"What are you doing, man?"* as he pounds on the steel door, hollering for the night guard.

I calmly reassure him, "Dude! Stop! Seriously! I can't even get down deep enough to hit a vein and make it count, so don't worry. I'm fine. I'll just wrap it up, and I'll be fine."

I put the razor down and start to wrap my wrists in towels when I notice a stream of blood running under the door out into the quiet day room.

Chuck's screams for help pull me out of the rabbit hole. I look around, registering what I've just done. I'm a mess. Blood is everywhere. I blow it off, telling myself it looks much worse than it actually is but here come the guards, and off I go to the medical ward for stitches.

With my wounds cleaned, stitched, and bandaged I'm taken to the suicide ward and placed in an isolated, padded cell. Every ten minutes, someone checks on me. The walls are padded in this cell, but the bed has no padding. There is no bedding, no pillow, no sheets, no covers—just a cold metal slab. I wait and wait. I wait some more. I sit for a while. I stand for a while. I lie down for a while. I pick at the bandages for a while. I stand back up for a while. Twenty-four hours later, they escort me to see a psychiatrist. I tell him my story, and he gives me a professional diagnosis of my problem. "You're not crazy," he says. "You're just stupid."

I know I'm not crazy. With that statement, he sends me back to my cell.

I don't want to go back to my cell. Chuck woke up the entire pod banging on the door yelling for help. I'm sure everyone knows what I did. I'm embarrassed to face them now and afraid I've lost their respect. For months, I've maintained a high status here. What will they think of me now? Suicide is something only the weak attempt. I cannot be viewed as weak.

My body tenses as the heavy metal doors clang shut behind me when I step back into D-pod. I force myself to stand tall as I walk to my cell, staring straight ahead and swinging two bandaged arms. No one speaks to me, and I speak to no one. I sit on the edge of my bunk and look down at the bandages. My wrists hurt, my head hurts, my heart hurts. Everything hurts.

Looking around my cell, I realize I have no choice. I have to do my time. Taking a deep breath, I shut my eyes and encourage myself, *I will not let time do me!*

Forcing myself to move forward, I mentally repeat over and over, *To hell with her! To hell with her! To hell with her!* until I no longer care.

Weeks pass, and I find that no one seems to care about what I've done. Criminals come in and are released from jail daily, creating a quick turnaround of people. Now most of them don't even know about my attempt. Because of the news coverage, they recognize me and know exactly why I'm in. In a room full of criminals, what does a criminal want to learn? They want to learn how to do something better than other criminals. Like any job, you climb your way to the top. As a result, I am still treated as royalty in my pod.

With my leg healed, I fall into the rhythm of daily walking the upper tier back and forth for hours on end at a constant nervous pace. At any given time, I have three to four people with me on this path, different people at different times throughout the day. Many have tried unsuccessfully to cook meth, so they ask about my recipe, my formulas, my contacts. They want to know what I know. I answer question after question while walking and burning up my nervous energy. I'm going crazy stuck in this sunless concrete pod.

Once a week for one hour, I am allowed to go to a concrete room with no ceiling. Basketball hoops are attached to all four walls. I have slept and purged my way through meth withdrawals and have put on a few pounds. It feels good to be in the sun, to move, to shoot hoops. For sixty minutes, I almost feel human again. Guards take us back to the pod, and I walk back through the door for another long week of no doors, no windows, no knowledge of whether it's cloudy, windy, sunny, or raining. Never in my life did I think that my access to sunshine would be restricted to one hour a week. I miss freedom. There are one hundred and sixty-eight hours in a week. One hour of sunshine, one hundred and sixty-seven hours of confinement in a concrete block—that's my life.

I need to talk to my kids. It's been weeks since I've made an attempt to call Mikki, so I sit down and fill out the paperwork to call Carol and get Mikki's number. Then I fill out the paperwork to call Mikki.

I'm surprised when she answers the phone on my first attempt to call. I can only say one word, *"Why?"*

She replies in a low, hushed tone, "I called your lawyer as soon as I arrived in Arizona, Darwyn. I asked her if you were going to be home by Christmas. She told me yes, in about twenty years. At that point, I realized I couldn't do this. It doesn't matter how much I love you...I have to think of the kids. They'll be in their mid-twenties before you're released. I'll be in my forties. Right now, I'm still young. I have my entire life ahead of me. Our children need to live their lives. The thought of waiting twenty years for your release is unbearable. I had to move on, Darwyn. You know I did."

As hard as it is for me to accept it, she's right. I was a fool to think anyone would wait twenty years for me. Understanding her doesn't take away my shame, guilt, and frustration as the consequences of my choices unfold before me.

County jails are designed for short-term incarceration while waiting for trial, usually no longer than ninety days, and certainly not *twelve months*! Not only does Mohave County Jail have no windows, this entire compound is made of cinderblock walls with concrete floors, both of which hold a dank, musty smell. The longest twelve months of my life has passed, and I'm still waiting for a trial date.

On the flip side, there is a good reason for this delay. I have many charges pending in multiple counties, so my lawyer keeps postponing my sentencing, trying to get all the charges from each county to run concurrently rather than consecutively. I no longer have a public defender—Mom managed to rake up twenty thousand dollars for Marsha's retainer. She's my new lawyer. I know I'm going to be staying in "Hotel Arizona" for at least twenty years, but I do not want to stay one day longer.

Fourteen months in, I get a visit from Marsha, like so many times before. I walk into the visitor's room and see her behind the glass partition. Talking loudly enough so that I can hear her through the window, she smiles and tells me, "You're going to want to sit down for this!"

I sit down, concerned, but she's smiling. Confused, I pick up the phone.

"I got the DAs in each county to agree to run all your sentences concurrently!" she explains. She pauses for my reaction.

I tilt my head and stare at her, trying to understand exactly what this means.

Her smile grows as she continues, "You are not going to do twenty years. You won't even do ten. If they run them all concurrently instead of one after the other, the longest sentence you will have is seven years! This means the *most* you will do is seven years! You will still have a life!"

I watch her lay everything out on the desk. We go through it all—six years at Mohave County, five years and a four-year in Coconino County, seven years in Maricopa County, and two other counties dropping all charges against me. I look at her and smile, realizing she is worth every penny!

I'm ready for prison; it has to be better than this jail. I've been told that in prison, you can see the sun every single day. My final sentencing is over, and I stand in front of the sally port desk waiting to be taken back to my cell. I remember standing here over a year ago. Glancing up at my reflection in the security mirror, again I'm shocked at my appearance. One year ago, I stood right here and was surprised to see my scrawny meth body. Now I'm looking into the eyes of an overweight blob! Fourteen months in county jail has taken its toll on me, and I've gone from meth skinny to downright fat. My skin is pale, pasty, and scaly from lack of the sun's vitamin D. I've gained at least sixty pounds eating slop, and I can see every ounce of it. I don't know which is worse, skinny meth-head or pasty blob.

I am so anxious for all my paperwork to go through. My lawyer stops by for another visit again, smiling from ear to ear. She tells me I will be eligible for parole in half my time. That's not all—I've been given credit for my time served here at Mohave County. That's *still* not all! She explains to me about the first-time offender kick-out program. All first-time offenders, of which I am one, will be kicked out six months early for good behavior. My brain is figuring, adding, and subtracting, and I realize that what I thought was going to be a twenty-plus year sentence could possibly be only a little over a year! *Unfreakingbelievable!*

As I'm escorted back to my cell, I keep reminding myself not to get my hopes up too high. I mean, there are many who don't make parole. I don't want to be disappointed if I'm not out next year. Seven years is still *so* much better than the twenty I thought I'd serve, and that's enough to keep me going.

It's May 1995, and the day has finally come for me to be transferred from Mohave County Jail to the Department of

Corrections. First, I'm taken to Alhambra, where every Arizona inmate is sent for processing before being transported to their designated yards to serve the remainder of their sentence. Upon arrival, I'm placed in a ten-man cell with thirteen other men and only five sets of bunk beds. Four mattresses are thrown on the floor. Quickly surveying the crowded area, I grab an empty mattress on the floor. I have no idea what to expect here.

Guards come periodically to get men for processing procedures, so when my name is called, I get up and follow them down the hall like I've seen the other guys do. They administer an IQ test, and during my physical, I'm questioned about the scars on my wrists. When I explain, they assign a counselor to me. The counselor and I discuss my scars extensively along with each of my crimes.

After multiple lengthy conversations, he evaluates the nature of my crimes to determine my risk assessment. This will decide what level of security yard I will be assigned to. Three weeks of counseling, assessments, and evaluations determine I am going to Meadows. Meadows is a level three, medium-security yard. Sounds like a country club to me. How bad could a prison called Meadows be?'

With twenty other men, I ride in the prison van in my bright orange county jail scrubs. The shackles around our waists and ankles hang down, clanking against the floorboard with every move, every bump. We're driven out to the middle of the desert, fifty miles outside of Phoenix, to a town called Florence. Florence has ten prisons—Meadows, North Unit, South Unit, East Unit, Central, and I don't know the others.

Still shackled together, we exit the van, shuffling in sequence toward a waiting guard who escorts us inside. I'm surprised and relieved when they immediately remove all our shackles and hand us real clothes. I walk in line with the others as they ask our size and hand us blue jeans, a denim shirt, and a property bag. It has been fourteen months since I've worn real clothes, and just holding them gives me hope!

The guard points to a dressing room. I walk in, sit down on a bench, and look through my bag. Inside are several changes of clothes, socks, underwear, and a pair of boots along with toiletries. Putting on clothes, especially denim, makes me feel human again.

Even though I haven't seen my cell, I'm already happier here than I ever was at Mohave. When everyone's dressed, they send us to the front guard station where all new arrivals check in. The guard checks our IDs and points to the housing unit where we'll live until our sentence is over. My bunk is 539. The guard points to a building and tells me to check in with the guard there. I walk out into the sunlight and look toward my building. It's one of eight rectangular cinderblock buildings in a circle. All eight buildings face inward around a prison yard. The prison yard consists of a ball diamond and athletic field.

It feels strange to me to be in prison wearing blue jeans and shoes with no handcuffs or waist shackles. I'm clean now—I've been drug-free for almost a year and a half. I walk out into the sun and take a moment to close my eyes, lift my head to the sun, and breathe, feeling more relaxed than I have in years.

Scanning the premises, I notice how immaculate this place is, far cleaner than county jail. I walk into my building and slide my ID under the screen of a steel mesh enclosure the guard sits in. He checks my card with some papers then reaches over and triggers a buzzer. I hear a loud click then a large metal door to his left opens wide. "Your bunk is all the way down on the right."

I ask, "Where is everyone?"

"It's two o'clock. Everyone's either working or in class. You will be, too. No one gets to just lie around all day."

With my property bag flung over my shoulder, I step through the huge metal door. A loud buzz sounds as the door electronically shuts and locks behind me, and then I walk toward my new home.

There are no cells, just cubicles lining the aisle. Fifty on both sides, each the same as the other. I find bunk 539 and toss my bag on the bed. I have a locker, two shelves, and a writing desk with a chair. Since I don't have much, it takes less than five minutes to unpack. Exhausted, I lay on my bunk to shut my eyes for just a second.

Awakened by the sound of a buzzer immediately followed by a loud click, I hear the large metal door unlock and slowly drag itself across the metal frame. Footsteps and voices are getting closer. I sit up and look down the aisle to see a parade of guys coming in. Work shift must be over, which means I've been asleep for at least two hours. This is my first time seeing my cellmates, and I watch the bunks fill up one by one, wondering who will be directly across from me.

The cubicle across the aisle is the closest one to me, the only one in full view. Whoever is in this bunk, we'll be seeing each other every night before bed and every morning for the next year. I wait, watching as all the bunks fill up, but no one yet across from me. Then I see a figure down the aisle. "Oh *no!*" I mutter under my breath,

I watch as the ugliest creature I have ever seen strolls down the aisle toward me. He must be at least six foot two and three hundred pounds. His bald head sits directly on top his shoulders—he has no neck. He reminds me of Jabba from *Star Wars* except this guy is much uglier. Every inch of exposed skin except his face is covered in tattoos. One single tooth overlaps his bottom lip, and I'm thinking the eye shooting off to the left must be glass. Noticing his other eye is staring straight at me, I sit back in my bunk. *That dude looks just like a lizard!* I think.

Sure enough, this guy flops down in the bunk directly across from me. I shake my head. *Great, just great.* This is what I'm going to see first thing every morning. I don't know what to do or how to act, so I stare down at the floor. *Freakin' unbelievable!*

I have never before in my life had a problem sleeping, but tonight is different. I can't sleep with the image in my head of what is lying just two steps across the aisle. I'm afraid if I shut my eyes, he's going to eat my face! Slightly comforted by his loud congested snores that prove he's asleep, I lie awake in bed and listen to him all night long.

At six a.m. sharp, fluorescent lights blink on in the run, and a loud buzzer sounds, indicating it's time to get up. Looking at my itinerary, I see I have exactly fifteen minutes to clean up, make my bunk, and get to breakfast. It's Sunday morning, so everyone walks back to the run from the chow hall. The correctional officer announces over the intercom, "Chapel. Anyone wanting to go to chapel, line up at the front door."

I sit down on my bunk across from Mr. Ugly, who sits down on his bunk and stares at me. Trying not to look at him, I glance down the run and notice a few guys holding Bibles lined up at the door. I look back over at Jabba's one-eyed stare. I can't just look away because that would show fear, so I take the opportunity to try and break the ice, display some bravado. I nod toward the men in line and say to him with a hint of disgust in my voice, "Look at those lames lining up for chapel!"

He slowly looks toward his shelf and leans forward, reaching for something. God help me! This is it! He's gonna grab his shiv and shank me!

Eyes wide, I watch as he pulls his hand back. He's holding a Bible! I sit back and take a deep breath as he gurgles, "You got something against chapel?"

Eyebrows raised, I don't say a word. I watch him stroll on down to the end of the line. He turns and motions for me to follow. Without a second thought, I stand up and join the line, not because I want to but because I don't want to offend this dude any more than I already have.

After service, I walk back to the run, still following Mr. Ugly. He turns around and introduces himself. "They call me Tiny."

Of course they do, I think, but simply say, "I'm Darwyn."

Tiny asks, "Dar What?"

"Darwyn. My name is Darwyn."

He stops and looks at me. "Dude! You got to change that! You can't be walking around a prison yard telling everyone your name's

Darwyn!" He steps back and looks me up and down then walks beside me. "Everyone in here goes by a nickname. Why not go by Dar? It has kind of a medieval ring to it." He looks at me for approval then encourages me, "Better than Darwyn any day!"

From that moment forward, I am Dar.

Tiny and I hang out together, and I soon find he's eighteen years into a twenty-five-year sentence for second-degree murder. He's been denied parole six times. He tells me, "When I first came in this place, I was a knucklehead! I was young, only nineteen years old, so I got myself in all kinds of fights. I made my time here harder than it had to be. Then I found Christ about six years ago, and everything changed for me. I now have peace and freedom. Not the kind of freedom the world is searching for, but true freedom from inside, freedom that can only come from God."

Normally, I get irritated when someone starts preaching to me, but I find Tiny captivating. He gives me a Bible, and I start reading it. Memories of my childhood, of Mom and Grandma, flood back as I read, and I can't seem to stop. I read late into the night until I fall fast asleep. When I wake up, I start reading again.

I'm given a choice to work or take some college classes. I sign up for a few computer classes and excel with a 4.0 GPA. My biggest problem right now is I can't stay awake. It doesn't matter how much I sleep at night, it's never enough. I've been told that's normal coming from county jail because of the boredom, inactivity, and food they serve, all of which lead to depression. I understand that, and it makes sense, but I should be past all that by now. I've been here long enough I should be feeling better. Every single day, I wake up tired, sit in class fighting to pay attention and stay awake, go to chow, and then go straight to bed. I sleep twelve hours a day and still wake up tired!

I've lived the majority of my life pumped full of speed. I'm starting to understand why. What is wrong with me? If this is my normal, it *sucks!* I don't want to go back on drugs. I have one other choice—learn to deal with it.

I am allowed one phone call on Monday, Tuesday, and Wednesday, and that's it. Today I call my kids, and Mikki answers, saying, "I've got some bad news."

My heart sinks not knowing what's coming next.

"All of our stuff got stolen. Well, your stuff."

I have no idea what she's talking about so I ask, "What stuff?"

"While you were locked up at Mohave County Jail, Carol and I packed up the entire house and moved everything into storage."

"Okay, I remember you mentioning that. What happened?"

"Someone broke into the storage unit and cleaned it out. I mean cleaned it out good. You won't even have clothes to wear when you get out." She snickers a little and continues, "Not that it really matters. Clothing styles will have changed by the time you get out."

I feel she's enjoying the fact that I'm in prison.

"Oh, by the way, Darwyn, you'll be receiving divorce papers any day now. Please sign and return them as soon as possible. Mike asked me to marry him."

She tells me this as if she's asking me to change the oil in her car. I mutter, "I just called to talk to the kids, but you've taken up my entire fifteen minutes. Tell them I love them, and I'm sorry I didn't get a chance to talk to them."

I hang up before she can say anything. Two days later, divorce papers arrive. I shove them in the back of my locker.

Not wanting to hear Mikki's voice, I don't call my kids for a couple of months. Finally, I sign the divorce papers and send them back to her. Good riddance!

I call and talk to Mom and Grandma every chance I get. I've talked to Grandma more in the last two years than I have in the last twenty years combined. Mom, Grandma, and I have good meaningful conversations that I look forward to. I tell Grandma about Tiny. She laughs, excited that someone's convinced me to attend church. I fail to mention he's a convicted murderer.

It's getting harder to stay awake in class. No matter how much I sleep, I can't stay awake. I know I need to see a doctor, but I don't want to see a prison hack. What will I tell him? I'm sleepy? He'll just laugh and tell me to get over it. I'm trying to deal with it. I mean, it's not like I have anything pressing to do with my days.

I force myself to start a daily workout routine right after class before complete exhaustion sets in. Starting with a fast walk, then an easy jog, by six weeks in, I'm running three miles. After my three miles, I finish with one hundred pull-ups, one hundred bench presses, and two hundred pushups, My pasty, fat county jail body has been replaced with solid muscle covered in firm skin tanned by the desert sun. I haven't cut my hair in over two years, so my bleached white ponytail hangs to the middle of my back. I am now in the best physical shape of my life, and for the first time, I'm starting to feel good about myself.

On Sundays, I go to chapel with Tiny, and throughout the week we talk about God. I knew God gave up on me a long time ago, but now I'm starting to wonder if it's possible that God would actually forgive me after everything I've done. Tiny keeps telling me God will forgive me, and Grandma keeps telling me God has already forgiven me, but none of this makes any sense. I keep asking myself why he would forgive me. If I were him, I wouldn't forgive me.

Out on the track, I hear over the PA, "Bryant, 113000. Report to the counselor's office." At once, I veer off track and run the opposite direction toward his office, wondering what's going on. Still sweating from my run, I check in and wait out in the hallway. The counselor sticks his head out the door and calls me in. With a stern look, he says flatly, "Your parole hearing is coming up in three months."

"Huh?"

It seems like I just got here, but yup, I was arrested in March of '94, and it's now December of '96. I add up the months. Yes, I am up for parole! Wow, did time fly!

My excitement is crushed by his next comment. "Don't get too excited. It's rare that anyone makes parole the first time in front of the board. Especially someone with your list of charges."

I take a late evening stroll around the track while a million thoughts race through my head. Will I make parole? Most likely, I won't. The sunset has turned the sky a beautiful pink, orange, red, and blue behind the saguaro cacti, and as I walk, a calm peace enters me. I begin to pray, I mean really pray. I pray like I have never prayed before. "Jesus, I know you're the real deal. Your evidence is all around me. I should be dead, yet I'm not. Nobody consumes as many drugs as I have and lives. I should be in prison for the rest of my life, yet I'm coming up for parole in three months. At the most, I'll only do seven years. No big deal compared to the twenty-five I almost had to serve. I should hate my life right now, yet I'm at peace. In prison, I've seen many around me experience trouble—some even murdered—but I've had no trouble. Not only have I had no issues with anyone, I've met and become friends with better people here in prison than I ever did out on the streets. Your love for me is apparent. Please forgive me. I know I've been a piece of crap, the worst of the worst. God, if you give me a chance, I will never do drugs again. I will live my life for you, and I will do right by my kids and my family. I promise. Please come into my life and stay with me."

Three months later, I make parole!

Chapter 14
Val

My scheduled release date is in three days. I'm anxious, to say the least, and trying to be excited as I should be, but I worry about walking out into a world I'm no longer familiar with. I have not functioned without the use of drugs in years. I've always considered myself as "self-employed," having made my living from nothing but criminal activities that I alone choreographed since 1989. I don't know the first thing about getting a real job. As my release date comes closer, I question myself over and over. What exactly will I do out there? How will I survive?

Once I'm released, I still have four years of parole to get through, during which I am not allowed to leave this area. The idea that if I make one slip up, I'll be thrown back in prison weighs heavy on my mind. I have no one out there. My wife and kids are gone. All my family, all my friends are back in Illinois. Well, I do have many friends in Arizona, but if I am to stay clean, I can never associate with them again. Hours, minutes, seconds roll by as dread instead of happiness grips my every thought. This whole getting out of prison thing sucks!

My day arrives, and I walk out the prison doors with nothing but the clothes on my back and my property bag. They send me to Crossroads, a halfway house centrally located in Phoenix. I am relieved to find my new living quarters clean and decent. After checking in, I throw my bag on the table and lie down, falling fast asleep.

The next morning, I contact my parole officer., "So," he asks, "how do you plan on supporting yourself, Mr. Bryant?"

Shaking my head and feeling completely lost, I answer honestly, "I really don't have a clue!"

"Well, there's a company that just opened up not far from here. They need people, and I've checked it out—criminal background is not an issue with them."

Reaching across his desk, he hands me a paper. "Here's the address. Go see them."

Hesitantly, I take the paper and slide it into my back pocket, not convinced they'll hire someone with my background. Shaking his hand, I thank him and leave.

I spend the day walking around town, familiarizing myself with the neighborhood. This feels peculiar to me, walking the streets without constantly watching my back and strategically planning a swift exit. It feels good, too, but my mind still watches and plans. Pulling out the paper from my back pocket, I check the address and locate the building. Confidence stirs within when I stand out on the front sidewalk looking up at this *huge* place. I tell myself, *Okay, let's do this!* and then head back to Crossroads, mentally preparing myself for tomorrow. I'm exhausted.

The next morning, I dig through my property bag for my razor. I shave in anticipation of applying for work. I haven't applied for an actual job in years. As hard as I try to be positive, when I see myself in the mirror, my reflection looks back, berating me. *Give it up, chump,* it says. *There is no possible way anyone would ever hire someone like you! No possible way! You're tired...just go back to bed.* This infuriates me! I stand back and look sternly at my reflection, wearing his state-issued denim shirt and blue jeans, and I walk out the door, ignoring him. He's the fool! I won't give up!

Using the skills I've honed from my criminal background, I walk in the front door, acting confident. I offer my hand in greeting, successfully hiding all the fears simmering deep inside. After the interview, I walk back out to the front sidewalk and turn to look up at the building and its surroundings in disbelief. They freakin' hired me!

I am now a telephone operator for a long-distance directory information center called AT&T. I sit in a very large room with hundreds of others. When my phone rings, I answer, saying, "City and state, please?"

With a couple strokes on the keyboard, I locate their listing and transfer the call.

After ten minutes, I realize this is the most boring job on the face of the planet. Then I look around, acknowledging its perks. Yes, this job has some pretty decent perks!

Fresh out of prison and in the best physical shape of my life, I have testosterone oozing out of my ears. Right now, I sit among three hundred women and maybe only ten other men. Scanning the room full of hundreds of young women, I look up and whisper, "There *is* a God!"

Knowing I will not survive this type of work for very long, I enroll at a local technical school, ITT. My days are now structured and very fulfilling. I work six hours, hit the gym hard for two hours, attend evening classes for three hours, and am in bed by eight. Even though I am healthy as a horse, I'm still exhausted all the time. Ten to twelve hours of sleep at night should be enough, but I still fall asleep at work and in class. This isn't normal, but I don't know what to do. Other than fighting exhaustion, I have never felt better in my life.

Taking complete advantage of this job's perks, I spend every weekend taking a different girl out. I literally have my pick. It's strange for me, though, because I haven't been in the dating scene in over a decade. I admit, I'm nervous, but I've honed that skill which allows me to function and hide all my apprehensions.

Monday night at 8:15, I'm lying in bed, dozing in front of the TV when the phone rings. Grandma's familiar voice asks, "Whatcha doing?"

"Getting ready to sleep, Grandma. What's up?"

"Oh, nothing. I was just calling to see how you are. Did you go to church yesterday?"

Sighing, I answer her honestly. "No, Grandma, I didn't."

After an awkward silence, she lovingly scolds me, "Well, Darwyn, you better remember all those promises you made to God. It will do you good to keep them."

"I know, I know, Grandma. I've just been so busy."

"What are you so busy with on a Sunday morning?"

I don't have an answer for that, so I concede. "I'll go. I'll go, Grandma. I gotta get some sleep. Good night. I love ya."

I hang up feeling guilty, knowing I should honor my promises to God, but I'm enjoying life right now just as it is. I'm actually enjoying life more than ever before. I enjoy being drug-free, employed, and single. Getting involved in church right now would be a killjoy. This is a whole new life for me, and I will always be thankful to God, but I feel God's not in any great hurry for me. I'll get around to going to church, later.

Standing in the break area at work, I light up a Camel when I notice two young girls walk into the smoking area. They have to be new employees because I would have noticed them by now. The blonde is a short cute little thing, but that brunette, that brunette is drop-dead gorgeous! She has to be almost six feet tall, and she has long wavy brown hair down to the middle of her back. She's wearing a loose spaghetti strap top and shorts that are not so short as to be tacky but short enough to show off a pair of long, beautiful legs. As I take a deep, lingering drag, she catches me looking at her and grins, giving me a slight nod. I don't know who she is, but I intend to find out.

The following morning, my boss calls me into his office and offers me a new position. I've been promoted to Floor Coach. My new job is to walk the floor and assist new hires or help when anyone encounters a problem or has a question. I shake his hand, thanking him for this promotion, but what's really on my mind? The tall, stunning brunette. She's been on my mind all night. I'm hoping she'll need an assist!

I walk out of his office and back to the main room, glad to no longer sit in a chair answering phone calls for hours on end. I scan the room of hundreds, looking for the brunette. There she is, sitting at her workstation right next to the blonde. I should check to see if they need anything. Hey, it's my job now!

Turning into the row where they're working, I saunter leisurely toward them, looking around and just doing my job. Not wanting to pass them without saying something, I lean over and ask, "You ladies doing okay? Have any questions?"

Disappointed when they both shake their heads without even looking up from their computers, I turn to walk away then hear one of them snickering behind my back. I smile, thinking, *Oh yeah! Game's on!*

Soon I'm taking my breaks at appropriate times in hopes of winning over this beautiful young woman. We're all outside smoking on the last break of the day, and I decide to go for it. Not paying any attention to the blonde sitting on the steps, I turn toward the brunette and say, "Hey. Name's Dar."

She smiles and says, "Val."

My peripheral vision picks up on the blonde's stare burning a death laser through my skull. Val holds out her hand, and I quickly switch my cigarette to the other hand, gently taking her hand in mine. She turns toward the death stare on the steps and introduces me to the blonde. "This is my sister, Deanna."

Aha! That explains it, a protective sister!

I've been at Crossroads for nine months now, and it's time for me to move on. Carrying a 4.0 GPA from ITT, I'm due to finish ahead of schedule, and my parole officer is happy with my progress. I make decent money. I'm not rich, but I'm doing okay for right now. It's time I get my own apartment. I put the word out that I'm looking for a place to live, and my supervisor at work hooks me up with a great place, but it's way more than I need at 2,500 square feet with three bedrooms. Man, it's nice! I walk through it knowing it's too big for me, but I don't want to let it go, either. Did I mention how nice it is?

I tell a couple of long-term residents of Crossroads about this place, and we decide to move in together and share expenses. Three clean, sober bachelors living in a bachelor pad—life just keeps getting better. I now have a place I can bring my kids for weekend visits.

Val and I talk during breaks at work, and I've noticed there's definitely an age difference between the two of us. I'm thirty-six, and I'm guessing she's probably around twenty-six or seven. A few days later, I decide the age difference isn't that bad, so I ask her out. She immediately shoots me down. "Sorry. I don't date guys from work, and besides, you're a little too old for me."

Ouch! Shot dead and stepped on.

She quickly notices my despair and tries to comfort me. "Don't take me wrong. I like you. I think you're cool to hang out with and talk to, but that's as far as it can go."

I drop my head, searching for words, and she continues, "Plus, I'm going through a divorce right now, and I have an eighteen-month-old daughter. I'm sorry, I just can't date you, but we can hang out here at work."

I look her in the eyes and quietly say, "That's fine. We'll hang out here at work."

She grins. "Cool. I'd really like that. To be honest, Dar, I'd like to have you as a friend. I just moved from Reno, and I don't have many friends here."

Lying in bed at my new place, I think of Val's words. I'd pretty much given up as soon as she said I was too old for her, but I really like this girl. I don't know exactly what it is. There is something other than the fact she's a knockout, something that draws me to her.

Dating different women every weekend, some good-looking and some not so much, right now all I'm interested in is having a good time. So when I find myself looking forward to Monday to get back to work so I can hang out with Val on breaks, it surprises me, confuses me. She's different than the others. I want to get to know her, talk to her. I'm interested in what she says, thinks, and feels. She intrigues me. I ask her at break, "You have a daughter?"

"Yeah. Kendal."

"I have to ask…you said I'm too old for you, so how old are you?"

I wait for her answer. "Twenty-one."

Ouch, well, maybe I *am* too old for her. I nod and go on talking. "I have three, two girls and a boy. They're older, though. I haven't seen my oldest since she was two. She's twelve now."

Noticing the confused expression on her face, I feel the need to explain. "She lives up North in Illinois. My other two live with their mother in Mesa. Chris is nine and Nikki eleven."

Val looks surprised and asks, "Wow! What happened? Why haven't you seen your oldest in ten years, and how did your other two end up in Mesa?"

I simply say, "Divorced, twice" and then take a long drag, exhaling up over her head.

"Oh. Got it," she says as we stand in awkward silence.

After spending all my breaks for the last two weeks with Val, I hand her a paper with my phone number on it, hoping she'll call. It works! She calls me every evening before bed just to chat. Nikki and Chris have been spending weekends with me, so I invite Val and Kendal over to swim, figuring with all the kids, she'll feel more comfortable. She accepts!

The five of us are having a great time hanging out poolside, but man, seeing Val in a swimsuit is not helping the "let's just be friends" issue. I invite her to stay for dinner, and the next thing I know, we're all sitting around the table eating, laughing, and talking. I look around, thinking, *Huh, we'd make a great family together.*

Nikki, her wet blonde hair sticking out in every direction after towel drying it, fresh from the pool, happily chews on a chicken leg. She looks at Val and asks, "So are you going to marry my dad?"

Instantly losing a mouth full of mashed potatoes onto my plate, I blush and look over at my daughter. "Nikki! Why in the world would you ask something like that? You just met Val for the first time today!"

Holding onto her chicken leg, Nikki looks up at me with her big eyes. With complete confidence, as if I'm a little slow, she informs me, "Yeah, but you've known her, and she's pretty and she's cool." She takes another bite, throwing in, "She even has dolphins painted on her fingernails! Dad, I think you should marry her." Chewing again on her chicken leg, she tilts her head and adds in a matter-of-fact tone, "You need to get married, Dad. Mom did."

Oh my! Out of the mouths of babes!

I have no words at this moment, so I look over to Val for help. Val smiles through a very red face. I can tell she's holding back a laugh as she blinks back tears and clears her throat. Val looks at my daughter and tells her in a most gentle tone, "Nikki, honey, your dad and I are just good friends."

Nikki quickly replies, "Yeah, that's what Mom and Mike said before they got married, too."

And with that, she takes another bite of chicken. I smile at Val as she avoids eye contact.

Later that night, Nikki and Chris are sound asleep after a fun day of swimming and playing. Val and Kendal are ready to leave. Standing in the doorway saying our good-byes, I seize the opportunity and lean in to kiss her good night. I come within an inch of her lips when she abruptly turns her head and sternly states, "No."

I watch her expression as she steps out of the doorway to wait for her ride home. Yes, I know she's seeing someone else more her age — well, I am too — but I just wanted a little kiss. No. That's all she said. No. I can tell she's a little nervous as we stand outside waiting for her ride, and when they show up, I watch her and Kendal climb in and drive away. I close my front door and tell myself, *I will marry that girl someday!*

Relentlessly pursuing Val for three long months, she finally agrees to go out with me — without kids! I've already fallen head over heels for this girl, so after a week of dating, I ask her to move in with me. I'm in love. I mean *really* in love. I am ready to take care of this woman for the rest of my life.

Finishing early at ITT pays off quickly with another promotion at work. I'm now a computer operator in the IT department. Finally happy with my wages, I'm ready for Mom to come out for a visit, anxious for her to see my new life. I've told her about Val, and I want the two of them to meet. Over the last two years, Mom's visits have been hard for her, seeing me strung out behind bars. I'm doing great now, and I want her to be proud of me again.

Mom and Val hit it off immediately. "I really like her, Darwyn!"

"The age thing, it doesn't freak you out?"

"No, honey, not at all, but what does her family think?"

"Her dad seems cool with it, but her mom hates me."

Mom smiles, touching the side of my face as I look to her for guidance. She says, "Well, Darwyn, that's understandable, now isn't it? Give her time."

Prepared to be rejected with Valerie's classic "no" that I've heard so many times before, as soon as her divorce is finalized, I ask her to marry me.

"Yes."

I watch her expression as she reaches for me. She said *yes!*

It's been a year since my release. I am now an educated, tax paying, law abiding, and productive citizen with a home, a family, a good job, and a fiancée. I feel normal for the first time in my life. It's great! Val and I settle into a comfortable routine. We both work forty hours a week, spend evenings at home, go out on weekends, and I get my two youngest kids every other weekend. Religiously working out at the gym, I have physically grown into something only in my dreams before. My shoulders are wide, my chest stretches every T-shirt I own, and my arms are as big around as my legs. I am 240 pounds of solid muscle. I love taking Val and the kids hiking up Camelback Mountain, laughing when they tire out halfway up while I feel great, enjoying the stamina of a child. Life couldn't be any better.

As the lead computer operator, I work the graveyard shift alone. My shift is almost over, all my tasks are completed, and I walk to the back room for my last break of the night. I've been apprehensive lately about my approaching marriage to Val. I love her. More than anything, I want to marry her, but the thought that this is my third marriage keeps rolling through my head, nagging at me. I shake it from my mind, and there it is again. I blow it off as normal marriage anxiety and sit down to sip a cold glass of iced tea. Exhaustion overtakes me.

I wake up lying in a hospital bed and look over to see Mikki sitting at my bedside. She looks at me with concern, asking how I feel. I don't answer her. This is too much...something is terribly wrong! Mikki looks just like she did early in our marriage back when we lived in Illinois. I look around for Valerie. Where is she? I want Val. I need Val. Where I am? My head hurts. My chest hurts worse. Feeling the tug of unconsciousness, I allow it, even welcome it, hoping when I come to again, this pain will be gone, and everything will be back as it should be. I should be at work in Phoenix. I'm marrying Val in a few days.

Consciousness tugs at me, trying to pull me back, wake me up. I'm rising, pushing through...water? No, it's thick and foggy. The higher I rise, the easier I breathe and move. Opening my eyes, I look for Val, but there's Mikki! Why am I in a hospital bed? What is Mikki doing here? Where's Val? I turn my head toward the window—trees full of green leaves, grassy lawns, and a hilly street are in full view. I recognize this city. I'm back in Illinois! Shocked and confused, I ask Mikki, "What in the world are you doing here?"

"What do you mean what am I doing here? I'm your wife, doofus. Why wouldn't I be here?"

I don't know what to say. A million thoughts course sluggishly through my brain. I ask, "Well, first...ah...this is not...I mean...I mean... Where's Valerie?"

"Who's Valerie? What are you talking about Darwyn?"

I stare at Mikki, trying to wrap my mind around what's happening, trying to figure all this out, when Mom walks in and right up to my bed. She looks great even though she is a little mad at me and reprimands me as I lie in bed staring up at her. I interrupt her, asking, "Mom, what are you doing here?"

She asks me the same. She looks so much younger than the last time I saw her. I look back at Mikki. My mind seems to be clearing, but absolutely nothing makes sense. I ask her again, "Mikki, seriously, where's Val?"

Mikki, annoyed with my questions about Val, asks sharply, "Who is Valerie?"

I look her straight in the eyes and say, "Mikki, you and I are no longer married! We divorced years ago! I'm marrying Val in a couple days, okay? Now I want to know why she isn't here, but you are! I want to know why I'm lying in this hospital bed, and I want to know why in the heck my chest hurts so bad!"

Mikki replies with concern, "Oh man! This has really affected you bad."

Dumbfounded at her response, I ask, "What are you talking about?"

"Don't you remember, Darwyn? Yesterday you left the studio to come home. As soon as you walked outside the mall, you passed out on the front sidewalk. Your lungs collapsed, cutting off oxygen to your brain. You stopped breathing, Darwyn! You were not able to breathe until the hospital inflated your lungs again. You've been in a coma ever since. It was touch and go for a while. We've been so worried about you and didn't know if you were going to make it. The doctor told me there could be some brain damage due to lack of oxygen."

It's been *years* since I've worked at the studio in Mineral Springs Mall. This couldn't have happened just yesterday! I stare at her, slowly shaking my head in disagreement as she continues to fill my head with words, sentences that don't make sense. I ask her, "What year is this?"

"It's 1985, Darwyn, come on now."

In a loud, stern voice, I get up on my elbows and set her straight. "No, no, no, Mikki! It's 1998!"

In a quiet, calm voice she whispers, "Darwyn, lie back and relax, you're hallucinating." She strokes my forehead and looks up at Mom. They study me with concerned expressions. Mikki continues, "It's the oxygen deprivation. You're going to be fine, Darwyn. Lie back down, relax."

"Where're the kids, Mikki?"

"Kids? Nikki's fine. She's with Mom and Dad."

"No, Mikki, you and I, we have two kids. We have a son, Christopher, a little brat. Where is he? Where's Christopher?"

Mom paces back and forth at the end of my bed, talking under her breath. "I knew it. I knew something was going to happen to him. I knew it." She stops and places her hand on Mikki's shoulder whispering, "He's lost his mind."

I'm shocked. I don't know what to say. There are no words to express how I feel right now. I have lived thirteen years longer than Mom and Mikki at this point in time! Mikki and I have two children. I have lived in Arizona, I have been arrested and sent to prison and have served my time. Mikki and I are divorced. I'm marrying Val soon. All these things are true! They are real! I have seen it, touched it, felt it, and lived it!

Trying to convince Mom and Mikki about a future they don't believe in does no good, so I stop talking and remain quiet, absorbing all that is going on around me. My brain races, thinking, figuring, analyzing, and trying to make sense out of any of this. Looking at them, I decide to just work on the facts that I can grasp here and now.

Fact—Mom and Mikki are at my bedside in an Illinois hospital looking younger than they should. I can't understand why they both look so young. I wonder, are they telling me the truth? Mom wouldn't lie to me. Could it all have been a dream? Is it possible that I've never lived in Phoenix, was never a criminal, never went to prison? Am I not yet the horrible person everyone talks about? Is it really possible that the last thirteen years of my life have been just a dream, lived only by me in my mind during the last twenty-four hours while in a coma? Could it be? Is it possible I can start my life again from 1985? Do you know what this means? I've done nothing wrong!

Hope surges through me at the thought of a second chance, but then I think of Val. My heart aches for Val. I cannot fathom living without Valerie or with the idea that she doesn't exist. Val is too much a part of me. She has to be real!

Fact—Mom and Mikki are real. I look out the window. Fact—I'm in Illinois. I look down at my body. Fact—there is a tube inserted into

214

my throbbing chest. Reality sinks in. Arizona, drugs, prison, parole, and no, I don't even want to think it possible, my son Chris and Val—could it really all just be an elaborate hallucination, a dream, a fantasy conceived in my comatose state of mind? I don't know! I just don't know! My heart aches. I slowly look away from the window and back to Mikki. I love Mikki. I will always love Mikki, but I am no longer *in love* with Mikki.

The doctor releases me the day after removing my chest tube. Weak and obviously a little foggy-headed, I still can't make any sense out of my life at this moment. While Mikki drives home, I look around, taking in all the familiarity of my hometown. I am extremely cynical of it all. I feel this right here is a dream, and my coma the reality. Actually, I want my comatose life back. I'm not proud of the choices I made in Arizona, but I am very proud of what I'd turned my life into, how hard I worked to rise above, how I became a man that a woman like Val would marry. Then it hits me—Mom's right, I'm crazy! Shutting my eyes, I lean back, resting my head lightly against the headrest. Mikki reaches over and turns on the radio. "Don't You Forget About Me" by Simple Minds is playing. I think of Val.

I wake up the next morning, still in freakin' 1985! Okay, roll with it again, Darwyn. Mikki makes small talk as I sip coffee and make plans to get back to a studio that closed years ago. As crazy as all this is, part of me feels good to have seen my future. I now understand not to travel down the same dangerous paths I've traveled before. This idea also scares me—if I don't follow the same paths as before, how will I ever meet Valerie? I'm losing it! I'm really losing it.

Sitting at the kitchen table, I stare out the window, thinking of Val, when Nikki wakes up and pulls me back to 1985. Listening to her play in her crib makes me anxious to hold her again as a baby. I walk into her room and find myself looking around for Chris. Another hole in my heart...I need Chris.

After a few phone calls, the decision has been made that I should rest a few more days before getting back to the studio. Not exactly my decision, but I'm tired of arguing with everyone about my state of mind. I need to stay busy. When I'm idle, my mind spins and rolls, jumping back and forth from 1985 to 1998 and questioning the validity of every second in between. Mikki suggests I stay home while she and Nikki run to the store. I kiss Nikki's chubby little cheek, trying to get her to wave good-bye. She doesn't wave, but I know for a fact she will soon.

Let's see, if it's 1985, Valerie was born in 1976 and should be around nine years old right now. I remember she told me once she lived in a very small Mormon town just outside of Salt Lake City during her grade school years. If my crazy futuristic lost years were actually just a dream, she won't be in that little town. I have to settle this. I have to try and find her.

My wife is not happy when she returns home to find I've booked a flight out of St. Louis to Salt Lake City. She tells me it's a stupid idea and I shouldn't go, but after we argue, she senses I am not backing down and reluctantly gives up. Handing Nikki to me, she quietly puts groceries away with a concerned look on her face. Bouncing Nikki on my lap, I think to myself, *I'm going, and that's that.*

My chest is still sore, and my thoughts? I can't even begin to straighten out my thoughts. When the plane takes off, I sleep soundly the entire flight, leaning against my closed window as the woman next to me reads.

The car rental place is out of compact cars, so they upgrade me to a family car, and I climb in, shivering. Turning up the heat and hoping this cold car warms quickly, I drive toward Midvale, Utah. Since I don't really know exactly where I'm going, my plan is to drive up and down each road of this small town looking for Val or something that might lead me to her.

Groggy and confused, I drive around aimlessly until I notice a small white Latter-Day Saints church on the right side of the road. I pull into the parking lot in front of a brick elementary school encased in a chain link fence off to one side of the church. I hear the laughter of children and see them running and playing in a playground close by.

Still weak from my hospital stay, I walk up to the fence, sliding my fingers through the chain links to steady myself while surveying the schoolyard. I notice one isolated child on the other end of the yard who looks so much like Kendal, Val's three-year-old daughter, but older. She has long brown hair braided into pigtails and is wearing a dark blue parka. Mittens dangle from her sleeves. Oddly, she's not talking or playing with the other children. She is the saddest-looking child I have ever seen. Amazed at how much this child looks just like Kendal, I watch as she slowly scans the yard, watching the others play, and then she notices me. Our eyes lock from across the playground. Immediately, she moves toward me, walking slowly through the other children without breaking eye contact. Walking up to the fence, she reaches up, placing her hands on top of mine. With a confident yet meek voice, she says, "Don't worry. When you're ready, I'll be there."

Blown away, confused and speechless, I can only stare down at this little girl. I jolt when the school bell rings. Val—yes, this is Val at nine years old, I know it is—turns to join the other children and runs back into the school. I watch in amazement as she keeps glancing over her shoulder at me while moving across the yard. She looks at me again and then blends in with the others hustling through the door, and then she's gone, just like that. I stand for a minute, shivering in the cold wind, burning this memory in my mind before walking back to the car. Slowly driving to the airport, I drop off the car and sit at the gate, waiting to board the flight back to St. Louis. So much to think about. None of this makes sense.

Buckled up and waiting for takeoff, I analyze everything that's happened. Fact—Val is real! I just have to wait for her to grow up, but what am I thinking? I'm married! I am a married man! She's a child, for heaven's sake! None of this makes any sense at all, and it's gone on far too long. I can't seem to grasp my reality. I'm losing it! God help me, I'm losing it!

Frustrated and confused, I stare out the window as the plane takes off. Flying through stratus clouds, I look up toward outer space, up toward heaven, up toward God and plead, "What am I supposed to do with this? Tell me! What am I supposed to do now?"

Surprisingly, I get an immediate answer, and I listen to a voice in my head, to God, as he explains, "You may go back to 1985, to

Illinois, to Mikki right now and live out your life as Darwyn without worrying about prison, drugs, or any of the bad choices you've made. You now know what your decisions will bring, and you can choose better paths from here on out for you and for your family. Or I can send you back to 1998 to face the decisions you've made to that point, to continue your life as Dar, to be Valerie's fiancé."

My immediate thought? I can't imagine having to wait for Valerie to grow up or chance living my life without her.

Instantaneously, I'm pulled violently in another direction as I watch my drink hover for a brief second then soar behind me. I look around to see luggage falling out of the overheads, hitting people as they scream. Passengers are pushing on the seats in front of them for stability. Oxygen masks fall from the ceiling, swinging in circles as the cabin loses pressure. Children cry, and flight attendants shout out instructions over the chaos. Shutting my eyes tightly as our plane spirals uncontrollably in a nosedive toward earth, I scream silently, *No! No, dear God, No! Please! I haven't lived yet! There's so much to do! Please!*

Dizzy, nauseous, and scared to death, I force myself to peek out the window one last time. The Earth with all its neatly organized circles and squares spins, rises, grows larger and closer as we shoot through sporadic clouds. We're going to hit!

My last thought is *I'm sorry! Please forgive me.*

I wake up with a powerful jerk in the break room at AT&T and check the time, realizing my shift is over. Standing up, I rub my eyes and push my hair back over my head, scratching my neck. Then it hits me. I touch my chest, checking for a wound. Nothing. Shaking my head, I throw my tea in the trash and walk out the door, shivering in the cold desert night air. Pulling my jacket tight, I walk home, thinking about what a crazy, vivid dream that was. I stop and look up to the stars for a brief moment. Drawing in a deep cleansing breath of fresh air, I lift my hands and give thanks, vowing to never again question my decision to marry Val. I walk home in silence. Thank God, it's 1998!

The next evening, I eat dinner with Val and her mother, Liz. From the dining room window, I watch a Gila monster stroll sluggishly across the rocks as I sip a glass of red wine, laughing at their stories of life, mistakes, childhood, and oddly enough, dreams. The conversation is interesting, the food is great, and I'm feeling happy and relaxed. I have not mentioned my dream to Val or anyone yet. It was so lifelike, so real, and when I think of it, relive it, I'm not quite sure if it was just a dream or if God has actually given me this choice.

It could be the wine or just being in the presence of those I love, but I feel it's a good time to reveal my dream to Val and her mother. I tell them a shortened version about falling asleep at work and waking up thirteen years earlier in the hospital with Mikki. I tell them that I flew to Utah to try and find Val, and that I did indeed find her. I tell them what Val as a nine-year-old said to me with her little hands on my fingers through the chain link fence.

Val and Liz sip from their wine glasses, encouraging me to continue. I explain to them that there are times when I'm not sure if it was just a dream or if it really did happen, if God did indeed give me this choice. They look at each other and burst out laughing, quickly setting their glasses down before spilling. I can't stop laughing, either, but I try my best to scold them, "I'm pouring out my heart, and you laugh at me?"

Regaining my composure and their attention, I continue, "Now just wait a second, Val! You were there! You were! You were in a schoolyard beside a little white church. You had on a blue parka with mittens hanging from your sleeves! It was *you*, Val, pigtails and all!"

I'm laughing along with them as I describe the school and what Val looked like when all of a sudden, I'm the only one laughing, so I stop and ask, "What?"

Liz and Val look at each other then back at me with puzzled expressions. So I repeat louder, "What?!"

Val's mouth is agape as her mother takes a sip of wine and looks me straight in the eye with a serious and somber look. She tells me, "You just described the exact place in Utah—the school, the church, the playground where Val went to school. Val was always losing her gloves, so I sewed them onto her sleeves. Dar, I braided her hair in two long pigtails every morning before school. Midvale is a Mormon town. Mormons don't associate much with anyone other than their own, which left Val with no one to play with." Liz looks down at her glass, shaking her head as she continues, "Val was so sad living there. She didn't have a friend in the entire school. All of them were Mormon, and we weren't."

Liz looks up at me. "You couldn't have known any of this, Dar! How do you know this?"

Waiting for me to answer, she looks over to Val. "Val, do you remember that little blue parka? Do you remember how mad you were when I'd sewn your mittens to your sleeves?"

Color drains from their faces as we look at each other. Then it hits me—I just accurately described what Valerie's life was like when she lived in Utah at nine years of age. Val and I have never discussed her childhood in detail.

Was it a dream, or not?

On August 31, 1999, I marry the love of my life in a little wedding chapel in Mesa. We honeymoon in Vegas. I did it! I've accomplished something that a few years ago I never dreamed possible. I have a great job and a beautiful wife and family. I'm working, making my way under my own name without fear of always watching my back and being recognized. Mom comes out to visit when she can, and we vacation in Rocky Point, Mexico once a year. Four years fly by, and I am off parole. Life is good! If I were any more normal, I'd have to change my last name to Cleaver.

Chapter 15
Adderall

September 1, 2001 is my forty-first birthday, but I do not feel anywhere near my forties right now. I feel better than I have ever felt in my life. I've been on the graveyard shift as the lead computer operator at AT&T for about four years now. It's a gravy job, and I've figured out a routine that works for me. Most nights, I work alone only having to check the TC/IP monitors every couple of hours for errors. This gives me time in between to head to the gym for workouts or take a much-needed nap. No one ever checks on me because I do my job well, taking care of the monitors and fixing all errors that pop up. My routine starts when I clock in at work. When the last shift leaves, I check the monitors then head to the gym. After that, I head back to check the monitors then take a two-hour nap. After checking the monitors when I wake, I have everything fixed before the morning shift arrives. When they arrive, I go home. It's awesome!

On September 11, 2001, Lanny and Perry come in to cover first shift, and Lanny asks, "Hey, did you hear? A plane just flew into the World Trade Center!"

I stare at him a moment, absorbing what he said, and then I ask, "How in the world did that happen?"

Shaking his head, he answers, "Don't know. It's probably a little Cessna and the pilot decided to get even with his cheating wife who works on the floor he decided to fly into."

I stare at him, detecting a little venom in his voice. Perry walks over and turns on the TV. I'm still looking at Lanny, contemplating what he said, when he asks defensively, "What? That's what I'd do if I had the chance!"

Lanny, obviously in the middle of a nasty divorce, has recently mentioned more than once the different ways he'd like to see his wife meet her demise. Shaking my head, I pat him on the shoulder and walk over toward the TV. I cannot believe my eyes when I see a gaping hole in the side of the tower with smoke billowing out. I say, "That wasn't a Cessna that made that hole!"

As we're watching the news footage in shock, all of a sudden, as if in slow motion right in front of our eyes a commercial airliner flies right into the side of the second tower! Perry screams, "What the in the world just happened?"

Forgetting about his cheating wife, Lanny watches the news and says, "This is bad. This is real bad."

As we stand in front of the TV with our mouths hanging open, warning signals start popping up across the boards all around us. All hell breaks loose as our monitors blow up, warning us of excessive call volume coming into the center. We look at each other, frozen for a brief second, then Perry yells out, "Doesn't look like you're going home yet!" He leans over to adjust a monitor. "Stick around and give a hand, will ya, Dar? I have a feeling this is going to get crazy."

We immediately sit down in our chairs, regulating the monitors fixing problems, trying to stay on top of them, but errors just keep popping up.

Our company provides long-distance directory information, and everyone around the country is calling for phone numbers in New York, mainly numbers for offices located in the World Trade Center. All of a sudden, we are the conduit between individuals in those towers and their concerned loved ones trying to contact them.

Val, having just arrived for her shift, immediately sits down at her station with the other operators answering calls. I look out over the floor, watching our operators struggling to keep hysterical callers calm, but it's so hard for them when most the callers are scared to death and frantically trying to contact a loved one in the tower.

I stay for hours, helping as much as I can, but I'm exhausted and finally decide to go home. Before I leave, I need to check in with Val to make sure she's okay. Out on the main floor, I scan the room looking for her, feeling completely dismayed as hundreds of operators sit at their stations on the phone crying and wiping tears from their cheeks as they handle each call the best they can. Some can no longer take the pressure, feeling unequipped to help in this situation. They stand up and run out the door.

I walk up behind Val and kiss the top of her head, whispering in her ear, "You okay, babe?"

Frazzled, she looks up at me with tears in her eyes. I ask if she wants to leave with me, but no, she wants to stay and help as long as she can. She squeezes my hand and then lets go, picking up another call and calmly helping another hysterical parent.

Living in central Phoenix only two miles from Sky Harbor Airport, on any given day, all day long, the sky is full of air traffic with planes taking off and landing. Not today. Walking outside, I'm hit with an eerie, surreal silence in the city that I have never experienced before. I look up—there's not a plane in the sky. The usually busy Phoenix streets are vacant as well. Exhausted, I slowly walk home, sensing the world will never be the same.

January 2002, my boss walks in early and catches me sound asleep at the end of the graveyard shift, again. This falling asleep issue, it's getting worse. I even heard him coming in this time and couldn't open my eyes. He doesn't yell, but he smacks my desk, jarring me out of my stupor, and in a loud voice says, "Dar! Wake up! I need to talk to you."

He looks over to Perry, Lanny, and the rest of the first shift crew, "I need to talk to all of you."

I jump up saying, "Sorry, I must have dozed off."

He stands for a moment looking at all of us then starts, "They're cutting the center back, moving the bulk of operations to Canada. I would advise you all to start looking for other employment."

My heart sinks, but then he pulls me aside along with Lanny and Perry telling us, "Except you guys. Your jobs are safe. They still need the mainframe hub maintained here, but unfortunately the other three hundred employees are out of a job." He looks over to me. "That includes Valerie, sorry."

Then he pulls me aside with concern, asking, "This morning is the fifth time I've come in early and found you asleep Dar. What's going on with you? Don't you sleep at home?"

My excessive exhaustion is getting worse, and I tell him, "Man, I'm sorry. It doesn't matter how much sleep I get, I'm always tired. I do sleep at home, much more than normal, but I'm still sleepy all the time. It's getting worse. The other day I fell asleep sitting at a stoplight on my way home! It scares me. It's like there's times I can't keep my eyes open no matter how hard I try."

"Okay, I want you to take some time off and get this taken care of, Dar. We have a great insurance plan, and you're allowed a short-term disability period until the doctors can figure out what exactly is happening. Dar, I can't have you on the job if you can't stay awake, and you're too good of an employee to fire, so take this time off and get well!"

Three doctors, two neurologists and a sleep study later, I'm diagnosed with narcolepsy. I ask, "How did I catch it?"

The doctor explains, "You didn't catch it, Mr. Bryant, you were born with it. But it doesn't manifest itself until later in life. However, your case is unusual." He looks up from his clipboard. "It usually raises its sleepy head during the teens rather than the forties."

Reflecting back on my life, I think about how I've always struggled with this but never thought it important enough to have it checked out. I mean, I'm not sick, just tired. Then again, most of my life, I wouldn't have ever known if I was sleepy or not with all the stimulants I took on a daily basis.

I ask him, "Okay. Now what?"

He explains the protocol. "We'll start with a prescription that should help you stay awake. Most likely, we'll have to try a couple different combinations before we find one that works for you. Every case is different, but you can't go back to work until we've stabilized your medication. Oh! And you can't drive, either."

I blurt out, "What? I can't drive?"

Tilting his head, he looks at me, asking, "Really, Mr. Bryant? You're going to question this? You can't stay awake. Think about it."

Frustrated, I walk out the door with my written prescriptions, but I also feel kind of good that maybe I will finally get a grip on the constant exhaustion that has plagued me for years. Narcolepsy! Who knew?

Val drives to the drugstore so I can fill my prescriptions. It feels so weird having her drive. Makes me feel like an invalid. I open the bag, and when I read the name on the bottle, I almost drop it. Adderall! This is basically dexedrine, a cousin to the very drug I started using in junior high school. This is what started it all! This is what I used to get high on, to take for energy and to stay awake throughout my teens and twenties. This is the very drug that started my journey down the rabbit hole. Cradling the bottle in my hands, I fear it and am thankful for it all at the same time. My head spins with a million thoughts as I hold this old friend/enemy.

I probably should have mentioned to my doctor about my addiction, but at the time, it really didn't cross my mind. It was so long ago. I look over to Val and can tell she doesn't understand the connection. Val wasn't even born when I first started taking speed. She knows nothing about that life or that world. She wasn't around back then and can't possibly grasp the intensity of it all. Don't get me wrong, I've told her all about my background, drugs, prison, and addictions. I had to because, well, it's a part of my past, but unless you've lived it, you really can't comprehend it.

I don't want to explain any of this to Val, about what these pills are and what they mean or about my fear and my solace just holding this little bottle. She's so innocent, so pure. She wouldn't know the difference between dexedrine and amoxicillin. Having lived a life of endless research, experimentation, and discussions on drugs, I avoid conversation about any of it as much as possible, and nowadays, the subject rarely comes up.

I walk into the kitchen and place the bottle in an upper cabinet out of reach of the children. All evening, my mind spins, rolls, thinks about that bottle of pills even though I carry on as normal and cover up, my best skill. The prescription bottle instructs me to take one in the morning and one in the afternoon, and I think, *Ha! I remember taking at least twenty to thirty of these a day!*

One side of my brain frantically screams at me to throw them away, to tell Val, to call the doctor and explain to him about my past, my addictions, my fears, but then the other side calmly chimes in, *Oh, come on now. You'll be fine! For heaven's sake, your doctor prescribed it. It's not like you're buying them on the street. Just go ahead and take what's prescribed. What could possibly go wrong?* The latter wins.

I wake up the next morning and immediately take my pill. I don't feel a thing, but I'm not sleepy, either! This is good. I can do this! Early afternoon, I take another. I am wide awake until nine p.m. Perfect!

All week long, I take Adderall as instructed, and all is good—except for two pills a day this week is not doing for me what two pills a day last week did. I have an extra busy day today, so I pop an extra pill, telling myself, *No big deal. So I'll be one short at the end of the month.*

Two weeks later, I grab my bottle to take another and realize I've used up almost an entire month's supply. Bright side, I haven't been tired at all. It feels awesome getting through a day without feeling the need to take a nap every few hours, without having to push myself so hard, without living in a constant lethargic fog. It's all good—except I'm almost out.

While on disability, I start up a little eBay business to bring in more money. I have a wife and four kids now. Buying merchandise at auctions and reselling it on the Internet turns out to be a great little venture producing some really easy money, and I'm good at it. There's a big auction this weekend, and I need to be alert. They're auctioning off delinquent storage bins. Hoping to find something good, I pop the last couple pills to stay awake. It feels so good to be alert again. I can't bear the idea of going back to where I feel like I'm walking around in a haze.

I got it! Nikki and Chris are spending the weekend. I'll take a few out of Chris's bottle when he comes over tonight. He's on the exact same prescription I am for his ADHD. Mikki won't notice, and I'll figure something out later for long term.

At the auction, I score a pallet with thirty used Dell computers for $200. I can easily get a $100.00 a piece for them. I run a classified ad in the newspaper advertising them and quickly get to work installing new memory. As I'm working, someone calls interested in buying one. I tell them, "It'll be ready in a couple hours."

He asks, "Where are you located?"

I give him my street address, and he replies, "You're just a mile away. Would you mind bringing it by this evening? My wife has the car and will be at work until eleven."

Writing down his address, I tell him, "No problem!"

Two hours later, I pull up to a run-down little shack. I knock on the door and a very familiar-looking dude about my age completely covered in prison tattoos answers the door. I say, "Here's your computer."

He looks at me, surprised. "Dar!"

As soon as he says my name, I recognize him from prison. I throw out my hand and ask, "How you doing, Dave?"

He smiles, steps to the side, and invites me in. "Good! Good! Come on in, brother."

I step in his house, setting down the computer, and ask, "How long you been out?"

"About a year. You?"

"I've been out almost five."

He replies, "Wow! It's been that long?"

"Yep."

That's all I can think of to say. We stand for an awkward second, and then he says, "Well, it's good to see you, and thanks for bringing the computer over. A hundred bucks, right?"

"Yeah. That's right."

He looks back in his house and points to a mirror on his coffee table with four fine lines of what is obviously meth and asks, "Hey, brother, wanna do a bump?"

Quickly silencing the screaming voice in my head, without hesitation or a second thought, I smile and say, "Sure!"

Laughing at my enthusiasm, he passes the mirror to me and says, "Go ahead and do two! One for each nostril. You don't wanna walk around lopsided."

And there it is! I inhale that second line, succumbing to a familiar rush I so desperately desire. Oh, how I have missed this feeling. Man, this feels good. They can keep those dumb pills!

It's all good, I keep telling the screaming voice within. Dave and I hang out talking, doing more dope, and he asks, "So what are you doing now?"

I tell him my story about my wife, my job, going on disability, narcolepsy, eBay, auctions, blah blah blah.

With interest, he replies, "Man, those storage bin auctions are a pretty good racket. I wouldn't mind getting in on that. Mind if I go with you?"

"No! Not at all."

Before I leave, I score an eight-ball, giving him back the hundred dollars he just gave me for the computer.

I tell him, "I'll pick you up at seven tomorrow morning. The auction starts at eight."

"Okay. I'll be ready."

We shake hands, and I leave.

"Where've you been?" Val asks with concern as I walk in the house. I tell her about taking the computer to Dave's house, about knowing him from prison, about picking him up tomorrow for the auction. I tell her everything…leaving out the part about drugs. Val looks at me with a teasing smile, "Well! You really seem like you're in a good mood. If I would've known that finding a friend for you to hang out with was going to make you this happy, I would've insisted on it a long time ago!"

She leans her head against my chest, giving me a hug, and I smile, pat her on the back, and get to work. I have a lot to do.

Later that night in bed, Val falls fast asleep as I lay beside her wide awake. Luckily, Val sleeps like the dead, so I slip out of bed and tiptoe out of the room, no longer able to just idly lie around. I'm amped. I need something to do, to occupy my mind.

I sit down at the computer and research anything and everything I can on my old scams. Reading up on checks and IDs, I see it's a tough game now—a lot has changed in ten years. For the last five years, the Valley has been plagued with identity theft and check fraud. Checks are now printed with magnetic ink and read with a check reader upon cashing. Since 9/11, security checks at the DMV have become so stringent that my old method of making fake IDs is now obsolete, but I tell myself there are no problems, only solutions. This'll just take a little more work.

Looking up from the computer, I stare at a picture hanging on the wall when it dawns on me—the monster has been unleashed. It's like it's been held captive, buried deep inside my subconscious and anxiously awaiting rebirth. It has picked up right where it left off like it never stopped. Following along the wall to another picture, our family portrait taken of the six of us when Alisha came out for a visit, I realize I have to figure out a way to keep all of this from Val. I love Val more than I have ever loved anyone, but I miss this. I miss this high. I miss this energy, this lifestyle, the adrenaline rush from outsmarting cops, the easy money it brings. I miss it all. The game may have changed, but it's still just a game, one I play well. My life in the last twelve hours has taken a one- hundred-and-eighty-degree turn.

Val may be innocent, but she's not stupid. In just a few short days, she starts questioning my erratic behavior. Falling back on my well-honed skill of excuses, I explain to her, "I took a couple more pills than I probably should have. I had to, Val. Dave and I are picking up a load from the auction, and it has to be sorted by tomorrow. I'll have to burn the midnight oil."

Believing me, she kisses me good night, saying, "Well, I'm glad you have someone to help you. I'm going to bed. Don't be working all night again. It's not good for you!"

Wondering how long I'll be able to bluff this woman, I reassure her, "I won't! Night. Love you."

Out in the garage, Dave and I search through boxes we just purchased from a government auction. Unbelievably, we score an ID making machine! It's outdated because it doesn't produce the hologram needed to pass through a TSA checkpoint, but we'll be able to make authentic-looking driver's licenses good enough to pass for check cashing or buying merchandise in stores, most anything but a cop's scrutiny.

Searching the Internet late one night while Val is sound asleep, I order a magnetic toner. The Internet is a criminal's shopping mall. Now all I have to do is load the toner in my laser printer, and with my photoshop program, I should be able to make the best-looking checks ever. I am officially back in business!

Dave tells me about his runners that will run the checks for a 50/50 cut. It's a good idea. This way we keep our hands clean, supplying them with checks and IDs while they take all the risk. Dave and I tell them where to go and what to buy, and we act as a fence for the merchandise they bring back. It's working great until one of them gets greedy and decides not to bring our merchandise back.

In just ninety days, I have completely slipped back into the abyss, a place it took fifteen years to get to before. It's different this time. My cravings are seven times worse, and I'm seven times more ruthless—no conscience, no empathy for others, and I have no fear of anything. Although my love for Val and family remains strong, even they come in second to my addiction. I am no longer the man Val married, no longer a responsible citizen that just a few months ago held a top supervisor's position at a telephone company. I'm

Darwyn again, just seven times worse, and much bigger and stronger, a dangerous combination for anyone who ticks me off. Today, I am ticked!

Our minions supply our merchandise with our help, and I sell it on eBay, getting close to retail value, or send it to local auctions. If it's unique or identifiable, I have out of state outlets I move it to. I don't know where most of this stuff comes from, and I don't care. It pulls in good money.

Jeff, one of our capricious runners, was instructed to purchase a Rolex watch. We know he scored it. His driver informed us he had it but asked to be dropped off at his house, said he had something to do. After waiting on him all evening, Dave and I decide to pay him a little visit. He's not home, so we drive around town looking for him. The longer we look, the faster the blood pulses through my veins. By the time we find him at another fence's house, I've had it. Driving in Dave's old pickup truck, we turn off the lights and roll to within a few yards of Jeff's car. We sit and wait. When Jeff walks out and climbs into his car, I whisper to Dave, "Let's get him!"

Dave fires up that old beast of a Ford. Popping the clutch, he punches the gas pedal to the floor and rams Jeff's car on the passenger side. We quickly jump out, and I reach in through the driver's side window, grabbing the front of Jeff's shirt and easily pull his skinny little body out through the window. Jeff is screaming for mercy as I hold him against his car with my forearm across his throat. His feet dangle a few inches off the ground. Dave clocks him with a straight-on violent punch to the side of his head. Blood spews across my face as two of Jeff's teeth fly from his mouth onto the pavement. Nose to nose, I growl, *"What are you thinking trying to rip us off!"*

As Jeff pleads, blood bubbles ooze from his mouth. "Man, you cut my percentage down to thirty percent! I get sixty percent here!"

"Who supplied your check and ID, you idiot! You think I do it for free?"

"I know, I know, I know. I'm sorry, man."

"Well, guess how much you're gonna make now? Zip! Nada! Nothing! Empty your pockets and give me every penny you have or I'll rip your head off, and Dave here's gonna crap down your neck!"

Wiping his bloody mouth with the back of his hand, Jeff surrenders all his cash without another word spoken. Dave and I jump back in the Ford and drive away, deciding it's time for a new hustle. We don't need that lame. We have our own band of thieves—six other guys who will do anything we want as long as we give them a fair cut and keep them high. Well, five guys and one very ugly woman, but she's tough as nails and more fearless than the rest of the guys combined. We call her Dixie because of her deep southern twang.

I arrive home and walk in the front door to find Val and Kendal sitting in the living room. Val is trying her best to hold back tears as Kendal sits beside her, leaning against her shoulder. I ask, "What's wrong with you two?"

Val stares at me. Kendal does the same. Then Kendal speaks up in her raspy little six-year-old voice, "Mommy's really upset with you, Daddy."

Kendal is now the same age as Nikki was when I was arrested in Havasu. Kendal didn't like me at first—most children don't like their mother's new boyfriend. Over the years, though, she and I have become very close. I am her daddy, and right now she's as concerned about what's going on with me as her mom.

In a broken voice, Val speaks up, "I don't know what is going on with you, but you're going to tell me right now!"

I assure her, "Nothing's going on, Valerie."

She spits out, "*Bull!*" as she stands up and stomps into the kitchen. I watch her and then look down at Kendal. She looks up at me, shaking her head, and her expression says it all—*Wow, you've done it now, buddy.*

I can't just ignore this. I have to at least say something to Val, so I walk in the kitchen and ask her in a tone implying this is all her fault, "What exactly is your problem?"

She is all over that question. "You've become weird, Dar! You never sleep. You act like you can't even sit and have a conversation with me anymore. You're different and secretive about everything. I don't even know you anymore. What has happened to you?"

Wiping tears from her cheeks, she looks at me with complete love and concern and quietly demands, "I want my husband back!"

I brush it off, saying, "Oh, good grief. You're overreacting."

Definitely not a good choice of words because now she makes it a point to overreact. "Overreacting! Are you kidding me? How can you look at yourself in the mirror and tell me I'm the one overreacting? You look like crap, Dar!" Choking to get her words out, she continues in a tone I have never heard from her before. "I used to see love in your eyes, Dar, but now I only see evil. Go look in the mirror. You look evil, and you act even worse!"

Ouch! Trying to smooth this over the best I can, I explain, "Things have just been stressful, babe, since you lost your job at the same time I was placed on disability. I'm trying to deal with all this the best I can. I'm trying to make enough money to keep us afloat, babe. What else do you want me to do?"

She looks me straight in the eye. "Dar! You're taking too many of those pills. They're making you crazy. The scariest thing is, you don't even see it!"

Pushing past me, she heads to the bedroom, slamming the door shut. I stand for a second thinking, then I turn to look back at Kendal in the living room just in time to see her stomp off, slamming her bedroom door as well.

Shaking my head, I take a deep breath and push my hair back out of my face. I walk into the living room and just stand for a moment looking back and forth at two closed bedroom doors hiding two people I love dearly. What am I doing? Val is the best thing that has ever happened to me. The one person in this world meant for me. No one has ever loved me the way she does, and I'm blowing it. I walk back into the kitchen, pop open a beer, and chug it down. I'm not an evil person, but why do I do such evil things? I feel like Dr. Jekyll and Mr. Hyde. The good me is trapped deep down inside watching the bad me who is in total control and doing all this stuff without repentance. No wonder they call meth the devil's multivitamin. I really do hate myself right now, but not enough to stop.

Sitting down on the couch, I finish my beer and elect to just leave the girls be. Sleeping is out of the question, so to occupy my mind, I decide to watch a movie. Leaning over the cabinet under the TV to search for an action-packed DVD to satisfy my need, I notice it. Again? Impossible! There is absolutely *no way!* Confused, I pick up a Bible, almost dropping it when it feels warm to the touch! I shake my head, thinking, *It's just your imagination. This is just a Bible and not a living being.* Needing to open it, I slowly unzip the familiar zipper as I have so many times before. *No!* I have never unzipped this Bible before! All my belongings were stolen out of the storage unit. The only thing they left was dust. This can't possibly be *that* Bible.

Sure enough, there's Grandma's handwriting. "From Grandma Ruby, 1969." My knees give way, and I fall back on the floor in front of the TV holding a warm Bible with Grandma's inscription. How does this keep happening? How does this Bible keep popping up so many times in my life in the strangest of places at the strangest of times?

I think back to the last time I saw it in Lake Havasu, right before my arrest. After my arrest, Mikki packed up everything and put it in storage. All of it was stolen a few months later. The only thing I came out of prison with were the clothes on my back. That was it. Nothing more.

I look around my home at those two closed bedroom doors and at everything I have acquired since that day so many years ago. I look down at the Bible in my hands. It's clearly impossible...yet here it is! Thumbing through the fine, thin pages, it falls open to a scripture: Mark 11:23. *"For verily I say unto you, That whosoever shall say unto this mountain, 'Be thou removed, and be thou cast into the sea'; and shall not doubt in his heart, but shall believe that those things which he saith shall come to pass; he shall have whatsoever he saith."*

This is the one and only verse in the entire Bible that I had circled back when I was a kid, probably twelve. I remember the day I marked it. Grandma told me this would be a scripture I could turn to when I needed strength. She told me I would need the power of this scripture to have victory over trials I would face in life.

I slowly read the scripture again, lightly running my fingers across the page. Confused and a little freaked out, I gently close Grandma's Bible and place it back under the TV, grabbing a Chuck Norris flick.

Five movies later, Val wakes up a little calmer than when she went to bed, so I ask her, "Do you know how that Bible got in the TV cabinet?"

"What Bible?"

"The one under the TV. The one Grandma gave me when I was a kid."

Val stops dead in her tracks, turns to look at me, and in a sarcastic tone I've never heard from her before, she asks, "You... have a *Bible*?"

Taking a deep breath, I exhale through closed lips, shake my head, then simply say, "Never mind" as I walk out the door and head to Dave's house.

Driving to Dave's, I think about the Bible. It's so strange, so very strange. I pull into his driveway, pushing it from my mind. I have too much to do today and don't need any distractions.

Dave and I are working on a new hustle I heard about in prison. I don't know if it'll work, but I figure I won't know unless I try. Using fifty one-dollar bills, we lay them flat in an 8"x 14"x3" Pyrex baking dish. Dave fills the dish with a solvent to remove all the ink, supposedly leaving the paper intact. We let it sit.

Six hours later, we have fifty blank pieces of rag paper. Rag paper is the type of paper used to make paper money. It's made from cotton and linen fibers. When merchants test a bill to see if it's counterfeit, it's actually the paper they're testing with the detection pen, not the ink.

When the blank bills dry, we load the rag paper into a printer using the template of a hundred-dollar bill from the year 1989. In five minutes, we print enough bills to total $500,000! This is just too easy!

From the year 1990 to the current year, a magnetic strip has been woven into every hundred-dollar bill, so long as our bills are dated pre-1990, it's all good. Using a counterfeit detection pen, I test a few, and sure enough, they prove to be authentic. Within a week, we pass $10,000 in bogus bills. Now that's a good return!

Dave calls, upset his old lady just up and moved to Tucson. "I have to go find her."

And with that, he's gone, leaving me in total charge of all his minions. Now this little band of thieves all work for me alone.

With ten of the fake hundred-dollar bills in my pocket, I have Rob drive me to a grocery store. He pulls into a parking spot where he can easily watch the doors in case things go wrong and I need to make a quick getaway. I jump out, reminding him, "I'll be right back. Keep your eyes open."

My plan today is to successfully purchase a carton of cigarettes paying with a bogus hundred and pocket the change at ten different stores.

I ask the cashier for a carton of Camels. She retrieves one from customer service and rings me up. I hand her a hundred-dollar bill, and with a charming smile, I say, "Sorry, I don't have anything smaller on me."

She holds the bill up to the light and looks back at me. With a quick "excuse me," she walks back to customer service and hands the bill to the store manager. As I'm watching this, I notice a police officer working store security standing by the front door. Within seconds, the store manager walks to the cop and hands him the bill. They both check the bill and look up at me.

I've been passing these counterfeit bills all over town for a couple weeks now. This morning I had a feeling this game had run its course. Standing in the checkout lane watching them examine me, I ask myself, *When will you start following your gut instincts?* I knew I should have stopped this a few days ago, knowing those bills have hit the banks by now. I'm sure they've put up red flags all over the Valley.

The cop motions for me to join him as he walks toward me. Needing to escape without alerting him of my intention, I assess my options. There's a lady blocking the aisle behind me with a cart full of groceries. The closest exit is the front door about thirty feet away, but the cop is about fifteen feet away and directly in between. He looks about 5'10" and maybe 145 pounds, probably why he's working security at a grocery store. I notice he's not even wearing a gun. That's good. I make a split second decision, taking my 6'4", 230-pound frame three steps toward him. In a quick move, I lower my shoulders in a sprinter's run, and with more speed than I knew I had, I lunge at him, hitting him midsection with my left shoulder and lifting him up and throwing him off his feet. He lands backward on a Rug Doctor display as dozens of carpet shampoo bottles tumble down on top of him.

Bolting out the door without slowing down, I run across the parking lot as Rob starts the car and throws open the passenger door. I jump inside yelling, *"Go! Go! Go! Get out of here!"*

Speeding off, he makes a right and a quick left when I yell, "Stop the car!"

"Why?"

"Because! Because they're looking for two guys in a car, not one. They only saw me. Let me out and go back to the house. Tell Val I got tied up, and I'll be home later."

He pulls the car over about six blocks from the store. I climb out, and he pulls away yelling, "Be careful!"

Walking down alleys, I head east with plenty of time to think up a few good explanations before I face Val. I love her so much. I hate having to lie to her, but what else can I do?

I check the house for the girls, and they aren't even home. Flopping down on the couch with a beer, I relax a little. *Huh, no explanations needed after all.*

Thinking about the evening, about Val, about how much my life has changed in just a few short months, I realize I am totally subservient to my addiction, to this evil that controls me. Yes, it's evil. I know it's evil. If I live long enough, I will confront this demon. A cop might take me out first, or maybe I'll just lie down and go to sleep never to wake again I don't know. I do know that one of these three scenarios must happen before I have to face Val when she opens her eyes and sees me for what I've become.

There are times I see it, my end. It comes from the trigger finger of an overzealous cop because you see, I have *no* intention of going back to prison. Next time I'm caught, my trial will be held in the street. That's where it ends.

Val opens the front door, and Kendal pushes her way in, jumping on the couch beside me.

Chapter 16
Arrested

James, one of my minions, introduces me to a guy, Buddy, who is said to be good at getting merchandise, a professional shoplifter of high-ticket items. Buddy is different, though. He doesn't look like the rest of my thieves. Buddy looks to be in his early fifties. He has a shaved head and a silver goatee and is a clean-cut, healthy, respectable-looking guy with a pair of reading glasses perched on the end of his nose. He reminds me of a college professor. After James's introduction, Buddy says with a firm handshake, "Good to meet ya."

I ask him, "What kind of stuff can you get?"

"What kind of stuff do you want?"'

The word's out that I move merchandise quickly as long as it's not junk and they're willing to let it go for ten to twenty percent of its value. I have an outlet for almost anything—buyers for antiques, electronics, jewelry, bikes, and guns…whatever you want. I pay all my providers in cash or dope. Most want dope as Buddy does. I don't care if the merchandise was stolen or not. This is business—it doesn't matter to me where it came from.

I ask Buddy what he brought for me today. "I have a Cannondale Mountain Bike. It sells for over $1,000."

"I'll give you a hundred bucks or an eight ball."

"You're crazy!"

I set him straight. "Look, man, that bike is hot. I'll have to sell it out of town for only $300 tops. Do you know what that means? That means I'll have to risk handling it, storing it, moving it, and selling it for only $200. You understand? One hundred dollars—take it or leave it."

He shakes his head, disappointed, and says, "I'll take the eight ball."

For the next two months, Buddy and I work well together. He supplies merchandise I can turn quickly. Then he's arrested leaving Home Depot with a cart of stuff he didn't pay for. Val doesn't like my new group of friends, but she genuinely likes Buddy. I try to keep Buddy's arrest from her, but she finds out and screams at me, "This is all your fault, Dar! You put him up to this! Now he's in jail! Do you get it yet? You put him there, Dar! You did!"

Val and I go from bad to worse. Our relationship deteriorates daily. She acts like she can't stand the sight of me, so I do my best to stay away from her. Many times, she has threatened to leave if I don't stop "it," and she doesn't even know what "it" is. She really has no idea what I do, but she has assumed that it's illegal. Smart assumption. She thinks my drug problem is overusing the doctor's prescriptions. She has no clue. If she were to find out, she'd be out that door with Kendal in a second.

Mikki's figured it out. She's lived it. She immediately recognizes the difference in me and has decided after this last visit not to let Nikki and Chris come for weekends anymore. I don't argue with her. I can't have her making a big production that will end with her talking to Val about it, so I let them go. I let my kids go. No more weekends with my kids.

With all the new activity at my house, I know I'm on the cop's radar again. I see them drive by multiple times throughout the night. The patrol helicopter makes regular passes overhead, and I listen to them discuss my surveillance on the police scanner. None of this worries me because I'm not making or dealing drugs, just using and bartering them. If the police were to come down on me, they couldn't prove any of the stuff I'm buying and selling was stolen even though they know it is. I'm not the one out there stealing it. It all just shows up at my doorstep. How it was acquired is unbeknownst to me, and that is not my problem.

Turning up the heat hoping to gain incriminating evidence on me, the local police start pulling over everyone that leaves my house. They sit across the street for hours trying to shake me up. I peek out the window and listen to them on the scanner, knowing this is just as frustrating for them as it is for me.

Rob and I are "working" when he asks if we can pick up a battery charger at Kmart to jump his wife's car. He tells me he doesn't have any money, and well, I don't have any cash either, but I do have a book of stolen checks Dixie gave me! We turn the truck around and are headed toward Kmart when I hear a police siren. Lights flash behind us as Rob says in a low voice, "We're getting pulled over again."

He pulls over as I shove the checkbook in my back pocket, mumbling, "Just be cool!"

The cop asks for Rob's driver's license and registration of which he has neither, causing him to start sweating like a pig and acting nervous and sketchy. I watch him fall apart in front of the officers, losing his composure, and I mentally coach him, *Come on, Rob!* But sure enough, another cop opens my door and order me out, "Get out! Put your hands on the hood!"

I'm still not worried because I don't have any dope, so I calmly get out and place my hands on the hood. Assuming the position, I ask, "What's the problem, officer?"

"Your buddy there doesn't know how to use a turn signal."

"Okay, but why the search?"

"You tell me!" he replies as he pulls the checkbook from my pocket, asking, "Whose is this?"

Crap! The checkbook! The officer opens the checkbook, reads the name, and asks, "Mr. Bryant, what are you doing with Herschel Manuel's checkbook?"

"Hersh is a friend of mine. He left it at my house. I was on my way to return it when you stopped me."

He handcuffs me, laughing, "Sure you were!"

Both of us handcuffed, Rob and I are sitting on the sidewalk when my cop tells his cop, "Mike, watch these two while I go call this in."

He leaves to call the station, and when he returns, I can tell we're going to jail from the determined look on his face. Helping me to my feet, he orders, "On your feet! Mr. Bryant, you're under arrest for possession of stolen property."

I look over to Rob as his officer releases him. Rob drives away as I'm escorted to the squad car.

I'm booked into Maricopa County Jail on a low-level class four felony. My bail is set at $1,500. Lying on a bunk in the holding cell, wide awake at two in the morning, I'm surprised when Val shows up to bail me out. Tears roll down her cheeks as we walk out to the car. I have nothing to say, but she does. "I'm done, Dar. I can't do this anymore."

No words are spoken as we climb in the car. She sniffles and I watch her wipe tears away as she drives us home. I have nothing to say. I know the best thing for her right now would be to get as far away from me as possible. I love Val. I can't stand seeing her hurt like this, but she doesn't understand—I have to have meth like she has to have oxygen. I've been here before, and I know the score. I know what's ahead of me, and I don't want her to be around for it. At this point, there's only one way out for me—either get caught or die.

Dixie calls, wanting me to stop by. She answers the door laughing as she shows me her take from the night before. "I got 'er from a preacher. Lifted it right outta his hospital room while he was down getting' them tests or something."

"How do you know he was a preacher?"

"Well, open it!"

I pop the latches on a hard leather briefcase and find a Bible, religious pamphlets, a missionary book, a checkbook, a passport, a wallet, an ID, and credit cards. I look back at Dixie, and she says, "I kept all the cash."

"Okay, Dixie. We'll have to run these while they're still fresh before he reports it missing."

On the table next to the briefcase, I notice an envelope containing the cash Dixie took. The envelope is addressed to Nadine Rhodes who lives in Idaho. A letter sticks out from among the bills. I flip it open and read:

> *My love, I miss you already. Pray for me. I've had a slight detour while on this journey. I started having stomach pains, so I checked into a hospital here in Phoenix. My arrival in Guatemala will be delayed. I've notified the mission down there. I love you so much. I know you didn't want me to go, but please remember I'm doing the work God has assigned me to do. Give the kids hugs and kisses for me. I will see you all in a month or so.*
>
> *Love you forever and ever,*
>
> *Your husband*

Something stirs inside me. I slowly fold the letter and place it back in the envelope. I tell Dixie, "Hey, maybe we shouldn't do this one."

Dixie yells at me, "*Are you crazy?* This one's a gold mine!"

I concede, "Alright! Alright. I'll be back later tonight. We'll start it then."

I leave Dixie's house feeling uneasy.

It's been five days since my release from jail, and Val hasn't left me yet. She hasn't spoken a word to me, either. I've laid low this past week other than to run by Dixie's place and pick up Buddy from jail. Buddy's been given a work release allowing him to leave jail for eight hours a day to work. I have to have him back by eight o'clock every evening. Buddy learned during his interrogation that the cops are watching my every move. They have no idea what I'm doing, but they're determined to find out and bring me down. He goes on to say they're trying to squeeze information out of him about me, but he's smarter than that. Buddy's been around long enough to know that snitching on me isn't going to gain him a thing.

A little after 7 p.m., Buddy asks for a ride back to jail, so I take him, planning on stopping by Dixie's after. Buddy and I walk toward the door, and I stop dead in my tracks when I hear Val speak up for the first time since she bailed me out. "I pray you get arrested for whatever it is you plan on doing tonight. I should have never bailed you out," she says.

A cold chill runs up my spine as Buddy and I walk out the door.

I drop Buddy off at the front of the jailhouse. "See ya tomorrow, bro."

"Yep, later."

On my way to Dixie's, I think about what Val said when Buddy and I left. That preacher's letter weighs heavy on me as I think about what I'm getting ready to do to him. By the end of the night, while he's in the hospital trying to get healthy enough to go on a mission trip to feed the hungry, I plan on cleaning out his bank account and maxing out every single one of his credit cards. Wow, this is a new all-time low, even for me.

Lost in thought, I cut my wheel to the right, almost missing my exit. I run someone off the road as I cross over two lanes of traffic trying to catch it. Within seconds, I hear a siren wail and lights flash behind me. *Dang!* Apparently that someone I cut off was a cop.

I take a quick mental inventory of what's in the truck. Dixie has the briefcase, that's good. Slowing down, I quickly look around—it all looks good. Then I remember I have an eight ball in the coin pocket of my jeans!

I do my best to stall, pulling over while I analyze my options. If I eat this much meth, it'll kill me. I slip the eight ball out of my pocket and empty all three and a half grams on the dirty floorboard of my truck grinding it into the carpet with the sole of my boot. I pop the empty baggie in my mouth and swallow it just as I come to a stop.

By the time I stop, two more squad cars surround me. *It's all good*, I tell myself. This is just another routine pullover like so many others. I'm in the clear unless they bring in a drug-sniffing dog. There is no way they'll notice the dope mixed in with the sand, dirt, and gravel in my carpet.

It's apparent as they approach my truck these guys are on a mission! They know who I am, and they're dying to catch me with something. They order me out of the truck, asking if they can search it. With an air of annoyance, I grumble, "Go ahead."

Standing off to the side, I watch them search under the truck, under the seats and the visors. Then they check the glove compartment. Pulling out a stack of papers, one of the cops goes through every single paper. He pulls something out of the stack, holds it up, and asks, "What's this?"

I lean over and begin to sweat, thinking, *That blank money order wasn't in there before! I know it wasn't!*

The cop waves the check, showing the others. Arrogantly, he says, "This looks like one of those counterfeit money orders that's been passed around all over town."

I stand motionless, watching them. Then it hits me—this is a setup! They aren't going to let me go. This was planned. They were following me just waiting for a reason to pull me over, and I got sloppy and gave it to them. I'm out on a felony bond and just got caught with a counterfeit money order. Off to jail I go…again!

Back in the interrogation room, a detective informs me they've been watching me for months, waiting for this moment, "You're being charged with attempted forgery and possession of a forgery instrument."

"What are you talking about?" I ask. "How? Over a blank money order?" He stares at me without saying a word, so I continue. "Come on now! It's not even mine!"

Matter-of-factly, he replies, "You're right. A counterfeit blank money order that doesn't have your handwriting on it is only a class five felony. We need something to enhance this charge. Luckily, we found this."

Tossing a plastic evidence bag on the table in front of me, I stare at it in disbelief. The bag contains a single ink pen.

He smiles at me. "This was in the glove box with the money order. This is what we call a forgery instrument. Your class five felony is now a class three. Do you know what this means? It means you will have a mandatory three and a half to ten-year sentence.

Guess what else? Since you're out on a felony bond, there will be no bond for you. Your butt's in jail!"

I angrily protest, "Do you guys just make up laws as you go? You can't charge me for an ink pen!"

He grins. "Oh, but we can! You can't commit forgery without a writing instrument. This ink pen was found inside the glove box with the money order, proving your intent."

He leans in close, whispering in my ear so the recording doesn't pick up his voice, "If we can't get a case against you, we'll create one. You skated by last time, serving only three and a half years on a twenty-one-year bit. Well, guess what? Arizona has adopted an eighty-five percent federal rule. There will be no parole for you. You will serve no less than eighty-five percent of your sentence. Do you know what this means? You're toast!" He stands up and grins down at me.

I shout, "You're so full of it! There is no way the district attorney or a judge will allow this bogus charge! No way!"

Anguish and depression engulf my very soul when I soon find out how wrong I was. The charge sticks! I need a bump!

The processing starts, and I'm assigned to a bunk in Maricopa County Jail, run by the infamous Sherriff Joe. I am beyond livid. These punks are *so* incompetent! They can't even catch me red-handed on a real crime, so they went and made one up.

Twenty-four hours slip by, and I find myself again in jail with no dope, severely depressed, and crashing hard. No bond, no hope, no choice—I find my bunk and pass out.

"Bryant! Wake up! You got a visit."

I struggle to sit up, feeling like a zombie. They escort me down the hall to a visitation room, and I'm miserable. I just want to be left alone to sleep. I walk through the door, thinking, *This better be good.* I'm more than surprised to see Val sitting at the table. Instantly awake, I sit down across from her and just stare at her. She's so beautiful.

Val doesn't speak or even look at me. My heart breaks as I watch a single tear roll down her cheek onto the table, then another and another. I watch her in pain, and I can't take it anymore, can't stand seeing her hurt like this, so I plead, "Baby! I'm so, so sorry!"

I want to reach for her, hold her, comfort her, but with my hands cuffed to the table, I can't.

I stare at her, contemplating her expression as she tucks a strand of long, beautiful hair behind her ear then blows her nose in a tissue. She looks up at me and in a flat tone whispers, "You're kidding me, right?"

Getting louder and angrier, she continues, "You're *sorry?* After I begged you for months to stop doing whatever it is you're doing? I pleaded with you, Dar! I threatened to leave you! I tried everything I could think of to stop you, and now this is all I get? You're sorry?"

I sit across from her, ashamed, listening as she cries, "We had a good life! We *had* an awesome life! You just up and flushed it all down the toilet! And—" She looks at me with disgust. "And all you have for me is, I'm sorry?" Looking me dead in the eyes, she spits out, "You're going to have to do a lot better than that!"

I can't hide it anymore. "Look, Val, I have to tell you something. I know I should've told you already. My drug problem is a lot more than taking extra prescription pills."

"Come on, Dar, I'm not stupid! There is no way you could've changed so much in such short time without abusing something stronger than those stupid pills!"

I can tell this is genuinely coming from her heart, and it's killing me.

"You act downright demon possessed, Dar! You frighten me," she whispers. She looks me up and down and looks away. Tears roll steadily down her cheeks. I can tell she's trying to compose herself, and for a moment, she looks like she's ready to walk out, but then she looks at me and asks with concern, "How're you doing? You look like crap."

"Actually, I feel like crap."

Relieved she still cares enough to ask about me, I seize the moment while she's not reprimanding me to quickly throw in, "Look, I don't expect you to forgive me. I know you're going to leave. I don't blame you. I just want you to know before you go, Val, I love you. I really do." I look down at my hands cuffed to the table. "All of this has nothing to do with me not loving you."

Seconds feel like minutes as I watch her stare past me in deep thought. I don't know what else to say to make this any better, so I just sit and stare at her, burning her image into my memory, knowing this is probably the last time I will ever see her.

She shakes her head slightly and with a deep sigh says, "I'm not leaving you. I know the real you, and this person sitting before me is not the real you. I want the real you back. The one I fell in love with. By the way, your Mom's already hired a lawyer for you."

"She *knows?* How?"

"Dad told her. Aunt Laurie was working last night when you were arrested. She called Dad as soon as she got home."

Val's Aunt Laurie is a deputy for the sheriff's department. Looking down, hating the thought of Mom knowing. I mumble, "Oh man!"

Val looks at me. "She was going to find out sometime, Dar."

I glance around the room and say, "Yeah. I'll call her, just not tonight. I can't handle talking to her tonight. I'm hurting bad."

"Good!" she says gruffly. "You need to hurt." I stare at her as she explains, "Look, I said I'm going to stay with you and that I love you. Don't get me wrong. That doesn't mean I'm going to make things easy on you! I am *mad*, Dar! And I've been mad for a long time!"

A guard comes to take me back to the cell. I watch as Val stands up and walks out the door without hesitation or speaking another word or a glance over her shoulder. I feel she was glad to leave. I'm hurting, mentally and physically. As I walk with the guard back to the cell, all I can think about is sleep.

Forty-eight hours later, I finally rise from my stupor to face the burden of a familiar wave of emotions that I do not enjoy. Under the influence of meth, emotions such as guilt, remorse, empathy, compassion, and love are all replaced with greed, self-gratification, indifference, and lust. As soon as the devil's drug begins to leave my system, guilt and remorse rush in, engulfing me with unbearable pain. I need a bump! There's another emotion dominating my mind this time, *anger!* I know deep down inside I have no right to be angry, but I am. After all, I was set up! They broke the law to get a charge on me. Ironically, I feel victimized.

Everyone lines up at chow time for a dinner tray. I can hardly drag myself out of bed, but I'm hungry, so I make an effort. Because I'm the last one in line, when I turn to look out over the room, I see all the tables are taken. There's seating for maybe twenty-five with forty of us in this pod. No big deal. I walk back to my cell to eat. When I get there, I see a Hispanic dude sitting on my bunk eating his dinner. "Hey, hombre! You're sitting on my bunk. Moverse por favor."

This guy ignores me, doesn't even flinch, and just continues to eat on my bunk with his tray on his lap.

Holding a heavy, thick plastic chow tray, I yell, "Vi *pharsal!* Seriously! *Get up!"*

This idiot ignores me!

Feeling a rush of heat surge through my body, I fling my tray back, splattering my dinner against the wall behind me. Continuing forward full force, I swing the tray at this dude, cracking him right across the bridge of his nose with the edge of the tray. Blood sprays across my bunk and his dinner and across the floor. He grabs his face, running to the bathroom and cursing along the way.

Everyone stops and stares at me. I scan the room, letting them know I'm ready for a challenge. Bring it on. Even though I've used meth for the last eighteen months, I've continued working out, keeping my size and strength. No one seems interested in a fight as they go back to eating their dinner. I look over to the wall as my dinner slides down toward the floor. I wasn't hungry anyway. Changing my sheets, I lie down and go to sleep.

I recoup from the meth withdrawals much quicker this time than I did ten years ago while in Mohave County Jail, probably because I didn't use for very long this time. I also noticed there's a huge difference in the potency of meth between 1993 and now. It was much more potent back then.

"Bryant! You got mail!"

Wow! I'm excited and nervous when I'm handed a letter from Nikki!

> *Dad, thank you for getting arrested on my sixteenth birthday! Wow, what a great present! I will never forget this day and now completely understand just what you think of me. I hate what you've become again. I barely remember it last time, but this time, I will never forget! How can I ever forgive you for this, especially on my birthday? It was your choice, Dad, and no one else's, and I've made a choice. I never want to talk to you again!*
>
> *Good-bye,*
>
> *Nikki*

Her letter is handwritten on a single sheet of paper. My heart sinks as I fold it up, realizing just how badly I've hurt her. Dear God, I've let her down. We were always so close. As I hold her letter, I have an overwhelming feeling I'll be getting another just like this from Alisha. Alisha and I have only recently reconciled. It's only been a few years since her mom has allowed her to visit. The only few years I was clean. These last years with Val have been wonderful getting to know Alisha again and spending time with her, Nikki, Chris, and Kendal. We were a family, a good family. I toss the letter on my bed. God help me, I've blown it! There's no way Val will stick this out with me. I've blown it all to hell.

I wake up in the middle of the night to the snores of men across the pod, and the jail's dank, musty smell in my lungs. It makes me angry. My mind races with a million thoughts. Why would Valerie stay with me? We've only been together a few years, and we have no kids together. On top of that, I'm sixteen years older than she is. She's still young and beautiful. I'm in my forties about to be sentenced to prison for the second time. I have no future, no way to provide for her or my kids or even myself. By the time I'm released, I'll be so far behind with the changes of the workplace that there will be nothing for me when I get out again. Who would hire an old two-time prisoner with no experience? Mikki and I were married over ten years with two children, and she couldn't even last a few months. Darwyn, you're a fool if you think you have a chance of a future with Val.

Three and a half years! That's the best deal my lawyer can get for me, or so he says. I don't care—it just doesn't matter to me anymore. I've been deteriorating in jail for four long months now. I can't drag this out like last time, waiting on a better deal. Get me to a prison yard so I can at least get some fresh air and sunshine. I take the deal.

Back in the pod, I lie in my bunk reading a book and awaiting transport to prison. For no particular reason, a guy who's at least in his mid-thirties comes over and starts harassing an eighteen-year-old kid in the bunk above me. The older guy is twice this kid's size. He wants him to give him his dinner tray, but this kid's hungry and isn't giving it up. The jerk pulls the kid off the bunk above me and starts pounding on him furiously right next to me. I stop reading and watch for a few seconds.

Taking a deep breath, I stand up and reach down, grabbing this jerk by the hair at the back of his head. Yanking back as hard as I can, he swings around to throw a punch at me, but before he can land one, I take this opportunity to cut loose all my pent-up anger, letting it flow out of me with every punch on this guy's head and upper body. After ten jabs in rapid succession, I keep punching until he curls up on the floor screaming, "Alright man! Alright! Stop! Please!"

I pause, step back, and without a word, I calmly climb back onto my bunk. Picking up my book, I start reading again, ignoring him. The jerk limps off, holding his bleeding ear. The kid drops his head down from the top bunk and says, "Thanks, bro!"

I tell him, "No worries, but you better prepare yourself. You're gonna run into one hundred guys just like him when you get to the yard."

The 9 p.m. alarm sounds, and I listen to the shuffle of feet hustling toward the cells. Marking the page in my book before the lights go out, I set it down for another night in jail. The buzzer sounds as thirty solid metal doors electronically slide shut and lock. The lights click off. My mind rolls with thoughts, emotions, hurt, pain, and depression. I think again of my family and what I've done to them. The only ones who have stuck by me, never giving up on me have been Mom, Grandma, Sherri, and Tim. They have loved me unconditionally through it all. They always seem to believe in me, no matter how bad I mess up. I don't understand why. I roll over and try to sleep, but my mind won't slow down.

Then it hits me how lucky I am to have the family I do. Then why am I so angry? *Because the cops set me up!* I can't get past it. It's driving me crazy. I can't think about this anymore tonight, so I think of Val. I think of how beautiful she is, how much I love her, everything about her. Her statuesque physique, her porcelain skin, her serene blue eyes, and the most gorgeous long, wavy hair I've ever seen. She's simply stunning—and all this wrapped around a warm, gentle heart. Will she come back to visit? Will she be there when I get out? I am such a fool to think a woman like Valerie would ever stick with a guy like me.

Chapter 17
Prison Is Prison
And So It Begins

What can I say? Prison is prison. Once you've been in, there's nothing new other than faces when you return. It's the same rules, the same smells, the same noise, and the same politics—and there are some nasty politics.

Surviving in prison is all about how you carry yourself. If you come in riding a high horse and trying to act like you're something, you will be challenged, or "getting checked" as it's referred to in prison. If you walk around with your head down, acting afraid, you'll be taken advantage of. If you try to click with one group or another, you will end up in more trouble than what you came in with. If you're a sex offender or a snitch, you will be hurt if not killed unless you request protective custody.

The key to survival is to be indifferent, to walk with your head up without making eye contact. Mind your own business and only speak when spoken to, especially when it comes to guards. Respecting others is critical—disrespect will get you wrecked quicker than a New York minute. Also, you must act as if you care about nothing. Don't let anything bother you, and never show worry or excitement. Every day in prison is just another day regardless of who gets hammered or killed.

There are some differences this time, not with the prison but with me. Last time, I was grateful to serve only three and a half years of an almost twenty-plus-year sentence. This time, I'm doing three and a half years partly because of an ink pen. Last time, my wife left me within a few months. This time, it's been almost three years, and my wife continues to stand by me. Last time, my children were too young to understand what I'd done. This time, all four of my children completely understand and are mad at me. Last time, I was weak and out of shape. This time, I am bigger and stronger than I have ever been in my life. Last time, I made the best of my time, enrolling in college and self-help classes. This time, I'm just angry. Last time, I was humble, but this time, I'm a ticking bomb!

Since I'm diagnosed with narcolepsy, I'm not required to work. When I'm not sleeping, I spend my days working out, reading, and writing letters. I'm doing my best to follow the mantra "Do your time, don't let time do you."

Days, weeks, months drag by and I'm surprised every weekend when Val drives almost two hours into the desert to visit me. It kills me to know how hard she struggles out there on her own while I sit in prison accomplishing nothing.

What keeps me going? My family. I have never felt so loved by them than I do now. Val, Mom, Grandma, my brother and sister all talk to me on the phone, encouraging me and always trying to lift my spirits. I really don't understand why they haven't washed their hands of me. I've done nothing but shame them.

Before prison, I never really took the time to talk with Grandma, trying to avoid her endless questions about church. Now I can't wait to talk with Grandma and Mom, and I call them as much as I'm allowed. Mom flies down for visits when she can, and I feel bad knowing how hard it is for her to see me here. I discourage her from visiting even though I want to see her so bad and am always thankful when she doesn't listen and visits anyway. My family, they're great. What happened to me?

Another Saturday rolls in, and I wait patiently, hoping for my name to be called. It's visiting day, and I know that eventually one of these Saturdays will be the day Val doesn't show up, proving she's moved on. I try to be strong, preparing myself, then I hear over the PA, "Bryant, number 113000. You got a visit."

Breathing easier, I walk to the visitor's center one more time, knowing she hasn't bolted yet. Every Saturday without fail, Val has visited me. I know! I'm a lucky man! She has a perfect out. Nobody would blame her if she walked away. No one blamed Mikki.

During our weekly visits, Val has my undivided attention for four solid hours. On the outside, we never sat and talked that long.

You'd think we'd run out of things to say, but every Saturday right when we're in the middle of a great conversation, they interrupt us to take me back to the yard. Those four hours fly by, and as I watch her leave, I'm thrown right back to wondering if she'll be back next Saturday.

Another Saturday rolls in, and again I'm thankful to be visiting with Val, but today she's different. I can tell something's bothering her, and as much as I want to know before she leaves, I'm afraid to ask. She's extremely quiet. This is it—I know she's ready to drop a bomb on me. I've been expecting it for the last three years. Suck it up, Dar. You deserve this.

I look up at the time with just a few minutes remaining, and I have to get this over with. I have to ask, "What's wrong, babe?"

She looks away, saying, "I really don't want to talk about it. Please, let's just try to enjoy our visit."

I don't want to push her or start an argument during our time together, and I definitely don't want our visit to end on a bad note. Val changes the subject. "Buddy's been a great help to me since you've been in. He's been clean since his release from jail. Dar, I really don't know what I'd do without him."

Normally, this is something I would *never* want to hear from my wife while sitting in prison, but this is Buddy. You just have to know Buddy to understand. It's all good.

Mom bought a small apartment complex in Phoenix a few months before I was arrested. The deal was supposed to be that Val and I take care of her apartments in exchange for a place to live. It's win-win. Mom has an investment, and Val and I have jobs and a home. Now they're Val's sole responsibility. Buddy's been helping with the apartments while I sit in prison. I tell Val, "Well, I'm glad he's working out," still wondering why she's acting so strange.

Glancing at the time, I ask again, "Val, tell me what's going on."

"I can't, Dar. I promised I wouldn't say anything, but it's killing me. I want to tell you."

"Why? Why would you make a promise like that? Who'd you make this promise to?"

"Believe me, Dar, it's best if you don't know right now. You'll know soon enough."

I look up at the clock. One minute remains. I can't let her leave without telling me, so I plead louder, "Come on, Val, please! You can't leave me hanging here! I'll think the worst!"

Looking down, Val sighs deeply and whispers, "It's Nikki. I can't tell you what happened because I really don't know. All I know is something bad happened with her, and she left home."

"What do you mean something happened? What do you mean she left home? She's just a *kid!* Where'd she *go*, Val? Where *is* she?"

As I'm questioning Val, the PA announces, "Time's up. Visitation's over."

Val shakes her head, looking worried. "I can't say now, baby. I don't know. I just caught a little bit before I left. I'll try to find out this week. See you Saturday."

Val stands up and walks out of the visitation room as I sit with my mouth hanging open. This is killing me! I have *no* idea what's going on with Nikki! I have *no way* to find out! My imagination runs rampant with every horrible scenario as I head to the track, hoping to burn off my anxiety.

I hit the track sprinting before I lose my cool. Nikki weighs heavy on my mind. Nikki, my second child, is the most like me. She marches to the beat of a different drum, takes her knocks and owns them. She has her Mom's quick wit, but everything else about her comes from me. All my kids are awesome and so different from each other. Alisha, my firstborn, is strong and independent. We were estranged for eleven years, but then we had some great years up until I started using again. My son Chris, my only son, is only fourteen. I feel he needs me the most right now. I've failed him, and it bothers me daily. My stepdaughter Kendal is the youngest and just like one of my own. She is her mother all over, kind, smart, and good. Nikki, she worries me—she's just too much like me!

"Bryant. 113000. Report to the counselor's office."

I slow down and walk a few feet before heading off the track toward the office. *Now what?* I wonder. These summons are never any good.

In his office, the counselor hands me his phone, telling me I have an emergency call. Worried to death about Nikki, my heart sinks as I take the phone, wanting to know yet hesitant to say hello. "Hello? Mom! What's up?"

Mom chokes out, "Your grandma had a stroke last night. She's paralyzed, Darwyn. Completely paralyzed."

I can't talk as this information sinks in. Poor Grandma. Mom assures me it'll be fine, reminding me Grandma's bounced back from bad situations before.

Doing my best to hide my anguish, I walk back and sit on the edge of my bunk. I don't know what to do. What can I do? I need someone to talk to and look across the run. Tiny isn't there anymore. I look up in anger, mentally yelling at God, *What else? What the heck else are you going to throw my way? What? I know I deserve what you throw at me, but my family? Don't punish my family!*

Devastated, depressed, and feeling completely useless, I can't understand why, why Grandma? I think about how strong of a person she is even with all the struggles from her past. Grandma's been a devout servant to God and the church for over sixty years. She's faithfully served others her entire life. She lived on a small farm town in southern Missouri and was widowed in her early twenties when Mom was only eighteen months old. Two years before that, she lost her first born to pneumonia—he was only six months old. A few months after Grandpa died when Mom was only two, they were traveling down a country road on horseback when a rattlesnake spooked the horse, bucking them both off. Mom was okay, but Grandma broke her back. If anyone has a right to be mad at God, Grandma owns that right. She isn't mad, though, and never has been. Instead of being angry, she dedicated her life to raising Mom and serving God. For years, Grandma has cleaned the church and cooked meals for at least one hundred people every Sunday. She attends church four times a week and does whatever's asked of her. She never remarried after Grandpa died. She never even dated another man, stating that Grandpa was her one and only true love. Even today, Grandma still wears the wedding ring Grandpa placed on her finger years ago.

Millions of thoughts bounce around the inside of my head as I rock back and forth on my bunk. I can't just sit here. I have to do something. I look around at where I am, and...nothing. There is nothing I can do. I'm shaking uncontrollably, and my jaw locks tight, clenching my teeth so they almost crack. I do the only thing I can. I pray. "God, I know you don't owe me anything. I know I don't have the right to ask you for one single thing after the life I've led, but this isn't for me. You see, Grandma needs to see me again. She needs to know I'm going to be okay. I have to prove to her I'm going to be all right. It's been years since I've seen her. Please, dear God, I just want to give her one more hug. With nine months left to serve, please don't take her until I have a chance to see her again. Please!"

I call home to check on Grandma during the small timeslots I'm allowed, and I go crazy in between wondering what's happening. Mom has been at her bedside caring for her 24/7, allowing her to remain at home. Hospice makes weekly visits, but it's Mom who cares for her daily.

Grandma's been hanging on for several months, and every time I call, Mom holds the phone to Grandma's ear so I can talk to her. Grandma's alert, but she just can't talk. I encourage her, "Hi, Grandma! I love you. Hang in there, okay? Don't you be going anywhere, Grandma. I'll be home soon. I promise, Grandma. I promise!"

I hear a few grunts and gurgles as she tries to respond. As I hold the receiver listening to her, I pray. "Please, God! Don't take her, not yet."

Waiting at my desk for the rec yard to open, I notice someone new walking down the run with a property bag thrown over his shoulder. He looks familiar, and I stare at him. *Huh, that kinda looks like Sonny.* But naw, it can't be him. This guy is white-headed and about fifty pounds heavier than Sonny. He gets closer, and I realize, it is Sonny! My old partner in crime!

I haven't seen Sonny in years, not since Lake Havasu. I thought I heard he had died a few years back. I approach him, grinning ear to ear, and it's apparent he has no idea who I am. Second-guessing myself, I wait to see if he'll acknowledge me. Maybe this guy just resembles Sonny. But there it is—he breaks into a big ole familiar smile through that Fu Manchu mustache of his and yells, "*Dude!* I thought you was *dead!*" as he grabs me in a big bro bearhug.

"I thought you was dead, too!" I tell him, laughing.

He asks, "Well, now that that's cleared up, how ya been, bro?"

I look around and lie to him, "Other than the fact I'm here, pretty good."

Truth is, I'm falling apart worrying about Nikki, Grandma, Val, Mom, and the rest of my kids, but now's not the time.

"Yeah, me too. Man, it's good to see you!"

"Especially since we're both not dead, right?" I joke.

Sonny and I spend most of our free time hanging out, catching up on everything that's happened in our lives over the last ten years. He's shocked when I tell him Mikki left me while I was in jail and even more shocked when I tell him about Val. He can't believe I found a woman like Val who would actually marry a man like me. He tells me about his divorce from Tina, and we talk about our plans to ensure we never end up in prison again. We discuss everything while out walking the track. He tells me, "I'm done with this life, dude!"

"Me too. I just don't know what I'm going to do when I get out."

He chuckles, reminding me, "Well, Mike! You're gonna take care of that woman of yours. I mean, Dar! That's what you're gonna do! That's what I'd do if I was you!"

"She wants to move back to Illinois."

"Then move back to Illinois, bro. You better get out of Arizona! They have your number here, and if they dial you up again, man, you'll never get out of Hotel Arizona."

I understand what he's saying, and he's right. When I'm released in a few months, the Arizona law enforcement will do whatever they can to get me back. They want me off their streets, and the next time being my third time, I'll get the maximum sentence, most likely for the rest of my life. I'm here because they planted that check, saying it was in my truck. They'll do it again.

"My family wants me back home in Illinois. Grandma's doing bad. I want to see her before it's too late, but man, I don't know about moving back there. Illinois wasn't good for me, either. That's why I moved here."

"Yeah. But that was years ago, man," Sonny reassures me. "Besides, that's where your family is. If you're trying to go straight, no better place to be than with family."

His words sink in, and I'm thankful he is doing time with me. It makes it easier to do.

After chow, I walk back to the run. It's late January with just a few months left until my release. I hear over the PA, "Bryant, 113000. Report to the counselor's office."

Nothing good ever comes from this announcement. Bile fills my throat as I walk toward the office, wondering which of my many worries this concerns. The counselor doesn't say a word, just hands me the phone.

"Hello?"

After a pause, I hear Mom's broken voice, "She's gone."

My heart breaks, and as much as I want to, I can't talk.

Sherri takes the phone. "Dar, she's way too upset to talk right now."

"I know."

"Grandma went peacefully," she says.

I cannot cry, not in prison. Crying is unacceptable, no matter the circumstances. If I show weakness now, I'll pay later. Holding back tears, I stare at the ceiling, trying to dry my eyes before the tears fall. Doing my best to stay in check, I calmly assure Sherri, "I'm going to apply for a bereavement so I can come home for the funeral."

Sherri sounds hopeful. "Really? You can do that? That'd be awesome, Dar!"

"I'll let you know, sis. I love you! Please give Mom extra love for me, and Tim too! How's he doing anyway?"

Sherri pauses a moment. "Okay, I guess."

It suddenly dawns on me just how long it's been since I've seen my brother and sister. It's been years. I hang up the phone, feeling extremely homesick, and walk back to my run, dazed.

The next morning, I run the track alone, realizing after my tenth time around that no amount of physical action is going to calm my anxiety. I look up toward heaven and scream to God. *"Really, God? You couldn't keep her around for just a few more months? You had to take her now, before we had a chance to see each other again?"*

Then I plead, "Forget about me, what about her? Don't you think she deserved at least that? I'm almost out of here, for crying out loud!"

Having gotten that off my chest, I still don't feel any better.

The next day when I learn they denied my bereavement request, anger wells up inside, escalating to a dangerous rage. Controlling it the best I can, I phone home explaining they'll have to go through this without me, again. I'm smart enough to understand my state of mind right now and fight to remain cautious, knowing how easy it'd be for me to pick up another charge and prolong my release. But the enraged side has been awakened, and I feel it stir to life, waiting, wanting someone, anyone to say anything derogatory to me—guard, inmate, it doesn't matter at this point. I'm beyond livid, and I want to hurt someone. I'm furious at the system, at myself, and especially at God!

Fighting hard to stay in check these last few months, my release date finally rolls around, and as far as I'm concerned, it's too little too late. Before I roll out, I stop by Sonny's bunk to say good-bye. He doesn't have much longer. We promise to get in touch when he's released with the understanding we can't until our parole's up. Felons are not allowed to associate with each other while under the supervision part of release.

I climb into the transport van to start my trip across the desert back to Phoenix. Other than the razor wire prison walls, the scenery here is amazing. The desert's sunrises over the mountains are only outdone by the sunsets sinking into the valley. Rays of red, orange, and purple paint the skies with silhouettes of saguaro cactus in the foreground.

I should be excited, but I'm not. I should be over the anger of being in prison again, but it has eaten at me every single day for the last three and a half years.

We pull into an empty parking lot outside my parole officer's office at seven on Saturday morning. My parole officer won't be in his office until Monday. The van pulls away as I stand in my state-issued jeans with my property bag flung over my shoulder. Where's Val? She was supposed to meet me here. Seven fifteen rolls around, and no Val. I sit on the steps and wait. Seven thirty rolls around, and no Val. I walk the empty parking lot, kicking rocks off the asphalt. Finally, at 7:45 Val pulls in, and I snap, "Where've you been?"

"I wasn't sure where to go and got stuck in traffic."

"Come on now! How many days do I get out of prison? Don't you think you could've made a little more effort to be here on time?"

Val wastes no time straightening me out, "If this is the way you're going to be, you can go back to prison as far as I'm concerned!"

I climb in, realizing I've clearly agitated her, not a good way to start my first day of freedom.

Val and I have argued every single day since my release. I quickly grasp the fact that even though she waited for me and visited me faithfully, she put on a pretty good front and now has every intention of making me pay for what I've done by making my life a living hell.

I need to figure out a way to make a living without going back to my old way of life. Val goes through the roof when I decide to start buying storage bins again. "Great idea, Dar! Just go hang out with all the same people you did before!"

I try to assure her. "Val! They're in prison or dead by now."

She counters with, "Yeah, but that business draws tweekers, and you know it!"

"I can't help that, Val. What am I supposed to do? I have to make money somehow."

Buddy and I spend the next several weeks bidding on and buying storage bins and selling the contents at auctions. At least we're trying to. Something happened while I was in prison that has made this business almost impossible to turn a profit now. *Storage Wars! Storage Wars* is a reality show on TV about a group of people doing exactly what I've been doing for years. The show airs on A&E and apparently has many viewers. Now everyone wants in on buying storage bins, making purchasing the units at a good price almost impossible.

I used to bid against ten to fifteen others, picking up a unit anywhere from one hundred to two hundred and fifty dollars. Now I stand among two hundred people, watching bids soar between one and two grand per unit! Unbelievable. Thanks to that stupid reality show, now everybody wants these bins, hoping to find that one special unit with a Picasso buried in the back or a coffee can stuffed full of cash. I still keep trying, though, managing to pick one up here and there.

After a long hot day cleaning out a storage bin in one hundred and fifteen-degree heat, I walk in my front door, and there's Val, watching *Snapped* on TV. Nowadays, she's always watching *Snapped* or Forensic Files or some other reality crime show. I ask, "Why are you so fascinated with this junk? I can see watching it once in a while, but Val, you watch this stuff every single day. I don't get it."

Staring at the TV, she replies in a most serious and sinister voice, "Because, Dar, when I decide to kill you, I want to make sure I get away with it."

Feeling very wary of her at the moment, the only thing I can think of to say is, "Very funny."

As I walk past her toward the bathroom, I watch her expression—no smile, no snicker, no chuckle, nothing. She just sits quietly glued to the TV.

I shower, dry off, and take my new medication prescribed for narcolepsy, Provigil. It's only been on the market for a few months. It keeps me awake without any of the side effects of amphetamines. It's nonaddictive, too. It seems to be working as I can now get through most days without falling asleep.

I walk into the bedroom and dress, noticing a sharp pain in my back. Dang, I must have pulled a muscle earlier working in the unit. Val and I spend the evening as is the norm now, not speaking a word to each other. I guess it's better than arguing. Sitting beside Val, I watch fifteen minutes of TV and can't take another one of her stupid crime shows, so I head to bed, leaving her alone in the living room.

I wake at three in the morning drenched in sweat with the worst case of night chills ever. Shivering, I get up and towel dry, take a drink of water, and go back to bed as Val sleeps like the dead. When her alarm wakes me in the morning, I feel worse than I did before. Val gets up to get ready for work at her new job with an insurance company, and I take my temperature. The thermometer reads 103. I tell Val, and all she says is, "Well, stay away from me! I don't want to catch whatever you have" and then walks out the door.

I spend the day at home on the couch, feeling worse as the day goes on. Val comes home and starts cooking supper. I tell her, "Val, something's wrong. I'm really sick!"

She continues with supper, saying nonchalantly, "I don't know what you want me to do about it. I'm not a doctor."

I wait it out, thinking it's just the flu.

Several days later, I'm no better. I did see a doctor who prescribed a high dose of antibiotics to kill whatever this is. One week later, I'm worse than ever. My knuckles have swollen to the size of walnuts, the chills have intensified, I've lost at least thirty pounds, and my fever hasn't broken once this week. I wind up in ICU while they run tests looking for lupus, leukemia, and lymphoma. These possibilities scare me, and I'm relieved yet confused when after two days in ICU, the tests come back negative. An infectious disease team is called in, and in the meantime, I'm not getting any better.

I sit in daily ice baths to lower my temperature, and doctors keep asking me questions. "Have you been out of the country lately?"

"No."

"Is there a possibility you've come in contact with a foreign substance of any kind?"

"No."

"Maybe anyone close to you?"

Sick, feverish, and confused, I don't understand his question, so I ask, "I'm sorry, what are you talking about?"

He pauses, clears his throat, and explains, "Mr. Bryant, we have run every test we can think of. We've run all the standard toxicology tests, and there's nothing out of the ordinary on any of them. However, there is clearly something very wrong with you. It's only a matter of time before you'll experience organ failure. To be honest, you have all the symptoms of someone who's been poisoned with an agent that is not detectable on regular toxicology reports. If you have any information that might help us…we're grasping at straws."

She did it! *Val* freaking did this to me!

I calmly tell the doctor, "No, not a thing, but I'm not thinking clearly right now."

He shuts the folder with a snap "Okay. We're going to continue to do everything we can," he assures me and walks out the door.

Val walks in a few hours later with a sincere look of concern, and I think to myself, *Why the concern? This is exactly what you want.* In the soft, loving voice I used to trust, she tells me, "Dar, I had no idea you were so sick! I just overheard the doctors talking about you. I'm so sorry I didn't believe you, and I'm sorry I treated you so bad."

I look up at her from my hospital bed. Is she for real? She sure seems convincing, or maybe she's just learned to be a really good actor. Hardly able to talk and still not convinced she's on my side, I whisper, "I tried to tell you."

I don't have the strength to say anything more. Kissing my forehead, she whispers, "Dar, I'm scared."

With that, I pass out cold.

"What happened? What'd they do?" I ask, trying to wake up Val, who's sound asleep in the chair next to me. I feel good this morning, or at least a lot better since my fever broke. I call out to Val again. "Val!"

She sits up quickly, asking in a panic, "What's wrong?"

"Nothing! I feel better!"

My doctor walks in followed by a nurse and asks, "Mr. Bryant, nice to see you're feeling better. Let me ask you something…the list of medications you're taking, you listed them all, right?"

"Yes."

"This Provigil, how long have you been taking it?"

"A couple months."

"You haven't taken any since you've been hospitalized. Is that correct?"

"No…yes…I mean, correct."

"Okay, Mr. Bryant, here's what we're going to do. We're going to give you a dose of Provigil today."

"So what was wrong with me?"

"We don't know. We're still working on it. I'll check in with you later."

The nurse hands me a small paper cup with my prescription and a glass of water. I down the pills then lie back to relax, so glad to be feeling better.

Three hours after taking the Provigil, my fever is back along with all the other symptoms. We finally have a diagnosis—allergic reaction to Provigil. It had taken a few months to build up enough toxicity in my liver, but once it did, it kicked my butt. Provigil, being a new drug, had no other reported cases of allergic reactions. I am the first.

Within forty-eight hours, I am back to normal, well other than the fact that I lost thirty pounds. I'm weak and back to sleeping all the time. On the bright side, there are two things I'm relieved about—one, I'm not dying, and two, Val isn't trying to kill me. I am a fool for suspecting a thing like that from her.

Val's attitude softens a bit since she thought she almost lost me, but now I'm back to square one. If I can't take Provigil, how am I going to function, hold a job, drive, and care for a home, wife, and children? How am I going to survive in this world? Val's advice? "Well, you're just going to have to take naps."

What choice do I have but to take her advice? I fall asleep on the sofa, in the car, at the dinner table, and even in the storage bin while trying to work. I can't go on like this. Promising myself I will stick to the prescribed dosage no matter what, I sneak behind Val's back to get another prescription for Adderall.

Two months pass, and I've done good keeping my promise. I'm managing the meds just fine, and even though I constantly feel the tug to take more, I don't. Val walks in the living room while I sit on the sofa watching TV. Glancing out the window, she yells, "Oh *no! No!* This is *not* going to happen!"

I turn to look out the window, asking, "What are you talking about?"

Dixie's walking up the driveway, and Val turns to me sternly. "What is *she* doing here?"

"I have no idea," I reply honestly.

Next thing I know, Val storms out the door, confronting Dixie. I watch out the window, unable to hear what's being said. After an exchange, Dixie turns to leave. Val walks back in.

"She heard you were out," she tells me furiously. "She wants to get together with you about some business. I told her you were asleep. If she knows, all the rest of those people know, and it's just a matter of time before they all come crawling around here like a bunch of maggots!" It's clear Val's serious as she continues to reprimand me, "It's not happening, Dar, not again!"

"I have no intention of having anything to do with them, babe," I reassure her. "Buddy and I are doing just fine with the storage bins. We're keeping it straight and honest."

"We can't stay here, Dar. We have to move to Illinois."

"You're crazy! Do you know how cold it gets in Illinois? You've never spent a winter there. Besides, Mom bought these apartments for us to run. She bought them so you and I would have a place to live. We can't just leave. Who'll take care of them?"

"Dar if there's any chance for you and me to make it, we have to leave. We have to get out of here. If we stay, you know and I know you're gonna end up right back in prison. Dixie and all the others, they're not going to leave you alone. The cops will always be watching you, just waiting for you to slip up. You don't have a chance here. *We* don't have a chance."

Even though I shake my head no as I listen to Val, she's right. Everything she says makes perfect sense, but it's easier said than done. First of all, we can't leave until I'm off supervision, and that's three months away. Even then, how? How will we survive? We have no place to stay once back in Illinois. I will *not* move back into my high school room in Mom's basement or infringe on any of my relatives. I do understand that moving is absolutely the best thing for us to do, but it's impossible at this point. I can't just walk away and abandon Mom's apartments.

I feel my fate is written in stone. We're stuck here, and I'll most likely end up back in prison, and Val, she'll be gone for good. I have to face the facts. It's my destiny. It must be. Why would I ever expect anything more of my life? I don't deserve anything better. I don't even deserve what I have now.

Seven o'clock the next morning, my phone rings, waking me up. "Hullo," I say, half asleep.

Mom's cheery voice asks, "What do you think about moving back here?"

Rubbing my eyes, I look over at Val who's sleeping like the dead and ask Mom, "What do you mean?"

She explains, "Well, they're auctioning a house this morning just a couple blocks away from us. If I can get a good deal, do you want to move into it?"

Last night's conversation with Val rolls through my head, instantly sending words to my mouth. "Yeah, sure, if you can get a good deal on it. But Mom, have you ever bought anything at an auction before?"

"Well, no, but how hard can it be?"

"Be careful, Mom. It's easy to get caught up in the competition, and then you'll end up paying way too much."

"Well then, stay on the phone with me while I'm bidding."

"Okay."

This is going to be interesting.

"Opening bid of $45,000, do I hear $50,000? $55,000? $60,000?"

As I listen to the auctioneer in the background, I keep asking Mom, "Hey! Did you bid?"

"Yep! I have the last bid!"

"Don't go over $65,000, Mom. I looked the house up online, and it's valued right at $65."

"Okay."

"$65,000? Do I hear $70,000?"

I listen as someone bids over Mom, and I tell her, "Oh well, Mom. You tried. Thank you. I love you, Mom. Talk to you later."

Val's wakes up, so I ask her, "Have you talked to Mom lately? Did you tell her we were thinking of moving back to Illinois?"

"No. Why?"

"Hmmm, it doesn't matter."

My phone rings again. "Hello?"

"*I got the house! I got it!* I bought the house, Darwyn!"

"What? How much did you pay?"

"Don't worry about that. Just start making plans to come home. We'll close in two weeks, and it'll take a couple of months after that to get it ready for you. It's in pretty bad shape."

No way! I ask again, "Mom. How much did you pay for it?"

"Eighty thousand. But that's my business, not yours."

I cannot believe this just happened. "Mom, what are we going to do about the apartments?"

"Sell 'em!"

"Just like that? Sell them? For how much? Who should I call?"

"I don't know, Darwyn, just try to get what we paid for them and be done with it. Call a realtor. Let them handle it all."

"Okay, Mom. Hey, thanks."

Unbelievable! Just like that, Val and I start planning so we can be ready to move as soon as I'm off parole.

First things first, I have to sell Mom's apartments. They're located in central Phoenix just south of the Biltmore. Built in the forties, these apartments are very old and now sit among many new developments. No one's going to want this old place. I don't think Mom has any idea how hard it's going to be to sell them. She paid $225,000 for them right before I went to jail. That was almost four years ago. I'll start at $250,000. Maybe we'll get lucky and make a few bucks.

By late evening, I've talked to a couple of realtors and have a few more to call when there's a knock at my door. "Hi. Are you the owner of this apartment complex?"

"Kinda. Why?"

"I hear you're looking to sell this property. I'm prepared to make you an offer."

Seriously? Is this guy for real? I haven't even listed it yet.

"Yes, we're considering selling it, but we just decided to sell. We haven't even set a price yet."

He replies, "Well, that doesn't really matter. I work with a team of investors, and I've been authorized to make you a very nice offer."

"How nice?"

"We're prepared to offer you $750,000."

I stare at him as I let what he said sink in. "Excuse me, how much did you say?"

"Seven hundred and fifty thousand."

I don't know what to say. I try to keep my cool and contain my excitement at the thought we could possibly get that much for these old apartments, but I'm still not convinced this guy's for real.

"Um… Um, um, excuse me. I need to go call Mommy real quick. Um, she's the actual owner. Wait right there, or here, or there's fine. Just, just stay right there. I'll be right back."

I close the door and walk to the phone, thinking, *Did I just say Mommy? Oh geez, I did, but wait until Mommy hears this!*

Stopping to take a deep breath after misdialing Mom's number three times, I steady my hands and dial again. It's ringing. Dear God, please let it be her this time! "*Mom!* Are you sitting down? Then sit down. You ready? Someone at the door just offered to pay $750,000 for the property!"

"What are you talking about?!"

"*This* property, Mom! *The apartments!*"

"Oh honey, are you using drugs again?"

"No, Mother, I'm dead serious. I just don't know if this guy's for real."

"Well, find out, Darwyn, and call me back!"

Boom! This guy was for real! Just like that, Mom's apartments are sold within twenty-four hours of deciding to sell them without even listing with a realtor, and not only that, we profit $500,000! What I viewed as impossible only two days ago is now not only possible, it's happening! Val asks to move to Illinois, Mom secures us a house there, the apartments in Arizona are sold, my supervision is almost over, and I have an odd feeling that someone is pulling strings to make all this happen. Three days ago, I felt my destiny was set in stone. Overnight, everything has changed so fast I can't even think straight.

Parole is over, and it's time to head back home. Tim flies out to Phoenix to help us move. I haven't seen my brother in *years!* He is a sight for sore eyes. After an evening visit, we load up a twenty-four foot U-Haul the next morning and begin our long eighteen-hundred-mile journey back home...without Val.

At the last minute, Val decides she should stay behind to finish a project at work. She assures me she'll make the trip in a couple of months. I look at her in disbelief as I say good-bye. I have a gut feeling this is it, this is the end for Val and I, but Kendal is staying with my sister in Illinois, so Val has to come back to Illinois at some point in time to get her. I know Val—she would never leave her daughter.

Analyzing her expression as we say our good-byes, it's very apparent she's glad I'm leaving. I can't take my eyes off her as I climb into the passenger seat. I don't blame her. Just like every other woman in my life, I have dragged this woman through hell and back. Tim pulls away as I lean forward, watching her until it's no longer possible. I turn and stare straight ahead without blinking, drying my tears before they fall.

Approaching my hometown, I'm overcome with dread. I want to move back, but not like this, not without Val. I left as a pariah and am coming back feeling much worse. Tim drives the U-Haul across the Lewis and Clark Bridge over the Mississippi River into Illinois. Alton comes into full view as Mineral Springs and other memories flood my mind, making me feel even more uncomfortable. Although I am no longer the person I was last time I was here, no one knows it. I'll have to face them all eventually and look them in the eye, no matter what they think of me.

Tim drove the entire eighteen hundred miles, laughing when I offered to drive. "You're kidding me, right? You think I'm going to let a narcoleptic drive a twenty-four foot U-Haul while I'm sitting in it? No way, big brother."

Minutes later, we pull into the driveway of my new home. It's beautiful, much nicer than the pictures online advertising the auction. It's a 1940s bungalow, completely remodeled with a giant addition for a master bedroom and bathroom. I'm overcome with emotion as I tour my new house. Within minutes, Mom, my sister, nieces, nephews, Kendal, and Alisha show up to welcome me. Complete despair is replaced with pure joy when my daughters welcome me home with open arms. I have never felt so loved.

I walk around my new home, absorbing my family's love and wondering about them all. My nieces and nephews, they're excited to see me even though they don't really know me. Hasn't anyone told them what I've done? Someone had to have told them…how can they love me? Honestly, I can't figure out why any of these people would want me back in their lives. But look at them—they've made it clear they want me. Man, I wish Nikki and Chris were here, and Val. I miss Val.

Chapter 18
Home at Last
"That Bible"

I'm restless the first night in my new home, tossing and turning all night long and waking the next morning sleepier than ever. Fumbling through the nightstand for my prescription bottle, I down a few pills to jolt me back to life and notice it's almost empty. Lying in bed waiting for its effect, I flip through a phone book to look for a local doctor. I need to get this prescription filled soon.

Mom drives to the doctor's office, and I hand him my medical report, easily getting a prescription for Adderall. On the way home, Mom asks about the pills, and I assure her that I am not and would never take more than prescribed. Yes, I just lied to Mom.

I've been ordering extra pills online from an overseas pharmacy. I already need four to five pills a day just to stay awake. I know...I know where this is headed, and I've decided to just accept this fact. I am who I am. I am an addict. I always will be an addict. I'll most likely wind up in prison again, and there is not a thing I can do about it. What other choice do I have? I might as well quit trying to be something I'm not and deal with it, accept my fate.

For the last two weeks, Sherri and Kendal have been asking me to go to church with them. My entire family keeps talking about this new church they're involved with. I have absolutely no desire to attend this church—or any church for that matter. I don't want anything to do with church right now, and besides, I'm sure God doesn't want to have anything to do with me, either, so I just keep making up excuses not to go.

Kendal is twelve years old now and the spitting image of her mother. I've been working on trying to rebuild our relationship. She's still pretty mad at me for being absent from her and her mother's life for so many years.

Alisha is very forgiving, always has been. We've been able to maintain a loving relationship over the years the best we can with me being in and out of prison on the other side of the country. She has grown into such an impressive young lady. Ironically, she works in a hospital pharmacy. I now have a chance to live close to her and be her dad. I try my best to be a good dad to her, knowing deep down inside I'm bound to blow this, again.

Every day, I am surrounded by family. I'm enjoying it but also find it a little overwhelming. I'm not used to all this attention. Mom, my stepdad, my brother, my sister, and all of their families along with Kendal and Alisha join us for dinner every night. Many times, there's a group of twenty to thirty people trying to get seated at Red Lobster or some other restaurant. Often, my first wife Ann and her husband join us also.

I look at my family and am so grateful for each of them, but I feel like a fish out of water. I don't belong in their circle anymore. For so long, I've been in Arizona, miles away from everyone, living a life they don't understand. I don't know how to act, and I can feel I'm not acting right, always saying the wrong thing at the wrong time and offending people or quick to snap at others, especially a slow waitress.

Words fly out of my mouth before I can stop them in an extremely abrasive dialect that I never before noticed until I was back with my family. I'm different from them now. I'm acting, talking, and living like I'm still a criminal, always trying to keep the upper hand and feeling the need to protect myself by belittling others. It's what I had to do to survive in my previous world. I witnessed many who didn't survive in that world.

Mom sits down beside me, patting my arm, and she cautiously, lovingly points out to me that I've dropped the F-bomb thirty-two times in a ten-minute conversation. She says, "Dar, honey, people around here just don't talk like that."

Leave it to Mom to count the number of times I have cussed in a ten-minute period and then bring it to my attention. I can only stare at her, realizing that I just don't know if I'm going to be able to cut it here, acclimate back into this life. But then I look around and notice that none of my family ever condemn or judge me. They don't ask questions about prison or any of that stuff. They all know what I've done and where I've been, but they act as if it doesn't matter to them. Even though I'm no longer the person I was before, they seem genuinely glad that I'm home.

Letting Mom's words sink in, I look across the table at all my family. All of them see who I am now, what I've become. Could they really love me so much that my past doesn't matter to them? Is it possible? All of this makes no sense to me but also makes me wish Nikki and Chris were here soaking up this family's love. And Val…I miss Val.

I call Val almost every night. "When are you coming up?"

She responds almost every night with "I'm not sure yet. I'm still running this project at work. I can't leave until it's finished."

I hang up the phone almost every night, tormented by unfounded thoughts.

Waking up on a Saturday morning in December, I stew over the fact that Val is in Arizona enjoying a perfect sunshiny eighty-degree day, and I am in Illinois where currently the outside air is a painful three degrees. It's downright cold. I have forgotten just how frigid it can get here.

Not wanting to leave the coziness of my bed, I watch my phone vibrate on the nightstand. I quickly grab it then retreat to the warmth of my covers. Answering, I hear Kendal ask, "Daddy, would you please come to church tonight?"

Surprisingly, as my mind rolls around a few excuses to give her, my mouth without my consent tells her, "Yeah, I'll go, sweetie."

"Cool! Aunt Sherri says we can pick you up at six, okay?"

"Sure, honey."

I hang up the phone, confused as to how that just happened. *Oh boy, here we go,* I think, and then, *What else am I going to do tonight? I'm* so tired of being cooped up in this house, and if it makes Kendal happy, it'll be worth it.

After I reluctantly get ready for church, Sherri picks me up on time, and we drive out to Fosterburg Road, opposite of Castelli's Moonlight. It strikes me as odd when we pull into the church parking lot. This place looks nothing like a church. It's a large, nondescript building with an American flag waving on a pole out front. It reminds me more of a corporate building than a church.

As we're walking across the lot toward the front door, Sherri, sensing my nervousness, smiles at me and says, "This isn't anything like the church we grew up in, big brother."

Sherri steps through the front door into a foyer, and I follow her into a sea of people mingling about. I continue to trail her as we inch through the crowd toward the sanctuary.

Someone standing at the entrance door greets me. "Darwyn! How are you?" he asks with genuine interest.

This sets me back on my heels, and I look at him, puzzled. I don't recognize him, so I ask, "I'm sorry, have we met?"

"Yes, we have! My dad had a recording studio in Bethalto back in the eighties. You and your band rented some studio time from us."

Vaguely remembering recording at a studio in Bethalto after my studio at Mineral Springs closed down a lifetime ago, I shake his hand and ask, "How in the world do you remember that?"

A little blonde standing next to him chimes in with a slight southern accent, "That's just what he does. He remembers everything! Comes in handy when I lose my keys!"

He laughs, shrugs his shoulder, and introduces himself. "I'm Pastor Mark Church, and this is my wife, Jennifer. We're so glad you're here! Please stay after the service a minute so we can chat."

I nod at him while shaking his wife's hand. I walk on in, thinking to myself, *How could he remember me? I don't remember anyone from that studio.*

Still following Sherri, I sit down toward the front of the church next to Mom and take a look around. My huge family takes up the entire first three rows! Sherri's right, this isn't like any other church I've been to. The people here are very down-to-earth. I see elderly people, young people, young families, and people with tattoos and spiked hair. People are dressed very casually in khakis and blue jeans, with no one seeming to mind how the others look.

The music starts, and I realize this is definitely not like any church I've been to before. The sound is amazing, loud and powerful. I'm drawn to the band, excited about their rock edge. The band is incredible and honestly the best live music I've heard in a long time. The pastor's message is on point, relevant, and thought-provoking. I find myself really enjoying the service.

Pastor Mark looks out into his audience and says, "It doesn't matter what you've done. It doesn't matter where you've been. You don't have to try to change for him. Jesus will accept you just as you are."

A powerful and strange sensation washes over my body when I hear these words, and I hang my head, thinking to myself, *Oh Pastor, you have no idea where I've been and what I've done.*

The pastor's wife starts singing a familiar old hymn "Amazing Grace," Grandma's favorite song. I have never heard it sung like this before. It's incredible.

I notice a handful of people walk to the front of the church and quickly realize it's baptism night. My mind spins back, reflecting on when I was baptized at nine years old. I remember it like yesterday—being at the old church, the way it looked, the way it smelled, and the feeling of being dunked under water then pulled back up and feeling so new, so happy, so thankful, and so free as I wiped the water from my eyes. I remember smiling as I looked out at Grandma sitting in the first row smiling back at me with the palms of her hands together, her fingertips under her chin.

Thinking of Grandma and the old church, my mind races, spins with memories, thoughts, and feelings. I glance over at Mom standing next to me. I see it in her eyes. She's thinking of days long gone with Grandma, too.

Wiping my sweaty palms on the side of my pants, I nervously rock back and forth, trying to stay in check. My heart pounds, and I'm sweating. I'm getting dizzy, and tears roll down my cheeks. One part of me accepts this, but the other part is furiously asking, *What is going on? Stop it!*

These emotions take over my mind, and I have never felt anything quite like this before. The mad side of my brain tries to straighten it out. *You don't cry!* it says. *Stop it!*

It's true. I have not cried since I was a kid, and my angry side wants to know why I'm crying.

I try to silence it. I tell it, *I don't like this any more than you do.*

I do not like losing control over my emotions, and the mad side continues to berate me. *You're not a woman! You're not a child! So what's going on? Get a grip and just stop this nonsense!*

Feeling immensely vulnerable and broken, I look around at all of my family surrounding me then up to the ceiling, almost expecting to see Christ himself looking down upon me, ready to strike me dead for daring to stink up his house with my presence. I ask myself, *How is it I come from such a perfect family who live such perfect lives, and I turn out to be such a mess? How is this even possible?*

I look over at Mom. She's been the most loving and supportive mother anyone could ask for. She has never turned her back on me even at my lowest of lows. Shaking my head, I look down, feeling so guilty for hurting her like I have.

My ex-wives are both good women, yet I seemed to bring out the worst in them. Neither of them deserved what I put them through.

My children are all so different from each other, and each of them is ten times better a human being than I have ever been. I thank God none of them are like me.

How can I ever make up for the past thirty years? How can I make it right? That angry voice in my head stirs to life. *You can't,* it says. *You're wasting your time here. You're not worth the effort. Get out of here, and don't ever come back.*

It's decided. I really like this church, but I can never come back. I cannot deal with this much raw emotion. I feel like one big wound with a fresh scab that just got ripped off, all painful and sore. I feel exposed, naked. I can't do this.

I hibernate in my home for the next three weeks, feeling miserable and questioning my moving back here. I'm cold, alone, and missing my wife, wondering if I will ever see her again, and I'm always afraid to get my mail, expecting a package from her divorce lawyer. I find myself being talked into attending church again with my family. I really like this church. I feel safe here. There is something about this place.

The end of February rolls around and finally, *finally* Val comes to Illinois, but she is full of *attitude!* It's bittersweet. I love her. I want her. She's understandably a little angry with me. We have so much to work through. I tell her about going to this new church and that they have asked me to help out in their media department given my background in production. I tell her, "They think I'll prove useful."

Val looks at me with a scrunched face and scoffs, "You? You helping at a church? You have *got* to be kidding me." She walks out of the room. I watch her leave and have to admit to myself that it does sound ridiculous.

On a rainy Thursday morning, Mom is supposed to drive me to my doctor's appointment, but she is afraid to drive in stormy weather. I climb into the driver's seat, and she rides shotgun to make sure I don't fall asleep. The storm picks up fury as we head west on I-270 into St. Louis. Traffic is thick as always on this stretch of highway. Torrential rain blinds me cutting down visibility to just a few car lengths at best. I'm always surprised at how fast traffic flows in such weather. It's way too fast for my comfort, so I hold onto the steering wheel with both hands, leaning forward and straining to remain within the painted lines while staying with the flow of traffic. The windshield wipers furiously struggle to keep up with the falling rain. I'm getting nervous, so I tell Mom, "I've got to slow down. If they don't like it, they'll just have to go around me."

Before I finish my sentence, Mom grabs the dash and yells, "*Noooo!*"

I follow Mom's line of sight to the right just in time to see an older model Buick headed straight for us. *How is this car driving at us on the interstate?* I ask myself. It plows into Mom's side of our car, knocking her toward me. Fighting the wheel to keep from losing control, I see this same car spinning like a top. It hits us again and shoots us straight into the concrete median.

"Mom! We *have* to get out of here!"

We're on the inside lane, pinned against the median. Oncoming traffic is swerving at the last minute to avoid hitting us. Mom yells, "I can't get the door open!"

I yell back, "If we don't get out of here, we're going to get creamed by a semi. We *have* to get out or we'll die!"

A massive, dark, angry storm surrounds us as we're pinned against the median in the fast lane. We have to get out *now!*

Crawling out the driver's side window, I straddle the median before planting both feet on pavement and running toward the back of the wreck, hoping to ward off traffic until help arrives. Instantly drenched, I look toward the oncoming traffic, panic-stricken when I see a huge semi barreling straight at us. I hear Mom yelling from the car, "I can't get out!"

An explosive flash of lightning strikes across the sky followed by an immediate deep, rumbling roll of thunder. I stand frozen in the pouring rain watching the semi fly toward the car while Mom screams for help. In a matter of seconds, this semi goes from fifty to twenty-five to fifteen feet away from impact. At ten feet, it swerves at the last second into the other lane, barely missing us. I have to warn oncoming traffic!

Making my way to the back of the car, I pop the trunk. There are no road flares, but there's a red umbrella. Quickly opening it, I stand at the back of the wreck, furiously waving this bright red umbrella and hoping and praying I don't become roadkill. I'm yelling at Mom to get out, but she still can't. I don't see this turning out well, but then the police arrive with flashing lights, warning the oncoming cars and trucks and protecting us while the rescue team helps Mom out of the car. We're both taken to the safety of a waiting police car parked in front of the wreck. Hmm, this is the first time I've been happy to be in a police car. The officer asks if we're okay.

"Yeah, I think so," I tell him.

I look at Mom, who's wide-eyed and frazzled, her wet, windblown hair sticking out everywhere, She's clearly in shock.

The officer goes on to say, "Well, you two sure are lucky. It's not every day I see people walk away from a wreck like this." He looks back through the pouring rain at our car against the concrete median. "Not only did you walk away, but you did it without a scratch. Honestly, I don't know how you didn't get hit being in the fast lane at a dead stop, let alone in this heavy traffic and blinding rain." He glances back and forth from Mom to me, shaking his head. Shivers run down my spine when he says in a serious tone, "I have to say, you two must have a guardian angel or something."

I look back at our car as the officer cautiously pulls out into traffic. There is not one place on that car that has not been damaged from the impact. Another flash of lightening cracks through the air. A deep roll of thunder penetrates my body as a semi flies past, shaking the police car, and a very surreal feeling engulfs me. I'm alive, and I've just witnessed something…supernatural. I don't know how else to explain it.

The following Sunday, Val attends church with me. Sherri and her family are already there, and when we walk in, Sherri pulls us over to introduce us to someone. "This is my brother, Dar Bryant and his wife Val, and this is Ward Cusic and his wife Debbie." Sherri turns to me and says, "They just arrived from out of town and are here to help Pastor Mark." Sherri smiles, looking at us all. "You guys have something in common."

I look at him—he's about my age—and then I look back at my sister, confused, and ask, "Oh? What's that?"

"They lived in Lake Havasu also!"

I look over to him and say, "Wow. Small world. When were you there?"

"Debbie and I lived in Lake Havasu in the early '90s. I was a youth pastor at a little church by the river."

Chuckling, I tell him, "Well, that's wild. I was there early '90s, too. I doubt we crossed paths, though." Inside, I'm thinking, *I don't think our circles would have ever connected.* I walk away, feeling he's strangely familiar, but I can't quite put my finger on it.

After the service on the way home, I look over at Val. "Well?" I ask.

"Well what?"

"How'd you like it?" With complete lack of emotion, she continues to stare out the car window and simply shrugs her shoulders. Man, what do I have to do to melt this iceberg? "What? No comment?"

"It was church. What else do you want me to say? Did you expect me to see some miraculous sign or something? Did you expect me to suddenly see you as something different than what you are? I don't know what you want from me, Dar."

"Val, babe! I'm trying here, okay. I'm telling you, there's something that happens to me every time I walk into this place. It's a good thing. It's hard to explain. I just thought maybe you might have felt it, too."

"Nope, didn't feel a thing," she tells me as she gives me an icy cold stare. "How many pills a day are you up to now?"

Without emotion, I shrug my shoulders and stare straight ahead, choosing not to go there with her. She knows I'm seeing multiple doctors for multiple prescriptions just to stay awake. Getting them overseas is becoming more difficult. I can tell she's disgusted with me. Honestly, I have no idea how to fix this.

Over the last few months, I've made some new friends and caught up with a few old friends. Zach and Annalee had dinner with Val and I at Tony's Steak House in Alton. We had a great time catching up, but I have to wonder what they were thinking. They know I've served time in prison. I know they have questions, but they didn't ask, and I'm glad. I'm not ready to talk about it yet.

I've also contacted Cat, and we meet up as well. I'm hoping Val meets my friends, and if she likes them, she'll lighten up on me a bit. I soon find that Val likes all my friends—she just doesn't like me.

I look up my old friend and neighbor from high school, Kevin. We shared many stoned days and trips to the Keys together. Sadly, I find that he passed away from a drug overdose just weeks ago. He was only forty-seven. Kevin dying from a drug overdose, this hits me hard. He was one of the good ones. I really loved this guy.

Searching for other friends I used to hang out with in school, I'm finding many of them have died or are serving time in prison. Most are dead, never having even reached their fifties. Even TJ, my old friend turned nemesis, has died of a heart attack from doing too much coke. I wonder, *How is it I'm still alive?*

As I'm watching late night TV while Val is in bed sleeping, my phone buzzes on the coffee table. Wondering who would call this late, I pick up, and it's Dixie. "Dude! You want in on the score of the year?" she asks excitedly.

I take her down a notch. "Dixie, I'm not messing with anything that could send me back to prison."

"Who said this was illegal?" she asks innocently. "This is a no risk deal, sweetie. Totally legit."

"Then, why do you need me?"

"Because, honey, you know how and where to sell merchandise quickly!"

Shaking my head, laughing, I straighten her out "No, no, no, Dixie. This sounds like something that's anything but legal. I'm out."

"Look, just listen a second, would ya? This old man died. He owned a chain of restaurants all over Phoenix. He was what you'd call a high-class hoarder. He has this warehouse—and I mean a *huge* warehouse—full of stuff. We're talking cars, tools, guitars, antiques...anything and everything you can imagine! This old man has one kid. He's a customer of mine, a hardcore tweeker. I made a deal with him. I'll keep him supplied with as much dope as he wants for a year in exchange for everything in the warehouse."

"Dixie, that's stupid. That's the craziest deal I've ever heard of. This guy actually believes you're going to give him as much dope as he wants for a year?"

"Honey, I didn't say he was smart. I just need help selling this stuff, and you have contacts with the fences and auction houses. Believe me, I've tried dealing with them. They won't deal with me. Help me do this, and I'll split everything with you fifty-fifty! Come on."

"You do know I live in Illinois now, right?"

"Well, dummy, get on a plane!"

Sitting on a southwest-bound plane at Lambert Airport, I lean back in my seat ready for takeoff with Val's words ringing in my ears, "You go out there and do this, and I *won't* be home when you get back!"

I don't care. The way we're getting along right now, we're not going to make it. I've been down this road before. I know when a relationship has soured beyond repair. It's just a matter of time.

Dixie wasn't kidding. This warehouse is *huge!* I walk around in awe, checking everything out. Sitting down on a box to rest, I tell her, "Dixie, this is way too much for us to move."

She assures me, "I've got people to help."

Looking around, I can see there's money here, but we need help from someone more responsible, so I tell Dixie, "Okay, this sounds crazy, but I'm going to call my Mom and have her come out. Since we're not doing anything illegal, there should be no risks, and she can help in contacting auction houses, do some legwork, help clean the place out, and organize inventory. She's the only one I know of I can trust. Otherwise, Dixie, this is just too much stuff for you and me to keep track of, and if we hire someone we can't trust, we'll lose a lot of it."

Okay, so maybe I'm also a little worried about slipping back into the clutches of the meth monster. If Mom's here, it'll lessen those chances. Everyone Dixie has coming in to help is spun out of their minds, and I'm just one slippery slope away from the monster's grip.

"Are you sure this is legal?" Mom asks.

"Yes, Mom, I'm sure," I assure her. "I wouldn't get you involved in anything illegal. I just really need your help."

Mom flies out and dives right in, taking inventory of everything, packing, categorizing, and organizing so we know exactly which outlet we're taking each box or item to. Dixie's friends are helping sort and pack, and on the second night, Mom asks, "Where did those two people go who were packing those boxes over there?"

"Who?" I ask.

"The man and woman. I think they were together."

"Why?" I ask, wondering what's up.

"Because, Darwyn, I think they just ripped you off! There were two boxes that had paintings in them sitting right there. You stated how much money they were worth and told that couple to put the paintings in the truck. They're not in the truck. They're not in the warehouse. They're gone. So are the two who packed them."

"Where's Dixie?" I ask a tweeker standing close by.

"Don't know."

"Do you know where those people packing the paintings live?"

"They live in the apartments you sold a while back."

Our old apartments are currently boarded up and slated to be demolished soon to make way for new construction. The tweeker goes on to tell me, "They've been squatting there for a couple months now."

I look over at Mom. "I'm going to run over there and take a look. Stay here. I'll be right back."

"No, I'm going with you!" Mom insists.

I try, but there is no talking her out of it. "Okay, okay. Buddy lives close to the apartments. I'll give him a call and have him meet us there."

As we pull into my old apartment complex, I am struck by how dilapidated it looks. Windows are boarded up, and graffiti covers the entire outside of the buildings. It's a perfect setting for squatters.

Mom and I get out of the car just as Buddy pulls in with Dixie close behind. Immediately, I see a head peek out of one of the doors, so I yell, "Hey! I need to talk to you!"

A skinny little tweeker comes walking out with no shirt and wearing dirty jeans shorts and combat boots. I recognize him. It's the same guy Dixie had working in the warehouse.

Dixie speaks up first. "Where is it, James?"

He states defiantly, "I don't know what you're talking about."

I can tell from his stance that he's ready for a physical confrontation. I watch him clench his fists as Mom walks toward the apartments looking around and not paying any attention to him. Trying to keep Mom in sight, I tell him, "Hey, man. Just give us our stuff back, and we'll forget about it."

"Kiss my butt!" His statement is cut short by what sounds like an Indian battle cry. Turning toward this high-pitched, broken scream, I see a woman charging out of the apartments straight at Mom with a tire iron pulled back in striking position.

Dixie takes off like a bullet, hitting this woman with a full-on tackle before she can get to Mom. She knocks her to the ground, putting her into a chokehold and instantly rendering her unconscious. Mom stands wide-eyed, not knowing what to think.

Anger boils up inside me. I'm ready to turn my wrath on the punk standing behind me when I feel a sharp pain in my leg. Spinning around, I look at this guy in disbelief when I realize the little jerk just tried to kick me in the crotch with his combat boots, nailing my inner thigh instead. Now I understand why he wears those stupid combat boots—it hurts! Not as much as if he'd been on target, but it still hurts!

Too furious to care about the pain, I charge after him. He runs behind my car. I run left, and he runs to stay opposite of me. I run to my right, and he runs accordingly, always keeping the vehicle between us. People come out on the balconies of the three-story apartment building next door, wondering about the commotion then staying to watch the show and cheering us on. Someone yells, "The cops are coming!"

I don't care. All I care about is getting my hands around this little punk's throat!

Suddenly I feel a bear hug grip from behind. Buddy yells in my ear, "No! Stop right now! Get out of here! *Now!* Get your Mom and *go!* The cops are on their way. You know what's going to happen if they find out you're mixed up in this! Get your mom and go! *Get!*"

He's right. I can hear them coming. Screaming sirens are getting louder by the second, so Mom and I quickly climb in the car and flee. I feel defeated as we drive back to the hotel room.

Mom tries to calm me. "Just let it go, honey. It's not worth it. Just let it go."

"I know, Mom. I know."

My blood boils as I pace the hotel room floor, breathing deeply and trying to calm myself.

My surging adrenaline finally wears off, and I feel a crippling pain in my thigh. Dropping my pants to inspect the damage...wow! My leg is completely black from my knee all the way up to my groin. All of a sudden, it hits me like a ton of bricks, and I feel sick to my stomach—not because of the kick to my thigh, but because I almost got my mom killed! Throwing up in the bathroom, I tell myself this craziness has to stop.

I'm done with Phoenix, done with all of this for good!

Val calls later that night, and I downplay the incident. She asks, "When are you coming home?"

I laugh, playing with her. "Wow! It almost sounds like you might be missing me a little!"

"Miss you or not, Dar, I don't want you going back to jail, stupid. The longer you stay in Phoenix, the more likely it's going to happen." She pauses then goes on, "I do miss you, Dar. I love you. I just want you to be okay. I want *us* to be okay. Come home. Please!"

"I'm coming home, babe," I assure her. "I'm done with Phoenix for good."

Getting up early the next morning, Mom and I drive back to the warehouse to finish up then catch an evening plane back to Illinois without further incident.

It's been a month since I've been home from Phoenix, and Val and I are getting along better for a change. We're not arguing near as much, and things seem to be smoothing out between us. We attend church every weekend, and it's slowly growing on her. She's starting to enjoy it almost as much as I do. I still keep my guard up at church, though. I'm not ready to fully commit, and most likely will never be. I am making good friends here, and it sure helps that my entire family, all twenty-eight of them, attend also.

At seven in the morning, Mom calls. "Darwyn!" she says with a stern voice, "your daughter is extremely upset with you!"

Rubbing my eyes, I ask sleepily, "Which one? What about?"

"Well apparently, Darwyn, the pharmacy she works at, well, they just got a memo not to fill any more of your prescriptions. You've been red-flagged throughout the system for going to more than one doctor for your pills."

Wide awake now and pacing my bedroom floor, I don't know what to say. "Crap! Mom, I only take what I need to stay awake! Trust me! It's true! It's not my fault it takes four times the prescribed dose! What am I going to do now?"

"You're going to go see your doctor, and you're going to be honest with him! That's what you're going to do!"

"K, Mom." I hang up the phone, knowing there's not a doctor that can do anything for me. I'm in *huge* trouble. What am I going to do now? I can't stay awake without the extra pills. If I can't get them, what am I going to do? I know what I want to do—I want to get an eight ball and forget about everything.

Stumbling through my day, I worry as I take each pill. I wonder just what's going to happen to me when they run out…but I know. I know how this is going to end. Crawling in bed at night, anxious about my immediate future, I can't stop my brain from rapidly spinning a million thoughts over and over. It's eating away at my very being.

Tossing and turning for hours, I get up and walk through the house into the garage, pondering my situation and fretting over what life will be like without my pills. I know the routine, though. I know it well. If I hadn't been caught, if I hadn't been red-flagged, I'd have continued needing more pills and then more pills to stay awake until I was back on meth, killing Val, Mom, and my entire family. The dark side of my brain springs to life, reminding me how I've already failed them so many times.

Feeling weak, lost, and completely worthless, I wander around the garage aimlessly when a rope coiled up on a shelf catches my attention. I remember putting it there. I used it to secure my load in the U-Haul on my way here from Phoenix. It's a strong half-inch rope. My eyes involuntarily look up to the sturdy exposed rafters in the garage. I can feel the dark side of my brain silencing the good side that's screaming out to me.

Pulling the rope off the shelf, I cradle it in my hand as good battles evil in my mind. Holding onto the loose end, I toss the rolled ball of rope up and over a rafter, easily making it the first time. Silent screams are heard within, but I ignore them. Within minutes, I tie a slipknot, making a noose. Looking around, everything I need is right here, so easy and so accessible. I don't even have to look for any of this stuff, so it must be the right thing to do—or so I keep trying to convince that screaming voice buried deep within.

With a trunk and a couple of milk crates in view, I take my time stacking them perfectly on top of each other under the swinging noose. Climbing up on the cartons, I check the length of the rope in relation to my height, the crates, and the floor. It all has to be correct for this to be successful. I take my time adjusting the length and securing the rope at the rafters when all of a sudden, the bottom crate gives out, and I tumble down to the floor, cracking my elbow on the trunk below.

Man, that hurts! Sprawled out on the garage floor rubbing my elbow, I look around in disbelief at what I was actually contemplating. The screaming voice in my head is back in control, and I look over at the offending trunk while squeezing my elbow. Curiosity gets the best of me, so while I'm down on the floor, I open the trunk to peek inside. It's full of mostly unimportant stuff left unpacked from Phoenix, but off to the side, right on top in full view as if just sitting there waiting for me...*that Bible!*

Feeling a strong, deep tug at my heart, I begin to sob as the now calm side of my brain encourages me, *It's okay, Dar! You can cry if you need to, but you don't have to anymore. You're not going to go through with this now or ever.'* With shaking hands, I pick up the Bible and get to my feet. I tell *that Bible,* "This time I'm going to put you exactly where I know you are. No more surprise appearances from you."

I walk into my living room and place it in our glass curio cabinet in full view so I can keep an eye on it. I look up and question God, "Are you trying to tell me something? If so, could you please be a little more specific? You see, I'm not very good at figuring out your riddles. I don't want to be like this anymore. I never asked to be like this. Please! Please help me. If you make a way for me not to need these pills without being a walking zombie, I promise you I will *never* touch them or any illicit drug ever again. I promise!"

My neurologist sees me the very next morning, and I'm straight with him. "I'm sorry, Doc. I wasn't trying to play you or anyone else but what am I supposed to do? If it takes five to six pills a day to keep

me awake, and I'm only prescribed two a day, what's the solution?"
I sit back, waiting for his answer.

"Well, Mr. Bryant, there's a brand-new treatment we can try. It's
not any kind of stimulant at all."

I chime in, "I've already tried Provigil. It almost killed me."

"No, Mr. Bryant. It's nothing like that, I promise. It works in the
opposite way that stimulants do with absolutely no side effects
whatsoever. It's a liquid that you take at night right before bed. You
will have no need for any stimulants after a few days. You will still
want them for a while, but you won't need them."

I look at him skeptically. "Sounds too good to be true."

"I hope you have good insurance, Mr. Bryant, because this
prescription costs about $2,500 a month, but it'll be worth it. Now
you have to realize that with as many pills as you've been taking, it's
going to be hard to just quit. You're going to go through some strong
withdrawals."

I stare at the floor. "Yeah, I know. I've been through them before.
I'll have to go through them one more time, one way or another." He
doesn't get my meaning, but I do.

He writes out my new prescription, and I stop by the drugstore
on my way home to have it filled. I'm nervous knowing that I'll soon
be going through amphetamine withdrawals, not being able to get
out of bed for a few days. I'm also nervous because the last latest
greatest drug almost killed me. I don't even know if this is going to
work. My immediate future—feel like crap, lie in bed, and wait to see
what'll happen to me this time.

Nine at night, and it's already starting. I am dead tired. Reading
the label, I take the recommended dosage of my new meds, knowing
that tomorrow is really going to suck. Falling fast asleep, I wake up.
At least I think I woke up until I realize Grandma is standing at the
foot of my bed. Okay…I'm dreaming. But it—she— seems so real.
She smiles at me and says, "Just remember, Darwyn, he is always
faithful even when we fall short. He always holds up his end of the
deal. He loves you that much."

I wake up again and look around for Grandma. I'm truly awake this time as the morning sun gleams through my bedroom window, warming my face. I look around. Grandma's gone. Sitting up, I scratch the back of my head and think, *Wow! What a dream!* Then I realize something isn't right. I must still be dreaming. I should be deep into my withdrawals by now—exhausted, hurting, jittery, depressed—but I feel great! Fantastic actually!

I pinch myself and realize, yes, I am awake, and I feel great. So great I can't wait to get dressed and take the dog for a walk. My little white shaggy dog is dancing, wiggling at my feet, so excited while I hook him to his leash. He trots happily around the neighborhood with me as we enjoy this beautiful sunny morning. I am so thankful for a good night's sleep and to wake up feeling great that I look up to the warm sun and talk to God. "So this is for real? I made you a promise that if you would take away my craving for amphetamines, I would never touch them again, and you did it! You took away all my cravings just like that! Wow! Thank you! *Thank* you! I haven't felt this good since I was a kid. *Thank you!*"

Surprisingly, I have no cravings at all—not the first day, or the next day, or the next week, or the next month. I no longer want, need, or even think about pills anymore. It's like I've never had an addiction before in my life. I also no longer desire meth or any type of drug. I take my medication nightly, but I don't crave or feel I have to have it. I just take it because I know I should. Every morning, I wake up feeling great. This is incredible! Unbelievable!

Tuesday is my designated day to spend at church editing the previous weekend's service for the upcoming TV broadcast. Like most of these days, I'm in the building alone. Sitting at my desk going through the different video clips, I feel a twinge on the left side of my chest. Blowing it off, I continue working. My left shoulder starts bothering me, aching terribly, and my chest tightens. Again, I try to ignore it, but it's persistently getting worse until I'm doubled over in pain and barely able to sit up straight.

Reaching for my cell phone, I dial my doctor's number and explain my current situation. He interrupts me and asks, "Is there anyone that can get you to an emergency room? If not, I'm going to call an ambulance for you. Mr. Bryant, you have got to get to a hospital right now."

I lie, telling him, "I can get a ride."

I figure the hospital is less than five minutes away. I'll drive myself.

I question my decision to drive as pain sears through my body, steadily increasing by the time I reach the hospital. I'm in so much pain I can't even get out of my car. Grabbing my cell phone, I dial 911, pleading with them for help.

The dispatcher asks, "To what address do you need us to send an ambulance?"

"I don't need an ambulance! I'm right outside your door! I just can't getttt ouuuu..." I can no longer talk.

Within seconds, I'm on a gurney and rushed into a room with six or seven people buzzing around. They hook me up to all kinds of wires and check my heart. They ask questions I can't answer. The only thing I manage to say is "It hurts!"

I look down as they open my shirt. Someone rushes a cart through the door, complete with paddles ready to zap me! A nurse follows behind with two giant hypodermic needles, and I look at her terrified. She looks back at me and says, "Blood thinners," right before she stabs me in the abdomen with them. Two nitro patches are placed on my chest, and finally my unbearable pain starts to subside.

Now that I'm stabilized, the doctor checks me over and informs me, "Okay, we're going to start running some tests on you."

After blood work, a heart scan, and other tests I can't remember, I'm told, "We're going to admit you. You have a blockage. We need to perform an angiogram on you to determine just how bad it is, and then we'll talk about how we're going to take care of it."

They must have given me something strong because I see Val and Mom walking into my room, but I don't remember anything after that.

Waking up the next morning, I am comforted to see Val sitting at my bedside. We don't talk, but I'm so glad to have her here with me. Just her presence is everything.

There's a knock on the door, and Clint and Hank, two guys from church, walk in. They're both jovial, older gentleman that you just can't help but like.

Clint asks, "How are you doing, young fella?"

Shaking my head, I say, "I don't feel very young right now."

Hank laughs, telling me, "Wait till you're looking at eighty like me, then tell me how old you feel!"

Clint walks closer and says, "We heard you were here. We just wanted to come by and check on you. You know, to see if you're gonna live or not. You gonna live?" he asks as he winks at Val.

I lie through my teeth. "I'm sure I'll be fine. Thanks."

Hank asks, "Would you mind if we pray for you?"

"Sure," I say, feeling a little awkward but not wanting to say no.

Clint reaches into his pocket and pulls out a bottle of oil. He dabs a little on his fingers. The two of them lay hands on me, praying intensely. A few minutes later when they're finished, I thank them, and we say our good-byes.

When they're gone, Val looks at me and says, "That was really thoughtful of them."

"Yes. Yes, it was. They're a couple of really nice guys, huh?"

Before I finish my sentence, the doctor walks in and says, "Alright, Mr. Bryant. We're taking you up for your procedure in just a few minutes. First, we're going to take off your nitro patches. When we do, your chest pains will return. Don't be alarmed, though. It's normal, and the pain won't be near as intense as it was before."

At their complete mercy, I can only mutter, "K, Doc."

Val and I are talking fifteen minutes later when the doctor walks back into the room and asks how I feel. "I feel fine!" I tell him, having forgotten that I was supposed to start feeling chest pains.

"No pain at all?" he asks.

"Nope. None."

He turns to leave, but fifteen minutes later, he's back in my room again, asking how I feel.

"Actually, I've never felt better," I tell him honestly.

"Strange," he mutters as he flips through my chart. "I'm going to order another heart scan before we proceed with an invasive angiogram." He turns and hustles out of the room.

An hour after my second heart scan, the doctor walks back into my room looking perplexed. "Mr. Bryant, I'm not sure how, but there is no longer a blockage."

"Okay," I say nonchalantly, not really comprehending exactly what this means.

He stares at me, slowly shaking his head, "I don't think you understand, Mr. Bryant. Blockages don't just disappear overnight."

"So that's it? I can go home now?"

Nodding his head, he says, "Yes. That's it, as long as you're feeling okay. You can go home this afternoon. I'm going to keep you just a few more hours to make sure."

As Val and I wait for my release, what just happened starts sinking in. The rest of the day, the rest of the week, I feel a little confused. It doesn't make sense. I understand that what just happened to me was nothing short of a miracle, but I can't figure out why. Why me? I don't deserve any kind of special consideration from God. I'm not worthy of a miracle. Miracles are for all the good people on Earth. Miracles exist only for those who do good things helping others, not for people like me.

The days roll on, and I keep reflecting back to Hank and Clint as they prayed for me in the hospital with the exact same intensity that Grandma used to pray. Grandma, visiting me in my dream, rolls through my mind over and over. I don't know what's happening to me, but I know it's something huge. I can feel it, a change in me and all around me emotionally, physically, my attitude...everything is changing. I'm humbled yet strangely excited.

Sunday morning Val, Kendal, and I are hustling around fixing breakfast, caring for our pets, showering and dressing, getting ready for the morning service when Kendal asks, "Hey, since this is your weekend off from working media, Dad, why don't you guys sit with me this morning at church?"

Kendal always sits front and center at every service. Val and I— when I'm not hiding in the media box—we're more of back-row type attendees. It's uncomfortable up front. Kendal loves it, and I tell her, "I don't think so, sweetie. Why don't you sit with us?"

"Because, Dad, I don't want to sit in the back! Come on! Please! Paaleeeez, Dad!"

I can't say no to her pleading, but I can't say yes either, so I do what most dads do. "Ask your mother. It's up to her."

Val looks down at her daughter. "I don't care, honey. If you want, we'll sit with you." She grins back at me.

Regretting having sent Kendal's question to Val, five minutes before the service is scheduled to start, I follow Kendal to the front row. Grinning ear to ear, she keeps looking back at her mother and me to make sure we're following. As we walk, I can feel everyone's eyes upon me, watching me, and before I sit down, I look around at all of them. No one is looking at me. No one is watching me. They are all talking and whispering among themselves, and not one single person is looking my way or paying any attention to what I'm doing. Feeling a little foolish that I thought I was the center of attention, I sit down between my wife and my daughter and wait for the service to start.

The first few notes of the first song ring through my head, changing the atmosphere, and I can instantly tell that this service is going to be different. Song after song is beautiful and intense, speaking to me and stirring up feelings I can't even begin to describe.

Crumbling inside, I silently talk to God. *Why God? Why me? Why do you keep tugging at me like this? I'm not worthy of you. You know I'll only let you down. You should know better than anyone just what a messed up man I am! Why me? It's not that I don't want you in my life...I do. I just can't understand why you would ever want someone like me. I'm scared, Jesus. I'm so scared that if I surrender to you, I'll fail you.*

Confused, my minds starts spinning with a gazillion thoughts, weaving them together like a mini movie.

*Val waiting for me to get out of prison when she should have run.

*Mom buying a house at an auction even though she had never been to an auction before.

*The apartments in Phoenix that sold within twenty-four hours for three times the amount we expected.

*My entire family welcoming me home with open arms.

*Sherri introducing me to this church where I became instantly connected.

*Dozens of new friends.

*Walking away from a car wreck that we never should have walked away from.

*Delivered from an addiction that has plagued me my entire adult life without even going through withdrawals.

*Grandma visiting me in my dreams, giving me words of wisdom.

*A heart blockage instantly removed, puzzling the hospital crew.

Time and time again, God, you demonstrate how much you love me, but why?

Coming back to the present, I look around and realize the sermon is almost over. I catch a few moments of Pastor Mark talking about letting go of the past. His wife Jen joins him on stage to sing the closing hymn, "Revelation Song." These words are so powerful they penetrate my soul, causing every hair on my body to stand on end.

As I sit front and center taking all this in and absorbing every note, every word, the sweetest lady in the world joins Val and me. I had noticed her earlier, seated with her husband a few seats down. I don't know Barb, Pastor Mark's mom very well, but after only a few encounters with her, I feel honored to know this woman at all.

Barb stands in front of Val and me and puts one hand on Val's wrist and her other hand on mine. She starts to talk, but the music's so loud I can hardly hear her. Suddenly it feels like there's only the three of us. I can see everyone and hear the music, but Barb's voice is loud and clear.

"You know, I don't normally do this, but I have learned that when God tells me to do something, I should do it. Right now, he wants me to tell you something, Mr. Bryant." Looking up at me, she continues. "Apparently, he's been having a difficult time getting through to you." I listen intently to her words. "God wants you to know he loves you. He has never forsaken you. He has always been with you and will always be with you. God says you have a place and a purpose here, and it's time for you to come home."

She then asks me, "Do you mind if I pray for you?"

Before I open my mouth to answer, she begins praying.

I'm falling apart deep inside as Barb prays for us. I watch tears stream down Val's cheeks. Barb finishes with "In Jesus name, amen" then gives Val a hug, pats me on the arm, and returns to her husband.

The song ends, and Pastor Mark gives an invitation to anyone wanting to turn their life over to Christ. "Now is the time," he says, and I notice him looking directly at me.

I look up to the ceiling. *Alright, Jesus,* I say in my head, *this is it! You want me? You got me! I'm done! I surrender!* Shaking my head, I look to the floor. *I'm so, so very sorry for being such a self-serving scumbag jerk my entire life. Please, please forgive me.* Staring forward, I sit up straight and continue my private conversation with God. *I'm all in! No halfway, no riding the fence or just dipping my toes in the water any longer. I'm all in! I'm all yours! If you can do something with me, God, do it! I'm done with my old life, all of it.*

Realizing the chance I've been given, I gratefully look back up to heaven, giving thanks. *Oh, by the way, thank you for seeing something in me that I have never seen in myself.*

Driving home from morning service, I quietly ponder everything that's happened to me up to this point. I've attended the River of Life Church for one year, and suddenly it all becomes clear—God has paved a very explicit path to bring me right here, right now, to this point in my life. I am humbled and thankful beyond words. I feel I've been given a fresh start, and as I drive home from church today, I look at my path with new eyes. I am beginning the first day of the rest of my life on this Earth—and for eternity.

Late evening after a peaceful Sunday, Val is still skeptical of what happened at church this morning, but she is always happy for any kind of change for the better. Cuddling in close to me on the couch, she kisses me and says, "I'm getting in the shower. Let's go to bed early. I'm wiped out."

When I hear the shower start, my eyes are drawn to the curio cabinet. There it is, *that Bible.* I have to hold it. Sitting back down on the sofa, I run my fingers over the cover, and suddenly, it all makes sense. Jesus fills my heart and burns in my mind a knowing, a revelation of sorts for me to reflect on over and over again so I will never forget. In the most gentle and subtle of voices, he instills in me these words, "My son, when you were baptized and filled with the Holy Spirit at nine years old, your grandmother gave you this Bible. Just like this Bible never left you, reappearing in your life throughout the years, no matter how many times you left, forgetting it, it never once left you. So it is, my son, with me. Even when you leave me and forget about me, I will never leave or forget about you. You were sealed at the age of nine, and no powers on Earth can break that seal. This Bible your grandmother gave you serves as your reminder...I am with you always."

Chapter 19
Throw It All Out There!

I've served in the ministry at the River of Life Church for years now. After rededicating my life to Christ, I didn't change overnight. There were no spectacular bright lights shining down from heaven showering me in diamond dust, and I didn't even feel that much different, at least not right away. I did not sit down and write myself a bunch of do's and don'ts of everything in my life, things I thought needed to be changed. I never once said to myself, "Okay, now I've got to change." I left that burden on God, telling him, "Lord, if you want me to change, you're going to have to change me because I can't do it on my own."

Sitting in the front row with Kendal that day long ago, I did completely commit myself to God, and I am still completely committed today. I'm all in. I put it all out there for God, turning myself into a lump of clay and letting him design me, form me, and shape me into the person, the man, the servant he wants me to be. Over time, I did notice changes. I didn't try...it just happened. My language changed. The F-bomb is no longer my most used word. As a matter of fact, I no longer use any foul language of any kind.

My outlook on life has changed also. I now seek the best in people instead of looking for the worst. I no longer feel the need to have more and more material things, thinking if I can just afford the next latest and greatest item, I will be happy. I find I am happiest while working at church or doing something for someone else. For the first time in my life, I understand Grandma. I understand what made her tick—her faith, her drive, her love, and loyalty. Before, I'd always viewed her life of servitude as a sort of bondage, but now I understand. Nothing made her happier than serving others and serving the Lord. I get it! I get it now, Grandma. Thank you.

There's a line in a song that rings so true with me, and I think with my grandmother as well. "It's not what you get, it's what you give. It's not how you lived, it's how you live."

303

Like Grandma, I too serve faithfully, spending at least four days a week at church recording, editing, and producing our weekly TV show. I also spend a lot of time with Pastor Mark, his wife, and the rest of the pastoral team, especially Ward.

Every day, I grow spiritually stronger, and every year, Pastor Mark asks me to share my story about how God has worked in my life with the rest of the church family. I have to admit, I'm afraid to do it. Up to this point, I've only told the pastor, his wife, and Ward. No one, nobody else besides my immediate family, knows about my dark past, and there's not one of them that know everything. I feel it's best this way—just leave the past in the past. Why would I want to relive that horror? What good would it do to go there again? It's over and done, and no one would understand any of it anyway, most likely leading them to shun me. I love it here at my church, and I don't want to mess this up, possibly alienating myself. So every year when Pastor Mark asks me to share my story, I respectfully decline.

March 2015

Spending a little time in prayer before my weekly lunch meeting with Pastor Mark, I feel the need to convey something to God. "God, I've been serving you in the same capacity for the last seven years as the video director at church. If this is what I should continue to do, that's great because I love this work, but if there's something more you need from me, please reveal it to me. You know I don't pick up on subtle hints very well. I want to live my life according to your will. I owe *everything* to you, so please use me as you see fit."

Sitting at Casa Romeo's, our favorite meeting place, waiting for our lunch to be served, I look over at Pastor Mark and ask him, "So what're your plans for Easter service?"

I need to prepare for the TV production as this will most likely be the heaviest viewed sermon of the year. He looks down as the waitress places a hot plate in front of him. He gives her a smile and a quick thank you then clears his throat, looks me straight in the eyes, and simply states, "You!" as he scoops a bite of refried beans.

Confused, I tilt my head, thinking for a moment. Then I respond, "Me?"

I don't get it. I have no idea what he's talking about. He sets his fork down and puts his elbows on the table. In a calm, straightforward voice, he tells me, "Dar, it's time to tell your story. The Easter message this year is on Restoration, and I think your testimony will help a lot of people."

Setting my fork down, I sit back in my chair and look up to the ceiling, mentally questioning God. *Really, God? So soon?* But what can I say? I had just prayed this very morning, telling God I would do whatever he asked of me. I had asked God to make it obvious, and well, he can't get any more obvious than this, so I look back to Pastor Mark and agree to it. I am no longer hungry.

Gathering information about my story, Ward, the videographer, and I are in the church office going through material for the shoot. I've looked up and pulled out police reports, newspaper clippings, and online pictures. We've jotted down key points, anything and everything I can find on myself from the last thirty years.

Ward picks up the Lake Havasu police report clippings and says, "Oh man, I remember this! I remember when this happened!"

"What do you mean?" I ask. "How would you know about this?"

"I was there! I lived only one block away when this went down! I remember everything about that morning! I woke up early to all the commotion outside with sirens, police cars, rescue trucks, and media all lining the streets with some helicopters circling above. Debbie and I, along with her mother, went outside to see what was going on, and we immediately began to pray for the safety of everyone in your house along with all the officers doing their jobs."

Ward's words force me to reflect on that day. I've never really brought it to mind since it happened. I remember being surprised at how my arrest had been strangely peaceful. Normally, when police raid the home of someone on a top ten most wanted list, they're rough, slamming occupants in the home to the ground with a knee pressed into their back until everyone is handcuffed, asking questions later. I remember the police allowing me to stand up and turn around so they could handcuff me without incident. I remember one of the cops even thanking me for being so cooperative as they knew I had weapons in the house. I could have made things real ugly that day, and so could they.

Looking at Ward as he's flipping through my reports, I remember being overcome with tranquility after walking into the garage and taking inventory, considering flushing all those chemicals down the drain but then just going back in the house and taking my wife's hand and lying down next to her and falling fast asleep. I remember such a strange peace throughout the entire situation. I wasn't expecting it to be that way.

As Ward and I talk, God's work becomes evident to me, clearer than ever before. Ward tells me he used to have youth rallies on the riverfront in Lake Havasu at the same time MTV did their big production for spring break, and I suddenly remember a kid handing me a flyer for a youth rally on the riverfront at the gas station the day before my arrest. It dawns on me why Ward's name has always sounded so familiar to me. I'm aware Ward and I share common interests, but as we talk, I find we have much more commonalities than I could have ever imagined.

Ward had an eBay business, buying and selling at auctions, dealing in antiques just like I did. We're exactly the same age, and both of us were raised in Pentecostal churches in Illinois just a mile apart from each other, yet we'd never met until now. Growing up, his dad and my uncle were pastors at the churches we attended. We both backslid severely as young men, and we both moved two thousand miles away to the exact same town just one block away from each other where he witnessed my arrest and prayed for me and my family, people he didn't even know. Years later, we both moved back to our hometowns in Illinois. We started attending the same church at the exact same time, ending up good friends. For the last seven year, I had never put any of this together, until today.

I believe the point I'm trying to make, what I've taken from this experience, is that sometimes God's signs and miracles take a long time for us humans to make sense out of, and sometimes we will never see the fruits of our prayers while we're on Earth. That doesn't mean God's not answering them. God's always answering prayers, sometimes prompting us to pray for something or someone, and we may never understand why.

Ward had no idea who he was praying for the day of my arrest. I believe now that Ward's prayers may very well have saved my life and all the lives in my house that day. I'm honored to have such a friend who obeys God's will unconditionally. I now strive to do the same.

Easter weekend, I'm in the media booth preparing for Saturday evening's service. Ward and I have worked on my DVD for weeks, and now my video, my story, is about to be played on giant screens during Easter service for all the church to view. We've told no one about this, and I'm feeling excited, nervous, and worried all rolled into one. I've known this congregation for over seven years now. I've built great relationships and consider many of them my friends. This is my church family, yet none of them know anything about my past.

As the media director, I spend most of my time in this media booth, and right now, I'm thankful to be tucked away up here. It's a small glass enclosure that houses the recording station, camera switcher, control console, soundboard, communications system, and me. This is my box. From here, I control what everyone sees and hears, and I can see everyone, but they cannot see me. I like it this way, especially tonight.

Having arrived early, I've already performed sound checks and visuals to make sure it's all good. Alone in my box, I watch as everyone enters the sanctuary talking, laughing, shaking hands, and hugging each other on their way to their seats. It's Easter weekend, and I watch alone in my booth as the church fills to almost capacity while the band plays and people sing. I sit quietly in my box with my elbows on the desk, tapping my fingers together, watching, thinking, waiting. Pastor Mark gives the signal. Nervously, I scratch the back of my head then reluctantly reach over to start the video.

Looking out toward the front of the church, my face shows large across the screens as I start to talk, instantly sending me into a complete state of panic. That dark side of my brain questions me as I scan the audience for their reactions. What are they going to think of you now? All this time you've been deceiving them. They thought they knew you, and now they're going to feel betrayed when they hear your pathetic little story. You should have just left well enough alone, left the past in the past. Things had been so good, but now you've just blown it all away. Idiot!

Fighting to calm a mild trembling deep inside, I watch myself divulge my clandestine past to these people who have taken me in and loved me. I now wish I could stop it, but there I am up on the screen, exposing all my sins, my mistakes, my foolish ways. This is too much for me. What was I thinking? Oh well, it's out there now. When the service is over, I'll just stay right here hidden in my booth until the church clears out. I know I have to face these people sooner or later, but for tonight, I just need to slip out the back door and get to my car unnoticed. I have to disappear.

There it is. No turning back. It's done, over, finished, and now, everyone knows. I sit alone in the booth waiting, wondering, worrying, and when just a few people are left in the sanctuary, I open the media booth's door, ready to sneak out, but instead I'm greeted by a line of people waiting to talk to me! Surprised and not quite sure what they want, I stand frozen, holding onto the doorknob and looking at them, waiting for their reaction.

The first person hugs me, thanking me for sharing my story. Okay, that wasn't so bad. The next person wants to talk to me about their loved one who has spent time in prison, and the next person about their loved one heading that direction. Stunned, I listen, shaking hands and talking with people who are suffering the same pain as my family and I had suffered. Some tell me about their own encounters in prison or with their past and present addictions. I listen in awe as the stories keep coming and coming.

Presenting three services Easter weekend, I am equally surprised with the audience's response after every single service. Each is a repeat of the time before, people waiting outside my media booth wanting to talk with me. I never realized how many people in this church are hurt and affected, all with similar stories, all of them holding it in and afraid to talk to anyone about it as I had been afraid.

Following Easter weekend's services, phone calls pour into the church from people needing to talk, all of them asking questions and discussing their situations, hoping to find answers before it's too late, before their loved one or themselves are lost forever. It appears that by revealing my past, we have opened a dialogue for others to come forward and talk about something that was previously not appropriate to discuss. People now feel comfortable opening up about their darkest secrets. We all know that true healing comes not from pushing our thoughts and our fears deep inside our minds, but through opening up and talking them through, by listening and learning how others dealt with the same or similar problems. We can learn from each other. I shake my head as I sit at church answering phone call after phone call, listening, talking, learning, and growing with all these people. I'm amazed at the need for this dialogue in our area.

Soon other churches call asking if they can share my story, so we immediately send copies of my DVD out to them. Jails and prisons are also asking for my story. All of this, all of it happens so fast without even trying or planning. It's as if it has a mind of its own. I sit back in awe watching as a prison ministry is born right before my eyes.

The path has been revealed, and it's more than evident that God is providing, creating this ministry that is new to this church, something never before explored. We have passion, drive, and anointing. We just need the know-how, as Pastor Mark nor I do not have a clue where to take this next.

Two weeks after Easter, Mike Palagai and his wife show up at our church for the first time, walking in and introducing themselves. They are new to the area, and come to find out, they previously worked for an organization dedicated to helping people fresh out of prison get back on their feet. "Returning Citizens" as Mike calls it. I like the name. It has an auspicious and positive ring to it. Mike explains that he and his wife are relocating to this area and heard our church was starting a prison ministry.

"We would like to see if we could get involved. Do you need help?" he asks.

My mouth drops open as I stare at both of them in disbelief. "Wow, really?" Offering Mike my hand, I say, "Absolutely!" My mind is spinning so fast, and that's all I can mutter.

Just like God always does when you're doing something he has appointed you to do, he provides. I look up, and yes, I now see a ray of light sprinkled with diamond dust falling all around me. You may not see it, but I am engulfed in it, and it feels so good.

With Mike at my side, we get right to work with local pastors, our church family, and God's anointing. Together, we have launched an awesome ministry, reaching many people.

The Dream Center of Alton now helps returning citizens, struggling veterans, the homeless and addicted, and at-risk youth with basic needs, education, employment, and counseling. I'm asked to speak all over the United States, and my story on DVD is being used as a ministry tool in jails and prisons. We now work hand in hand with the DOC to help those who are serious about turning their life around.

Out of one small step of obedience, this ministry was born. I am humbled and honored to have the opportunity to utilize my mistakes to help others, giving the world something back. My past, my awful, disgusting past that I was so ashamed of, is no longer a waste. God has taken all that junk, that garbage, and He's turned it around into something magnificent! It's helping others to cope with their dark pasts or current situations. I am home now. I am where I belong. I am doing what I should be doing. I am truly blessed. Satan's plans didn't include a 360. That was God!

Epilogue

I am still married to Val, the most wonderful woman in the world, and I am father to three awesome children who are all grown now with lives of their own and stepfather to another child who is more like me than my other three natural born children. In addition, I have two beautiful granddaughters.

I feel that if God could spare me, protect me, and guide me through all the bad choices I made, providing me with this full and wonderful life I am living now after everything I did, he can and *will* do it for you as well. He can do it for the loved one that you're worried about. You see, I am the least deserving of forgiveness, yet he forgave me. He saw something in me that I never saw in myself.

God not only restored my marriage, he's brought Val and I closer together, making our relationship stronger than ever. Not long after rededicating my life to God, Val gave her life to Christ as well. God also restored my relationship with all four of my children, providing for all of us. Val and I have never been happier.

I've witnessed miracle after miracle in my life and in the lives of my loved ones, from Mom being healed of cancer two times to finding my dad against all odds.

For years, I have prayed for my father and that God would grant us one more time together. I haven't seen or heard from him in over twenty-five years; no one has. Many have told me I'm chasing a ghost and that he's most likely dead, but I can't give up. It isn't that I'm looking for a 'happily-ever-after' reunion, although that would be nice. I just want the opportunity to tell him I'm sorry for being such a crappy son. I know he blames me for his divorce, and I do feel partially responsible. I can't be the one standing in between him and God. I do not want him harboring bitterness in his heart or struggling with forgiveness or anything toward me that might cost him his salvation. So I continue to look for him and daily pray for him knowing I will never give up.

311

Word spreads around, and I get a lead about my father. My brother and I follow this lead, finding our father in a homeless shelter downtown St. Louis. As we expected, he is not happy to see us, but he does listen to what I need to tell him. I tell him I'm sorry, and I ask for his forgiveness. I remind him that he is my dad, always will be my dad, and that no matter what, I love him. That's all I can do. I leave with him my phone number, telling him to call anytime. I wish I could say he called, but up to this point, he hasn't. I had prayed, asking God to provide for me the opportunity to say my piece to my father before either of us died. My prayer was answered.

My friends from Arizona, Sonny and Buddy, have cleaned up their lives and moved back to my hometown in Illinois. Buddy lives with Val and me on weekends and works on the road during the week. Sonny manages an apartment complex for Mom and me in St. Louis.

I have reconnected and have close relationships with Zach and Annalee. Annalee is the cowriter of this book.

I see Cat often. She and Val have become close friends.

Alisha, my oldest child, still works in the pharmaceutical industry. She and her husband have blessed me with two beautiful granddaughters. I often wonder what would have happened to me if she hadn't brought to Mom's attention what I was doing. God was working that day. God bless you, my daughter, thank you. I am honored to be your father.

Nikki has paved a path through life not many could follow. Her accomplishments are so vast I can't even begin to list them all, from modeling to secret government work. She blows my mind. During my last stay in prison, she needed me more than any other time in her life, and I wasn't there for her. I'm so sorry, Nikki. God bless you, my daughter. Be safe.

Chris, my son, joined the United States Air Force and has already completed his term. I have never been more proud than watching him graduate from basic training. He currently lives in Arizona, his home state, and attends college. I missed out on so much of your childhood, Chris, and for that, I am truly sorry. God bless you, my son. I am proud of the man you've become.

Kendal is now a beautiful young lady. She is and has always been one of my most loyal supporters and is as much my child as the rest of them. She's the one who snapped the picture I've used for the cover of this book and for my DVDs. God bless you, my daughter, for always believing in me and setting me straight when I needed it. You make me smile, and I am proud to be your father.

I could not be more proud of every single one of my children. None of them ventured down any of those dark paths that I had taken early in life, and I thank God for that every single day!

Val and I have a close a relationship with my first wife Ann and her husband. They are two of our closest friends!

Mom, my brother, and sister, and their families are amazing. They never once gave up on me, criticized or judged me. They only loved me unconditionally. They are truly the best example of what family is all about.

I've also reconnected with friends from the old band days. Most of them are alive and well, and when they get together for a band reunion, I'm there listening to them play, enjoying great music and great company.

Mikki still lives out west with her husband.

Pretty much everyone else from my past is either dead or in prison.

Barry was convicted of manufacturing meth and sentenced to thirty-three years.

Dixie was arrested and sent to prison for an array of burglaries.

On a warm summer day, Pastor Mark calls to ask if I would mind taking him and Jen to the airport. On my way to pick them up, he calls again to tell me their flight has been delayed. He asks if I have something I could do for thirty minutes, otherwise come on over and wait. Immediately I think of something I've been wanting to do for a while, so I tell him, "No problem. I'll see you in thirty minutes."

Grandma is buried in a cemetery less than a mile from Pastor Mark's house. I haven't visited her gravesite in years. Pulling into the cemetery, I look around, overwhelmed by everything that's happened to me since Grandma died. I park and walk to her gravesite, knowing she's not really there. Grandma, right this very second, is with the Lord, I'm sure, bragging about the fact that she was right about me all along, just like any proud grandma would be. I smile down at her grave then sit down in the grass next to her. Visiting her grave is my time of reflection. Here, I can hear the sound of her voice. I can even smell her wonderful breakfasts all those Sunday mornings. Like yesterday, I remember her giving me *that Bible.*

Mom and I have always been closer than most mothers and sons, partly because we were business partners, and sitting here now, I realize just how lucky I am. I have a mom who is everything a mother is supposed to be, just like my grandmother was everything a grandma should be and more. Deep in thought, I'm brought back to the present by a butterfly that carelessly lands on a neighboring grave as I think about where I would be without my mother's support and Grandma's prayers.

Standing up to leave, and considering my life and all that's happened, I'm drawn to the butterfly as it takes flight again, landing a couple of graves down. Looking down at Grandma's grave, I tell her good-bye, then looking up to the heavens, I thank God for allowing me to have her in my life. Turning to leave, I glance toward the butterfly's beautiful, flapping wings and notice the inscription on the tombstone the butterfly is perched on—Rev. Joe Cusic. Could it be? Taking out my phone, I snap a picture of the tombstone and leave to pick up Pastor Mark.

Pastor Mark and Jen along with their luggage are all loaded up, but before I back out of their driveway, I pull out my phone and show him the snapshot. "Do you know if this is, by chance, Ward's dad?" I ask.

"Yes, that's him. Why?"

"He's buried close to Grandma."

I think to myself, *Huh, just another one of those commonalities?* as I drive Pastor Mark and his wife to the airport. We pull into a departing slot to unload. Pastor Mark thanks me and asks, "So what are your plans for the week?"

Pondering a moment, I tell him, "I think I'll write a book!"

Annalee: A Little about Darwyn and Me

I feel honored to be the cowriter of Darwyn's story. I've learned so much from his experience, and I thank you, Darwyn, for having the courage to share your story as others will learn and grow from it. The main things I've taken from this: don't judge, never give up, always lend a helping hand, nourish and listen to the "good" voice within, and stop worrying, just give it all to God.

Judging...that's a hard one for me, but I work at it daily. *Never give up hope* for what is right and good, no matter how despairing life becomes...never. We all need help at times, all of us, so be that helping hand for others, and also, when it's your turn, accept help with gratitude. There is and always will be a struggle between good and evil within us. Which side wins depends upon which side you nourish and give strength to. Pay attention to your surroundings and your friends. Neither you nor I have to save the world, so relax, love, pray, and let God do his thing.

My relationship with Darwyn as teenagers was pretty much how it reads in this book with many uneventful and good days left out, like our trip to Six Flags. I've always viewed him as a great big little brother, the kindest, nicest, gentlest person you'd ever know.

While working at IHOP, I noticed something in Darwyn change, and it scared me. I still viewed him as a good person but I sensed in him a loss of scruples, a lack of caring of the consequences of his choices. I witnessed the slow beginning of that part of Darwyn slipping away, for what appeared to me at the time to be by choice. Having openly spoken my mind then, and still today, I talked to him about what I saw. I suggested that he should maybe change paths. I suggested that he should maybe hang out with different friends. Realizing that day upstairs at IHOP when he collapsed on the floor from taking too many pills that my words were not sinking in, I distanced myself from him. I knew I wanted no part of the path he was taking.

Keeping him at a distance, as I watched his life unfold, I was mad at him for choosing this life, for going deeper and deeper into it, for risking his life and lives of those around him. I remember a visit right before his first arrest and prison sentence...his wife and children ate dinner at Red Lobster with my husband and children. I felt uncomfortable around him—he just wasn't *him* anymore.

I remember occasionally running into his sister and mother around town. They always remained supportive, loving, caring, and very protective of him. I could say that they are the reason he is back, the reason he is alive. I could say that without their love and support, we might have lost him into the abyss forever. Darwyn is very lucky to have the family he has. but when it comes down to it, it was Dar's decision to change that saved him, a decision we all have, no matter who our family is.

When Darwyn moved back home, he called my husband and I many times, wanting to get together. I'll admit, I stalled. Then after a successful dinner at Tony's, we agreed to spend New Year's at his house with his family and were surprised to walk into his home and see his first wife, Ann, and her husband, along with Val and all his family, celebrating the New Year in a most loving, fun, and safe environment. I saw my old friend again.

A few summers later, my husband and I met Darwyn and Val at the Grafton Winery. Alongside the Mississippi River, we ate, drank great wine, listened to good music, laughed, and talked about life, children, childhood experiences, and what a great book he could write. I offered to help him write it that day. He's back. Darwyn is back. I no longer look into his eyes and fear him. I'm proud of him.

I do not believe God chose this path for Darwyn. It was his to choose. I believe God gives us free will, and no matter how muddled our decisions become, when we allow it, God will make something great from it.

Not only is Dar back from the brink of oblivion, he now stands strong, helping others, people who've veered off track and need help finding their way back. I've always been told that God only allows in our lives what we are capable of handling. I am pleased to be a part of bringing to you the story of an amazingly strong family who are the epitome of unconditional love.

Oh, Mom and Dad, I know you're going to read this. Don't worry, Dar never had a chance of driving that GTX!

Dar, you are truly a blessing!

Always,
Annalee Banks

Annalee: A Little about Zach and Me

Growing up in Roxana, Illinois, I thought it was like any other small American city. Looking back, I'm shocked at the drugs that were readily available to anyone at any given time. Many of the so-called "good kids" were also using. Some survived, and some did not.

Besides playing with Hot Wheels in a dirt pile when we were maybe four or five years old, I had nothing to do with Zach because of his lifestyle and choices throughout our school years. Believe me, I was no angel, but I did not have a death wish.

In my twenties I found myself in a relationship I could not stay in. I became a single mother of a beautiful little two-year-old son. The man I had married was not the same man I left five years into our marriage. He had drastically changed three years into the marriage.

Zach joined a local health club where I was employed and attended daily, slowly winning over my trust, and I'll never forget his words. These are the words that caught my attention. "I don't know how to be a father, but I sure know how *not* to be a father."

He saw my struggles and realized my son deserved better. Even though he hadn't completely straightened out his life, I saw in him someone who was ready to move forward, as I was.

Many were surprised about my decision to marry Zach, saying it would never last. Only those who went to school with Zach and me would understand this. Over the years, my children have come home with stories of how people, when they find out who their parents are, are surprised. We are an odd combination. We were then, and remain today, complete opposites. Thirty-three years later, we're still hanging in there, each of us balancing out the other.

We were both in our twenties when we married, young and naive with a long road ahead to reach "normal." Drugs and alcohol surrounded us. Addicts surrounded us. We watched as more and more people succumbed, allowing drugs to alter them, kill them, destroy their lives, and send many to prison.

Zach and I, our marriage, our success derives from our life experiences along with our amazing children working together as one, and many prayers, always many prayers. My husband is clearly the hardest working man I have ever known. He may grumble, but he always drops everything to help out when one of us is in need. In the times I feel life becoming too hard, he always comes up with silly one-liners that we've all come to know as Zachisms, making us shake our heads and laugh, bringing it all into perspective and lightening the situation. Together we have raised three beautiful, successful children, and we are now the grandparents of three beautiful grandchildren. Clearly, we are blessed.